What People are Saying about *Rogue Angel*

"This story is fascinating, heartwarming, and almost too good to be true; yet it is. There are few examples of God rescuing a lost soul as dramatic and compelling as Mary Kay Beard's story. I recommend it to all . . . male and female, rich and poor, old and young. This book is a terrific read!"

—DRAYTON NABERS, JR., *Chief Justice, Alabama Supreme Court*

"Encouraging and inspiring, the story of the founder of Angel Tree® is evidence of the great good that can result from missteps and false starts in life. Jodi Werhanowicz does an outstanding job in her narrative of the transformations that reflect the life of Mary Kay Beard. This is a book for the person who questions whether his or her life can ever be used for good. Mary Kay Beard is a testimony to what God can do with a life fully surrendered to Him."

—ZIG ZIGLAR, *Author, Motivational Teacher*

"From robbing banks with class to creating Angel Tree® for prisoners, Rogue Angel is an awesome account of the lavish grace of God. You're about to meet an amazing woman who's story will awaken hope in the hearts of those who have forgotten that 'where sin did abound, grace did much more abound.' "

—KAY ARTHUR, *Author, Speaker, Co-CEO, Precept Ministries Int l.*

"What other inmates would see 'as the end of their life', Mary Kay Beard transformed into 'the rest of the story' for thousands and thousands of children who have parents in prison. Truly receiving grace herself, her life has been an extender of that grace through founding Angel Tree®. She has made a vast rippling difference in our world!"

—NAOMI RHODE, Author, Speaker,
CSP, CPAE Speaker Hall of Fame, Co-founder of SmartPractice

"Jodi Werhanowicz has given us a wonderful gift. You're going to love this story! You will laugh and cry; you will be shocked and amazed; and, because this is a true story—every word of it—you will be encouraged and motivated. I'm a cynical, old preacher who needs to see the real thing sometimes. Maybe you're like that too. This is the real thing and, if you sometimes wonder about God and what He's doing in the world, read this book. Then you will owe me for having recommended it to you."

—STEVE BROWN, Author, Professor, Reformed Theological Seminary,
Bible teacher on Key Life radio program

"This is a remarkable story of pain and of grace. Jodi Werhanowicz shows her readers how God can take a broken woman and reshape her into a life-changing healer to others. Mary Kay is an example to all of us of God's great power! Truly, nothing is too hard for the Lord!"

—DENISE GEORGE, Writer, Speaker, Teacher, Author

ROGUE ANGEL

The spiritual journey of one of
the FBI's Ten Most Wanted

BY JODI WERHANOWICZ

Foreword by Charles Colson

EZEKIEL PRESS
Phoenix, Arizona

Copyright ©2005 by Jodi Werhanowicz

Published by Ezekiel Press
PO Box 40152, Phoenix, AZ 85067
www.ezekielpress.com

Printed in the United States of America

ISBN: 0-9774294-0-7

Library of Congress Control Number: 2005935503

Cover Design and Typesetting: Peter Gross
Editing: Becky Beane and Mary Kathryn Christiansen

To all the mothers and fathers in prison
—and to their children—
God bless you!

—— And ——

To Grace, who truly made a difference.

By God's, grace you too, can make a difference.

maryKay
The Rogue Angel

FOREWORD

This is one book I didn't feel I needed to read. After all, I've known Mary Kay since shortly after she was released from prison. We've worked closely together over the years. I've heard her testimony many times. I thought there wasn't much more I could learn about her from her book.

Was I ever wrong. This book is a great read, very exciting and inspiring. As I worked my way through the pages, I found myself many times in tears, thanking God for this woman's life.

The first thought that came to me when I finished reading this book was that I wished every teenager in America could read it. It is a cautionary tale for juveniles, many of whom, like Mary Kay, are raised in dysfunctional homes. If only they could understand how important it is to learn the lessons of this woman's life.

Then, the more I thought about the book, the more I realized that it should be read by anyone who has encountered adversity in life (which of course is everybody—if you haven't yet, all you have to do is wait long enough; no one gets through life unscathed). This book gives tremendous hope to all of us that the worst things that can happen to us turn out to be the very best things in God's hands.

As everyone knows, I've discovered this paradox to be true in my own life. That's why I constantly say that I thank God for Watergate. In my brokenness, God could do more with me than I could ever do in the most powerful positions in the U. S. government.

And Mary Kay certainly illustrates this paradox. She was a bank robber, married to a criminal who, when Mary Kay became pregnant and was battling cancer, walked out on her and ended up in prison. When she couldn't raise the bail to get him out, Mary Kay, being young and foolish, helped him break out of prison. She sank about as low as anybody could in life, ending up behind bars facing a sentence of more than 21 years with no husband, no help, and no resources.

It was then, of course, that she met Christ. Her life was transformed, and she has gone on to do the most remarkable things with her life. This is truly the story of a life redeemed and then used by God for great work in His Kingdom. The best example in the life of Mary Kay is Angel Tree®.

I frequently run into people in airports and at public events who thank me for Angel Tree, for coming up with the program. Some will often say, "What a great idea you had!" I have to immediately explain that it wasn't my idea, that, in fact, I didn't even know about it when it began. It was 1982 when Mary Kay Beard, then a member of our staff directing ministry in Alabama, set up a single Christmas tree in a Birmingham, Alabama shopping mall. She knew the need, for when she was in prison, she had noticed that when the inmates received Christmas gifts—usually cosmetics, laundry items, and toiletries—instead of using them themselves, they saved them so that they would have a gift to give to their own children when they came to visit them. She realized the toughest thing about imprisonment was being separated from your own children. So when she was released, Mary Kay went back to the Julia Tutwiler Prison where she had been incarcerated, got the names and addresses of the kids of the inmates, and set up the first Angel Tree. Shoppers came by, took an angel off the tree, which had the name of a child and the gift desired, purchased the gift and delivered it back to the volunteers working at the tree. That first year, 1982, 556 kids who had a mother or dad in prison received presents. It wasn't until the next Christmas when Mary Kay set up a similar project, that I even heard about Angel Tree. My first encounter was to fly down and have a picture taken with Angel Tree children. And what an ironic moment that was for me, because Montgomery is the very city in which I had spent much of my prison sentence following Watergate. Here I was, back in the city, but now helping the children of inmates, seeing the look of joy that came over their faces when they realized somebody cared for them, and seeing their mother grinning from ear to ear that she was able to care for her kids.

But what started out as a good idea by Mary Kay Beard—and provided a wonderful, joyous day in a Montgomery shopping mall for me—resulted in a ministry that is now reaching well over half a million children every year, sending over 10,000 children to Christian camp, and enabling nearly 1,000 children to be mentored by loving adults. It has spread not only to all 50 states in the United States, but to 50 countries abroad. Hundreds of thousands, perhaps millions of kids every year are discovering that they are not forgotten at Christmas. They are discovering that their parents still love them, and they're finding out the real meaning of Christmas, not the sanitized, happy holidays version, but the one that talks about the Christ Child, God's greatest gift to humanity, born in a manger.

When Mary Kay puts her head on the pillow at night to go to bed, she has to be filled with joy and satisfaction. Just look at the way God has used the life of this very remarkable lady. She has extraordinary talents, as you will soon discover reading this book, and as you would be forever convinced if you heard her speak. She's eloquent, powerful, and moving. Those gifts, misdirected as they were for the first part of her life, are now being used mightily by God, multiplied many, many times over.

The great joy in my life is no longer hearing "Hail to the Chief" played, or flying on Air Force One with the President, or meeting with princes, kings, and presidents. Now it is seeing men and women whose lives have been transformed by the power of the living Christ, men and women who have been a part of our ministry who were once lost in prison and are now found and doing God's work in one of the most vital mission fields in the world. These men and women are what I call the living monuments of my life. I couldn't be prouder of them if they were my own children.

People frequently ask who is going to replace Chuck Colson when he's no longer able to do this ministry. The president of the ministry, Mark Earley, is taking my place. He is an enormously gifted leader. But Mark will frequently say that he isn't really replacing Chuck Colson, that I will instead be replaced by the legions of Mary Kay Beards, trophies of God's grace, those who will carry on this work well into the future.

I recommend a lot of books, but this is one I want to tell you that you must read. It is beautifully written; it will move and inspire you. Read this book, and no one will ever again be able to tell you that there is anyone beyond God's reach. No one ever again will be able to tell you that for some people there's just no hope. Mary Kay shatters those stereotypes—and lifts our spirits in the process.

Chuck Colson

INTRODUCTION

"Every happening, great and small, is a parable whereby God speaks to us; and the art of life is to get the message."
—Malcolm Muggeridge

There is something about a good story that grabs us and moves us. I know this a good story; I only pray that you find it well told. God is the author and director of Mary Kay's story, both the living one and the written one. Someone likened human life to a play; the script is written but the actors bring their own interpretation to it and are occasionally allowed to improvise.

In all of Jesus' parables, there is a nut of truth surrounded by a narrative shell. Our prayer is that you will find seeds in this story that will be planted in your hearts, nourished and watered by the Creator, and that they may produce fruit in the story of *your* life. Everyone's story is unique and different, yet there are similarities too. We all suffer, strive, seek, find, lose, want, run, hide, fall, then get up and keep going until the end of our own story.

> "The fact that hundreds upon thousands of children grew up with similar circumstances does not subtract from the pain and anguish and anger of any one of them. It simply echoes through hearts, from one corner of the earth to another corner and across time."
>
> *–Rick Bragg*

Mary Kay and I met in 1991 at the Arizona Women's Retreat; she was the keynote speaker and I was a counselor and workshop leader. At a luncheon before the start of the weekend, I sat next to her husband, Don. As we talked, he would occasionally exclaim, "You *have* to meet my wife. I know the two of you would click." We did.

There are similarities in our stories; we both had a biblically based, Christian upbringing. We were both rebellious and headstrong, which led to illegal, immoral, and unethical behaviors. But best of all, we both had devout and loving mothers who never stopped praying for us. Miraculously, the Lord lifted us both from the swamp of our own undoing and redeemed our lives.

Only God knows how I came to be the one to write Mary Kay's story. Others asked, and there are those who were surely more qualified. I am continually and immensely grateful for the honor. Thank you, Father God, first, foremost, and forever. And thank you too, Kay.

We collect other people's words and ideas like sticky notes in our minds. I tried not to openly steal another's words. If a mental sticky note or two works its way onto the page without giving credit where credit is due, please don't hold it against me. Count it as a compliment to the author that I thought it good enough to remember and repeat.

I must extend my deepest appreciation to Mary Kay's family. This book couldn't be published without their cooperation and blessing. A biography is not about one person but about all those whose lives are intertwined. To Jean, Joyce, Bill, Don, Connie, Tom, Ilene, Sean, Brenda, and Mama—thank you for letting me tell your story as well.

I don't think there is a single person who believes in Mary Kay (or this book) more than Don Beard, her husband. It is said that behind every great man is a great wife. Well, Mary Kay has a great husband behind her. I feel honored to call him my friend.

I was truly amazed and humbled that Chuck Colson agreed to write the foreword. I know it is because of his love for Mary Kay, but I am also grateful for his faith in me to tell her story.

In addition to Mary Kay's family, I interviewed many people who contributed to her story. I thank Betty Bostwick, Bertha Barfield, Ginger Cummings, Barbara Brown with the city of Peoria, Illinois, Sally Shanahan, Molton Williams, and Pastor Bob Curlee for their input and especially Nina Hamilton Kingery who chauffeured me and shared her home and her wonderful storytelling

My friends Carol Boley and Shirley Pinchoff and my family critiqued the book and helped me make the most of it. I am grateful for the prayers of my Bible study home group. Becky Beane edited every word and Mary Kathryn Christiansen contributed her expertise as an English teacher. My appreciation goes to Peter Gross for his creative book design, to David Carlson for his assistance, to Peter German for his advice, and to Mark Earley, Alan Terwilliger, Val Merrill, Sherrie Irvin and the whole staff of Prison Fellowship for their encouragement and help. I am indebted to Naomi Rhode who generously narrated the audio book—a huge blessing. Thank you all.

Special thanks go to the women of Arizona State Prison Complex, Perryville, Arizona, especially the Lumley Unit Monday night Bible study. Your openness, hope, strength, and courage are an inspiration to me. Never let go of the Lover of your soul.

Self-doubt was a frequent companion. My sister, Pat Lawrence, helped me keep that demon at bay by continually telling me that, yes, I was a good writer and yes, she was *sure* this was God's plan for me. Pat, you'll never know how much I needed that. My sister, Susan Hunter, did what she could from afar— she faithfully prayed and encouraged—invaluable gifts. Her husband Glenn and her children Alexandra, Wesley, and Gareth did too.

My parents, Mardy and Bill Lawrence, are my own personal cheerleaders. They'd call once in a while and offer to run errands, "so you can write." They also loaned their lake house to Mary Kay and me or to me alone when it was time to do marathon writing. They are a true blessing to me.

My husband, Victor, and sons, Casey and Jamie, are the meat and potatoes of my life *and* the icing on my cake: my special gifts from God. Victor took up the slack repeatedly so I could squeeze in writing. They all made do without me as I traveled to do research and then when I'd go off by myself for days to work. Though I know there were many other things they would have liked for me to be doing, they believed enough in me and this book to sacrifice without visible results for nearly four years. Thanks, guys, you're the best!

PROLOGUE

Twenty-one years and a day." The judge's words echoed in Sandra Marshall's head as she was led from the courtroom back to the jail. *The "day" must be for good measure*, she thought as she slumped onto the metal shelf that was her bed, couch, and chair in the county jail cell in Tuscaloosa, Alabama. Only nine months before, FBI agents had caught up with her; it seemed like a different lifetime altogether. This was only the first trial and sentencing; there would likely be more. Eighteen additional counts remained in Alabama, and three other states had issued warrants, not to mention eleven federal charges. One did not get on the FBI's Ten Most Wanted list for a few misdemeanors. How many years would they add to her sentence?

The force of that thought unsettled her long hidden emotions. *What is it about tears that make them so frightening?* She had learned long ago to show no signs of weakness and vulnerability; she was sure her survival depended on it. No one else was in the four-person cell, but the walls seemed to have eyes and ears. She shuddered at the thought of what would happen if other inmates saw any sign of weakness in her. It wasn't just the others that scared her; she could not maintain control and fall apart at the same time, and maintaining control was a way of life. Still, the thoughts pushed forward, dragging feelings with them.

I am not even thirty yet. How old will I be when I get out? She glanced at the small calendar she had made; June 18, 1973, her sister Jean's birthday. At the thought of family, the strength of emotions again threatened to overwhelm her.

"No! I won't do that!" She jumped to her feet, pacing the short, narrow space between the bunk beds. When the cell was full to capacity, two always had to be on their bunks; there was not room for four to be up at the same time. She often longed for company, but today she was glad she was alone.

1

The cell had two steel walls on either side, cement block in the back, and the front was solid bars. All were painted that hideous "institutional green." It was everywhere, broken only by the stainless steel of a toilet and sink. Years later when this became a trendy color, she couldn't rid herself of the memory of drowning in an unending sea of green and metallic gray. Vulgar graffiti screamed from the walls. To the right of the sink, a showerhead extended from the wall. Her feet ached from endless hours pacing the floor. She walked toward the drain in the sloping floor and picked up the plastic wastebasket from beneath the sink.

"I'll just keep busy."

She emptied the contents of the wastebasket away from the drain and filled it with water from the shower. She peeled off her only set of clothes and dumped them into the basket. Picking up the bar of Ivory soap from the sink, she washed her hair, her body, and her clothes. No curtain, no partition concealed her; anyone passing by in the hallway had a full view. She had become used to it months ago and no longer cared. She hung her clothes to dry from the chains that held the beds to the wall. She pulled the single, military-green wool blanket from the opposite bunk, wrapped it around her, and curled up on the flat, plastic-covered mattress. The rough blanket provided scant cover, and she hated pulling it too close to her face because of the stench of sweat, vomit, and urine. It was repulsive, but it was all she had.

She shook her head to drive away feelings that tried to sneak in whenever she was still. There was nothing left to do but to sit, to stare, to think while her clothes dried. Time, that precious commodity for which so many on the outside yearn, is a vast, barren desert in solitary confinement. The only book in the cell was a worn Gideon Bible. She perused it, trying to concentrate on the words, but her mind wouldn't focus. Too many unwanted thoughts and feelings battled for attention. She refused to give in to them, but the struggle was draining.

Frequently, she twisted around on the thin mattress, pulling the blanket more tightly around her. Although it was June and warm outside, the cell was a cool sixty-five degrees, or so the officers said. She wouldn't be surprised if it were fifty degrees. The thin, short-sleeved smock she'd been issued would not be any help against the chill, even when it dried. She wondered, not for the last time, if she would ever be warm again.

Part One:

Early Life

CHAPTER ONE

She had not always been Sandra Marshall. Twenty-eight years earlier, just south of the center of Missouri, she was born Mary Kay Petet; smack dab in the middle of nine kids: two brothers and two sisters ahead of her, and two brothers and two sisters behind. Her mother, Grace, was two inches under five feet, and over the years she grew nearly as round as she was tall. She was a sweet, caring woman who loved Jesus first, and then loved everyone else fiercely. Her brown hair was generously sprinkled with gray, even in her early thirties. Grace's face was remarkable; it radiated peace and love even though she had plenty of reasons to feel otherwise. Mary Kay's father, Bud, only two months older than his wife, was muscular, slim and handsome. He had the ruddy complexion of his Native American mother, but the startling blue eyes of his father. His hair was coal black and wavy; he wore it combed straight back from his high forehead. He was a charmer, but also, in the words of one of Mary Kay's siblings, "simply a mean, ole drunk."

Mamie Grace Crawford and Cleveland Francis "Bud" Petet grew up in the little towns around Springfield Wright County, Missouri. Grace quit school after eighth grade to keep house and take care of her younger brothers and sisters after her mother died. When her father remarried, her new stepmother said she could now do whatever she wanted—go back to school, get a job. Grace did what she wanted; she eloped.

Bud came from a well-to-do family. He was the youngest of eighteen children and spoiled rotten; he had a beautiful saddle horse and a car to drive, highly unusual for a teenager in the 1920's. His father was quite old when Bud was born. His mother was a full-blooded Choctaw Indian and a difficult woman to like. Bud's relationship with his mother was volatile and obsessive;

5

they fought fiercely and often, yet they defended each other just as fiercely to outsiders.

Jean, Mary Kay's oldest sister, says, "If my father really truly loved anyone, it was his mother." She remembers being made to stay outdoors when they went to her grandmother's house. When it became dark, they were allowed to come inside, but there was nothing to play with and they were required to sit quietly.

It is not surprising that Bud and Grace eloped; his mother would never have approved. Immediately after the wedding, they took off for California to escape her wrath. When they finally returned to Missouri, Grace was pregnant with their first child. They stayed for a while with his mother, but she was cruel to Grace. She would not let Grace leave the house, and when company came, she sent her to her room. When Jean was born, they moved to Idaho, where two more children, Joyce and Bill, were born.

Just before America entered World War II, they moved back to Missouri. Bud enlisted; his mother was not at all pleased. When he told her he had to report to the nearby base the following Tuesday, she stated, "Well, when you get back on Tuesday night, I'll fix you dinner."

"I'm not sure I will be coming back," Bud said.

"If you don't come home, I'll kill myself."

The next Tuesday, Bud did not come home. A month later his mother fell in front of a moving train. Grace thought it was an accident, but many thought it was suicide. All her life, Grace chose to believe the best about people and never allowed negative talk about anyone in her presence. She lived by the adage, "If you can't say something nice, then don't say anything at all." She expected her children to live by it, too.

Bud never quite recovered from his mother's death or from the war. When he came home, he was a different man—he had turned into a mean drunk.

And it was all Mary Kay's fault—hadn't Aunt Effie said it herself? Mary Kay was only four years old when she overheard the conversation in the kitchen. Her aunts were chatting as they washed and dried the supper dishes.

"Well, I do believe Bud really started drinking about the time Kay was born," said Effie.

Mary Kay's eyes grew round and then filled with tears. She ran to her room and grabbed her hand-me-down rag doll.

"It's all my fault," she sobbed. Aunt Effie's words were a hot brand on her heart. To her little child-mind, the message was clear: her father drank because of her; therefore, there must be something terribly wrong with her. From that day forward she set out to make amends and overcome whatever evil there was in her, but no matter how hard she tried, she could not. She thought she might make up for the wickedness inside by being smart. She taught herself to read before kindergarten.

Mary Kay was certain that she was not only bad, she was also ugly. The mirror showed a pale face generously sprinkled with freckles. Her brown hair looked mousy to her; she wished it weren't so fine and board straight. Bangs covered her wide forehead, but her face was long and thin. To Mary Kay, her grey-blue eyes were not nearly as pretty as the brilliant blue of her Dad or sister Jean, and no matter how much she ate, Mary Kay was always skin and bones. By the time she was thirteen, she could add her nose to the list of things that made her ugly. Her father had broken it—twice—and now it had a bump in the middle. Every time she looked at it, her hatred for him grew.

Bud rarely came home after work on Friday nights when he was paid; he stayed out and drank until the early morning. One night Mary Kay heard his car drive up to the house. Everyone else was asleep or pretending to be. At the time, they were living in a two-story, dilapidated farmhouse. The stairway was narrow, and the chimney from the stove went up through the bedroom Mary Kay shared with Connie and Ilene. When it was very cold, Don, Tom, and Ronnie also slept there because of the heat that came from the chimney.

Mary Kay listened as Dad stumbled in, woke Mama, and insisted she get him something to eat. Mary Kay had too many upsetting memories to trust her dad alone with Mama when he was like this. She went downstairs into the kitchen and stood by the old-fashioned wash table with its galvanized metal washtub. A dipper hung on the nail nearby and a medicine cabinet was on the wall above it. Mama was trying to get the wood fire in the stove going. Dad saw Mary Kay.

"You get back to bed," he barked.

7

"What good would it do? You're yelling so loud no one can sleep anyway," Mary Kay snapped back.

"I told you to GO TO BED."

"I'll go to bed when you do; then maybe we can all get some sleep."

Dad began to cuss. It always made Mary Kay cringe but she stayed put. She saw the fear in Mama's eyes; Mary Kay was not about to leave her.

Dad stood up from the table so fast, he knocked the chair back onto the floor. As he lunged toward Mary Kay, she backed up into the doorway, staring him down. She never knew if he was really going to do something or was just threatening. Abruptly, he turned and yanked the medicine cabinet off the wall.

"That was real smart, since that's where you shave, but what can you expect from a drunk."

He turned and threw the cabinet at her. She stepped aside, watching the cabinet fly by. She did not see Dad step toward her or see the punch coming. A sudden sharp pain ripped through her side, and all the air was knocked out of her. She struggled to catch her breath.

"Bud, don't! Leave her alone. Don't hurt her."

He turned and raised his arm to backhand Mama; she sidestepped and he missed. Mary Kay shoved him into the doorjamb and he crumpled to the floor. She backed away from him and Mama took her gently by the arm.

"Come upstairs, Kay," she said. Dad rose and started to follow them. Mama reached into the wood bin, chose a big stick, and turned to face him. Fierceness replaced the fear that had filled her eyes a minute before.

"If you take another step, I'll hit you upside the head with this." He gave her a furious look but stumbled to the table and sat down, his head in his hands.

Once she and Mama were safely upstairs, Mary Kay realized her side was hurting terribly. Weeks passed before the pain finally faded. Years later, when she had an x-ray, the doctor asked, "How did you break so many ribs?" She did not tell him the truth. Her father had not broken all those ribs that night; it took several more violent incidents to do that.

The greatest impact on Mary Kay's life that night was not the broken ribs but the sight of the terror in Mama's eyes. Mary Kay decided then and there she would conquer any fear that she encountered. *I am not going to live in fear.*

I am not going to let anyone control me with fear. I would rather be dead than give someone that kind of power.

Many people who grow up with violence think it was normal. Mary Kay never believed that. Violence always angered her. Somehow she knew that fathers weren't supposed to beat their families. He was wrong to drink. He was wrong to hurt her, Mama, and her siblings. He was wrong to use their money for booze instead of food and clothes and shelter.

I may be bad, she thought, *but he is worse!*

Soon she began to believe that his drinking and the resulting poverty, abuse, and unhappiness in their family were completely his fault, and so was anything else that went wrong in her life. Her anger spread like poisonous weeds. From the seeds of anger and rejection, grew a root of bitterness.

Over the years as her hostility grew, so did her sense of loneliness and isolation. No one in her family saw things the same way she did; no one understood, or so she thought. Years later she was surprised to discover that life with their father had been similar for her older siblings.

Mary Kay believed she was the only one who understood that her father's abuse was wrong; therefore, it was her duty to point this out—in front of him. Her brothers and sisters deliberately ignored her when Dad was around, afraid of drawing their father's attention to her; her words might set him off. When they ignored her, she felt invisible.

"In reality," said her sister Connie, years later, "I don't think anything any of us ever did made it better or worse. Everything depended on how Dad was feeling and whether or not he was drinking. Tom and I could be off playing and his car would come down the road. We would stop and watch. We could tell by how the car pulled into the drive and how he looked when he got out that, well, we knew how to plan our evening. We knew if we should go in, sit down, shut up, eat supper, and get out of the way. Once in a while, we could talk; sometimes he was a happy drunk. As I remember, Kay was very confrontational and always angry. If Dad was in a bad mood, he would start out by nitpicking at Mama. Then Kay would get in the middle of it and mouth back.

"I know she saw herself as always being the one trying to help Mama and stop the trouble; we saw her as one of the instigators. I remember thinking,

Oh, Kay, just shut up, shut up. Get off of it, leave it alone. I was just a little kid who wanted the trouble to stop. I don't know how accurate that was, but that's the way it seemed to me. I don't think she was afraid of him. She didn't appear to be, but that might just be because *I* was so terrified of him."

Mama's love and gentleness were a sharp contrast to Dad's rage and violence. She did not love people with "if only" or "because of" love; she loved with "in spite of" love. She loved her husband as she loved her children, without reserve. Her eldest child, Jean, said years later, "It was amazing to me how much Mother still loved Dad. She lit up when he was around. When he died, she had his body brought back to Eldon, so some day she could be buried next to him." Mary Kay's dream was to have a loving heart like Mama.

Because the family did not talk about the violence, neighbors did not intervene and help them. No one was willing to acknowledge that Dad was the kind of person he was. As with so many hurting families, the no-talk rule was firmly in place: "If we don't talk about it among ourselves, maybe we can believe it's not that bad. Certainly we don't tell anyone outside the family what is going on." Only many years later, after Dad had died, and they were all grown, with children and grandchildren of their own, did they begin to share their stories with one another.

Sadly, the no-talk rule meant that each child suffered alone. One heart-breaking story belongs to the eldest brother, Bill. When Bill was only eleven, Dad took him on an errand. They did not return for two years. No one knew where they had gone or when they would be back.

Bill never told anyone much about that time, not even his wife. On a cold, wintry morning, as he was interviewed for this book, he courageously opened the wound and exposed the hurt.

Dad and Bill, along with Mama's brother, Uncle Vance, had traveled to Idaho, far away from their home in Missouri. The two men were already drunk early one afternoon. They drove the winding mountain roads trading jokes and jabs, until finally his uncle went too far. Bill does not know what set his father off, but Dad suddenly pulled the car sharply to the side of the road and yelled at his brother-in-law.

"Get out! Now!"

Uncle Vance knew better than to protest or argue. He opened the door and drunkenly fell out, slamming the door behind him. Dad sped away. Eleven-year-old Bill sat in the back seat holding his breath. What would happen next? When would his father turn around and go back to get Uncle Vance? Time stretched to the point where Bill could stand the suspense no longer.

"Aren't you going to go back and get him, Dad?" Had he imagined his father's response, he would never have opened his mouth. His father again jerked the car over to the side of the road.

"You can get out with him," he barked. "Go on, get out, you're so worried about him. You can just walk with him."

Bill did not have a chance to protest or even think before he, too, was standing on the side of the road watching the car disappear. Scared, lonely, and lost, Bill stood there, not knowing what to do next. Soon another car approached behind him; he looked hopefully at the occupants. His uncle sat in the passenger seat. Like a kick when you are already down, the car's driver did not even brake. His uncle turned his head and looked straight at Bill, his lips shut tight. He said no word to the driver to help the young boy. Bill's little heart sank—he was all alone. What should he do? As one salty tear followed another down his cold, red cheeks, so one foot followed the other in the direction the cars had taken. Three long, lonely, and fearful days passed before he was able to find his way back to the place where they were staying.

CHAPTER TWO

Mary Kay's family moved every time that they owed rent they could not pay. They shuttled around the county moving into old houses no one else would live in—ones with paper-thin walls and no electricity or running water. In one house they woke up to find snow on top of the blankets. In most, they had to catch leaking rain in odd containers to prevent their few belongings from being ruined.

Occasionally Dad had one of his "straightening up" binges. It might last six months to a year. He was generally well liked in the community, and it did not take him long to find a job and turn things around—when he was not drinking. Once, they moved to a farm, which, to Mary Kay's delight, even had fruit trees. The family referred to it as "the house on the hill," and it was her all-time favorite. There was no electricity, but both the house and barn were in good repair. Dad was sober for more than a year there.

In addition to fruit trees, the farm had milk cows and vast acres on which to roam and play. Here, Ronnie, child number eight, was born. Jean, Joyce, and Bill had left home long before, but with the new baby, there were still six at home.

Tom and Ronnie stayed with Mama while Don, Mary Kay, and Connie attended a small, one-room school where a wonderful teacher, Mrs. Conlon, taught all eight grades. They walked to school every day, crossing Saline Creek before climbing up to the main road. They hopped across the water on rocks except in the spring, when the snow was melting and the creek overflowed its banks. Then Don hiked upstream to cross on a fallen log. Once on the other side, he ran up the grassy hill to knock on the neighbor's door. Grace and Edgar Vernon were surrogate grandparents to the Petet children. Edgar came out, always cheerful, and drove his tractor through the swollen creek to pick up the girls, drive to the main road, and let them off to join the other kids walking to school. When the creek was too full for the tractor, he rode his old mule across, hoisted the girls up, and carried them to the other side.

The house on the hill always provided lots of work for the family. They kept a large vegetable garden, and down in the woods large patches of blackberry vines and gooseberry bushes grew along the creek. Mama was a good cook, but she excelled in piecrusts. Mary Kay did not mind fetching a pail of berries for a pie, especially her favorite, gooseberry.

Dad worked in town and came home to do the milking at night. On Saturday evenings the family went to Edgar and Grace's; they had one of the first televisions in the county. The Vernons were a loving couple, and their home was a joyful place. In the summer they made homemade ice cream, which Grace served with cookies, and in the winter they made a big pot of chili. All evening the adults played Rook while the children watched TV. Life on the hill seemed like heaven.

They had lived in the house on the hill nearly a year when a man and woman drove up the driveway and parked near the fence one Saturday morning. Visitors were few and always welcome. Mary Kay was swinging on the gate. She greeted the strangers cheerfully, "Hi, come on in!"

"That's far enough. What do you want?" Mama had walked up behind her. Mary Kay had never heard her mother sound so unfriendly and unwelcoming. The child's mouth fell open. Without taking her eyes off the strangers, Mama told Mary Kay, "Get in the house and check on the baby."

Mary Kay was shocked that Mama had rebuked her for being friendly to visitors. She turned reluctantly and headed for the house. The anger in Grace's usually gentle voice sounded strange to Mary Kay's ears. She was stunned when she looked back over her shoulder and saw her mother grab an apple from the woman's hand and order them both to leave.

When Grace returned to the house Mary Kay felt she was looking at a stranger. A furious frown had replaced Mama's steady peaceful countenance. Something was terribly wrong. Not long afterward, they moved from the house. Years later, Mary Kay learned that Dad had lost the house in a card game to the man at the gate.

Mary Kay was crushed when they had to move, but not surprised. She always remembered the house on the hill as the one place in her childhood where she experienced security and happiness. Dad was now drinking again and often disappeared for a week or two. With Dad gone, everyone could relax; they began to laugh and play together again. But Mama grew quiet, and late at night she often sat in her rocking chair with an open Bible on her lap and tears on her face. Mary Kay prayed that Dad would never come home again. When he did return, she imagined ways to kill him. She swears the only thing that kept her from making a serious attempt on his life was the risk of losing Mama's love—and not being able to figure out where she could hide the body.

Car trips with Dad were an ordeal. Mama's father, Mary Kay's only living grandparent, lived less than a hundred miles south of Eldon in the little town of Hartsville. It was one of the few places they visited, and they usually went only after Mama received a letter saying her father was not feeling well. On Friday evening around six o'clock, they would set out. They rarely arrived at their destination before two or three o'clock in the morning because Dad would stop at a beer joint and leave Mama and all the kids waiting in the car. An hour or two later he reappeared and drove to the next one. The more stops they made, the drunker he got, and the more terrifying the drive became.

On one trip it was Mary Kay's turn to sit in the front with Mama and Dad. Usually the front-seat kid sat in the middle, between the parents, but Mary Kay would not sit in the front unless she could sit next to the window, far away from Dad.

"Can't you keep it in one lane?" Mary Kay covered the concern she felt with a derisive tone. "You can't even drive straight."

"You better watch out; you've got a good one coming." He said it so often that the warning was meaningless.

"You can't even keep it on the road much less keep it at one speed. You keep slowing and speeding up."

"You think you can drive better?"

"I don't have a driver's license. Why don't you prove that a license means you know how to *drive?* See if you can keep it at sixty and on this side of the road."

Her father accepted the challenge but he did not do well. Ahead of them was a railroad crossing with a train coming around the turn. They all expected Dad to hit the brakes, but he sped up. The train blew its whistle several times. Dad still did not slow down.

Mama cried out, "Bud, Bud, don't do it. Bud!"

Everyone screamed except Mary Kay. Her heart was pounding, but she did not make a sound; she would not let him scare her. They crossed the tracks, the train looming within feet of the passenger side of the car. Dad started laughing; he seemed to enjoy their fear the most. Mama was so traumatized she made him pull over and stop the car.

"That was real smart," snapped Mary Kay.

"I knew I had enough time."

"You didn't know any such thing." It was the last thing Mary Kay said that evening. She knew he had taught her an important lesson: do not talk back to Dad when he was driving. Even when he stopped at the next bar, she kept her mouth shut. Every time they were in the car, the children were perfectly quiet when Dad was driving, even if five or six of them were there at once.

In the midst of the fear and misery were two shining, glorious things in Mary Kay's life. One was Mama and the other was school. She loved both passionately.

Her mother was her source of security, her rock. Like the sun, Mama's love glowed warm and bright upon whomever was around her. She managed to make each child feel like her favorite in spite of coping with a drunk, abusive, and irresponsible husband. When Dad was drinking, Mama would go to work, usually as a restaurant cook. She provided food, clothing, and shelter for them all. And Mama never said anything negative about Dad.

When Mama went to work in town at a café, she left twelve-year-old Don and nine-year-old Mary Kay at home with Connie, age six, Tom, age four, and baby Ronnie. Years later, Connie asked, "Mama, how could you go to work and leave us way out there with no phone or electricity? Didn't it worry you sick?"

"Well, I prayed about it a lot," replied Grace, "and I told God I would stay at home with you children and trust Him to provide for us if He wanted, but we had to eat. If He gave me strength to find a job, then I would work if He would watch over you so none of you would be hurt. I was hired at the first place I interviewed so I figured He must want to baby-sit. Not one of you was ever injured or sick while God was watching you."

As deputy mom, Mary Kay was good at caring for the children; Mama trained her well and always left clear instructions. By twelve, Mary Kay could cook a complete meal, scrub the house, care for babies and toddlers, and still find time to read. Reading was her escape to a land where no one could find her. In a book, the real world and the real Mary Kay faded away. She did not own any books herself until adulthood, so she was a frequent visitor at both the school library and the town library. The librarian said she checked out more books than all the other kids put together. School came easily; she rarely brought schoolwork home, just books.

She and her siblings were not above squabbling with each other, but they were united in their commitment not to hurt Mama's feelings. Mama made sure they treated each other with respect. Whenever they were caught fussing among themselves, Mama sent the offenders out to pull the weeds that multiplied like cancer cells in the ditch by the drive. She believed there was no better way to make amends and iron out differences than working side by side.

Mary Kay's dependence on her mother was mixed with a strong desire to protect her. The desire to draw Dad's anger away from Mama was at the heart of many of her confrontations with him. Even as a small child, she believed she had to be strong, for her mother and for herself. Too many times Mary Kay lay in her bed in the dark listening to her Mama's cries, "Stop Bud, you're hurting me. Don't. Please stop."

Sometimes she put her pillow over her head to muffle the sobs. Other times she stood outside their bedroom door, put her finger down her throat, threw up, and told Mama she was sick. After caring for Mary Kay, her mother often crawled into bed with her "to comfort her." Mary Kay knew she had won, for that night at least. Mama's crying stopped and she slept in the safety of her daughter's bed as Dad ranted to the walls in the other room.

School is boring to some children who want to be elsewhere, burdensome to those who struggle to learn, and tolerable for many kids who enjoy the socializing but endure the instruction. For a few, school is like being an Olympic gold-medalist and visiting Disneyland, wrapped into one. Mary Kay was one of those children.

School was the one place she could forget the pain and poverty of home. She excelled in her classes, which pleased her teachers and often made her their pet. She loved school more than just about anything except Mama. She relished the sense of mastery, control, and admiration. Once on the way to school, she put home and Dad behind and opened a door to a different world. She was stepping out of hell into a cool, sweet breeze; that's how much it refreshed her.

The frequent change in schools did not bother Mary Kay; one year she attended three different ones. To her, it was an adventure. Another school was another opportunity for her to excel and impress new people. She never understood why new places and new people seemed to bother her brothers and sisters.

Like the house on the hill, the one-room school provided Mary Kay with the most pleasant memories. During one Christmas vacation, several small one-room schools were consolidated into a single district school. All of the children were bused into Eldon, and to Mary Kay's delight, her teacher was Betty Conlon, her teacher from Vernon School.

Mary Kay truly loved learning and won awards as a bright honor student. She was popular with the other kids, and she relished being away from home. But it was more than that. She wanted to know everything there was to know; she felt as though she could never learn enough. She hoped that knowledge would be her key to freedom, not only from her life of poverty and misery, but also from the darkness inside her. Despite all her accomplishments, she never lost the sense of being bad that had come over her in the kitchen that day when she was four, listening to Aunt Effie. The pain hung on for years like an old scar—sensitive and achy to the touch. The seething anger under the surface and the thoughts of murdering her father only reinforced her conviction that something was terribly wrong with her.

Escape was often on her mind. Her older sisters had left home before Mary Kay was old enough to start school. Bill went to live with their older sister Joyce soon after he returned from Idaho. Don, who was three years older than Mary Kay, started working after school at an early age and was seldom around. He, too, left when he was fifteen. Like so many children in dysfunctional families, the Petet children fled at the first opportunity. Mary Kay was sure that getting away would fix everything.

With the older children gone, Mama at work, and Dad in his miserable state, much of the care for the younger children fell on Mary Kay. When she was eleven, Ilene, her baby sister and the last of the bunch, was born. In those days, a woman stayed in bed for ten days after giving birth. Mary Kay stayed home to take care of Ilene while her mother recovered.

She hated to miss school; even when she was sick, she refused to miss a day. But she adored Ilene; she was her own living doll, and she wanted to help Mama. Her younger sister Connie brought home Mary Kay's assignments, but she yearned for the day when she could go back to school. When she finally did return to school, she missed her baby sister and rushed home afterward to little Ilene.

Mama had one ironclad rule in the house. No matter who you were, on Sunday morning everyone under the roof went to church—except Dad. No one dared tell him what to do. Mama's faith in Jesus ran deep, and she shared this faith with her children every possible way. She might not be able to provide other things for her children, but she gave each of them her very best, and the best thing she gave was her prayers.

Mary Kay did not mind church; to her it was like going to school. And just as in school, she excelled. She always knew her memory verses and always earned the perfect attendance award. Together her mother, the pastor, and her Sunday school teachers laid a foundation of truth in her early life.

The best thing about church and school was that Dad was not around. "If I can just get away from Dad, then I'll be all right," she told herself over and over. A time came when she thought they were actually going to live free from him. Bill had come home for a visit. Dad was drinking and turning mean. Mary Kay took little Connie and Tom into the bedroom to get out of Dad's way. Bill told Mama, "Get everybody in the car. We're going to go."

At that, Mary Kay told Connie and Tom to grab a few things, and they raced out to the car and jumped into the back seat. Mama did not argue with Bill and soon they were all in the car. He was barely fifteen and did not even have a driver's license, but he drove them all the way from Eldon to Barnett, where Mama's father lived.

Mary Kay was so glad to be there. Grandpa had a big yard, with several beautiful lilac bushes and some little goats. He had hummingbirds and seemed to know a lot about birds and animals. She thought he was the smartest man in the world. The best thing about being at Grandpa's house was that Dad was not there. It almost felt normal.

After only a few days, Dad sobered up and came looking for them. Mary Kay was playing in the yard with the goats when he arrived. As soon as she saw him, she ran and hid behind the well house, overcome with a mixture of anger, fear, and dread. Why didn't he just die and leave for good? Why did he keep showing up like some chronic disease? A tiny flicker of hope rose in her. Maybe this time they would not go back with him. Why, they could stay right here with Grandpa and go to school.

Dad and Grandpa walked outside. Dad looked hung over. Speaking in low tones, the two men came near enough to the well for Mary Kay to overhear. She sank deeper into the grass and flattened herself against the ground, hardly daring to breathe. She crossed all her fingers, squeezed her eyes shut, and pleaded silently, "Please, please, Grandpa, send him away. Do not let him stay. Send him away!"

Grandpa's voice was stern, "This is not the way it should be, Bud. You need to take better care of Grace and the children. This is wrong."

The flicker leapt to a bonfire of hope in Mary Kay's heart, "Yes, good, good!" Grandpa was going to save them! There was silence, and then her father mumbled something she could not hear.

"Maybe so," her grandfather replied, "but you'll get a job before too long. You always have. Now, you take them home and do right by them."

Mary Kay felt all the air escape from her lungs. She was crushed; she felt so completely betrayed she did not know what to do. Her heart had risen in expectation and desire; now it sank into despair. Tears burned her eyes, and she smothered a sob in the cool, damp grass. She loved her Grandpa, but he had made it clear that while he would plead on their behalf, he was not going to intervene. She lay there for a long time after they walked back into the house, bottling up the pain so that she could muster the strength to go back home. She never told anyone, least of all Mama; she did not want to admit that Grandpa had sent them back into that misery.

CHAPTER THREE

The bus passed the abandoned fire tower every day on the way to school. Each day as Mary Kay craned her neck to see the top of the tower through the bus window, her heart raced and her palms sweat. Everyone has some deep-rooted fear; hers was heights. Nothing could chill her spine like looking down from even a second story window.

Mary Kay knew that she would have to climb that tower, someday. She would not do it for the thrill. In her mind, she was certain any unchallenged fear would lead to her destruction—if not her physical death, then the living death of a life controlled by fear. She realized early in life that she could make herself do something whether she wanted to or not. She could tackle fear and toughen herself. She forced herself to endure pain just to show herself and others that she was strong. Fear was the same as weakness, and Mary Kay believed that weakness kept the family trapped in their misery.

Whenever she sensed fear in herself, she felt compelled to conquer it. Even before she was old enough to go to school, she overcame her fear of the dark by walking alone, her heart in her throat, her spine prickling, through the house, across the yard, and into the woods to the outhouse. She did this night after night until she could face the dark walk without fear.

Now, near their latest home, loomed the fire tower. It stood on the same ridge as their house, looking out over a beautiful valley. The tower was the tallest thing she had ever seen, taller than all the trees. Eldon, Missouri, had no skyscrapers; the tallest buildings were two stories. How tall was this tower? To Mary Kay, it seemed at least ten or fifteen stories.

I guess it might as well be today, she thought one day as the bus dropped them off after school. Fear moved into her stomach, turning it over. *No! I will not give in to the fear. I will do it and I will do it today!* she scolded herself. She stood looking in the direction of the tower, but her feet would not move.

"C'mon, Kay. What're you staring at?"

Tom's voice startled her out of her frozen state. She began walking in the opposite direction of her younger brother and sister.

"Hey, where you goin'?"

"You just go on and mind your own business."

Mary Kay did not say this meanly. She turned and gave a weak smile, waving them on toward home. Tom shrugged and began a race with Connie to their house. Mary Kay turned toward the tower. This was a secret thing, for her alone. She set her schoolbooks behind a bush and slowly trudged the quarter mile up the hill toward the tower. The hill shivered with leaping grasshoppers. Spring scents blanketed the soft air. Clouds moved across the sky like flocks of fuzzy sheep. Mary Kay did not notice any of it. Her teeth clenched with determination and dread. Her pace slackened and her feet were heavy as lead.

She arrived at the tower and stood for a long time staring at the lowest step, not daring to look up. She grabbed the rail of the rickety staircase and put her foot on the first step with the steadfast resolve that would be both a blessing and a curse all her life. She began to climb. After the third flight, she released the breath she had been holding in a sudden rush then gasped a huge swallow of air. She was careful to breathe every third step to keep from holding her breath again. It was slow going; halfway up, she stopped. Her head spun so fast she could not look; her stomach rocked. Now she did not have to force her breath; it came in short, shallow pants, making her lightheaded until she thought she might pass out. She sat down on the step and placed her head between her knees. How could she go on? She began a fierce dialogue with herself.

I can do this. Nothing and no one will ever control me. I am not going to let fear get the better of me! "I will do this!" The last words she said aloud and the sound of her voice forced her to stand again. She took a deep breath and started up again on rubbery legs.

She climbed stubbornly. The ground grew farther and farther away through the spaces between the steps. She tried to concentrate only on her shoes as they moved from one step to the next. At last she reached the platform at the top. She stood staring at her feet, gripping the handrail until her knuckles were white. Should she look out? If she didn't, would she truly have conquered her fear? She peeked out from under a damp strand of hair. The gentle hills of the valley rippled from bright green to smoky blue as they faded into the distance. Next time, she might look at the ground and trees so far below her. This time, the horizon was enough.

She did not linger to savor her victory, but went quickly down, watching her shoes as she went. When she reached the last step, she fell in a heap onto the ground and sobbed the fear and tension away. She knew she would have to do it again, just as she had walked into the night to the outhouse so many times. She would keep climbing it, over and over, feeling stronger each time, until she could do it without fear.

No time like the present, she told herself as she grabbed hold of the staircase rail and pulled herself up again. When she at last stood at the top for the tenth time, it was nearly dusk. She stared down at the ground far below with no emotion. The conquest was not satisfying. It was like the bittersweet triumph a soldier feels when he has defeated the enemy but lost his friends. As Mary Kay shut herself off to pain, she also shut out the joy of the beauty around her and the thrill of the victory. She felt nothing but dullness, and from that day forward, her father and the miseries of their life had less of a grip on her.

She grew proud of her tough veneer and sought ways to reinforce it. She faced down many more fears in the years to come without ever tasting the pure exhilaration of victory. Each time, her protective armor grew stronger and thicker, but in the quiet hours, it was simply a shell that hid a scared and lonely Mary Kay. Over the years, it became easier for her to acknowledge the toughened shell than what was hidden deep beneath it.

She was sure that if she just worked hard enough she could save herself; by overcoming her fears and learning to be tough she could keep from being hurt or controlled. And maybe, with enough self-discipline, she could overcome the bad she knew was in her. Whatever the answer, she meant to find it.

Mary Kay had reasoned that good people are weak and bad people are strong. Good people could not help being weak; it was part of being good. Mama was good, her brothers and sisters were good; she and Dad were strong but bad. Since early childhood, she had believed that some people were just good and some people were bad, and she was a bad one. A Christian turns the other cheek and since she did not do this, then either she was not a Christian or she was not a good Christian. She continued to look for ways to erase the guilt she felt and make amends for being bad.

Mary Kay built a protective wall with beliefs like these: "The strong survive but they are bad"; "If you conquer your fears, no one can control you"; "Submission only makes you weak and unhappy, caught in a trap under someone else's control"; "If you stop feeling, pain can't get in and you'll be okay"; and "You have to take care of yourself because no one else will."

One belief stood above the rest. She was certain that anything wrong in her life was her father's fault. With a different father, she would have been a different person, a good person. He was to blame for everything. Therefore, in order to be sane, safe, and happy, she had to be free of him. She had to get away. She did not realize then that her troubles and her walls would go along with her.

Then her fainting spells began. She was afraid she was going to die. She would suddenly awaken to find that she had been lying unconscious for up to fifteen or twenty minutes. What was wrong? This fear could not be conquered simply by climbing a tower or venturing into the dark night. She could not will away this fear; it haunted even her dreams. She was no stranger to doctors and hospitals; she did *not* want to go there again.

Mary Kay's first trip to the hospital had come after a long night of suffering from severe stomach pain. Mama finally convinced Dad to take Mary Kay to the emergency room.

"It is just plain foolishness. She isn't really sick; she's just acting up," her Dad fumed. Mary Kay curled up in the back seat of the car, her head in her mother's lap. "This is gonna cost a pretty penny, that's for sure."

"I'm sorry," she said weakly as Mama wiped her hot forehead with a damp rag. She looked up at her mother and whispered, "I'm so very sorry." She knew she was not worth the time and trouble. Mama quieted her and told her it was okay, but Mary Kay apologized and Dad complained all the way to the hospital.

At first, the doctors thought Mary Kay had appendicitis and prepped her for surgery. But as they wheeled her down the hall toward the operating room, the tests came back: an acute ovarian infection. They wheeled her back to her room and put her on antibiotics and pain medication. Dad was not convinced; he insisted she was just looking for attention.

That was not the only time Mary Kay was hospitalized. Once she had thrush and another time a severely infected tooth that led to blood poisoning. Then another ovarian infection sent her back to the emergency room. Each time she was taken to a different hospital in the county because Dad had not paid the bills at the last one. Each time he complained and she felt guilty, apologizing for bothering everyone. Years afterward, far away from Dad, she still felt pangs of guilt whenever she was sick.

Now, the fainting spells were filling her with unconquerable fear and guilt. She did not want to go through it all again but fainting was hard to hide. Mama insisted she see the doctor, but he was unable to find the cause. They could not afford the lengthy testing the doctor recommended. She would have to live with the fainting, the fear, and the guilt.

One place where she could escape the fear and hurt of home was her 4-H club. As she did in school, she worked hard in 4-H to excel, and she won several awards. She felt better at these functions, and oddly, she rarely fainted at school, church, or club except when she'd had a fight with Dad before she went.

One spring she spent long hours on the sewing machines at school making a skirt and blouse. She chose a difficult pattern and took care to make sure each detail was flawless. The county fair was coming; she planned to enter her beautiful garment.

She tried on the skirt and blouse and stood before the mirror on the door of the tiny closet in the bedroom she shared with her two sisters. She turned round and round, checking to make sure the hem was even, watching for loose threads.

It looks perfect, she thought, *even if I do say so myself. I think it has a real chance at the fair.*

Suddenly she heard footsteps in the hall. She recognized the drunken stagger of her father. Her heart froze, and she pressed herself into the closet. She was alone in the house; he mustn't know she was here. She reached for the handle on the closet door and tried to pull it quietly shut. The rusty hinges protested, and she released the handle.

Had he heard the door's squeaking hinges? She watched through the crack. Her heart leapt into her throat; there he was, coming closer. He pulled open the door and before she could run past, he pressed himself up against her. There was a ripping sound as he pulled at her blouse. In his intoxicated state, he lost his balance and stumbled. Here was her chance! Mary Kay shoved him backward out the door and into the hall as hard as she could. He grabbed her skirt as she ran past and pulled himself up, tearing it away from the waistband. She turned and scratched at his hands and arms, struggling to loosen his grip on her. He was too drunk to fight back. He cursed, let go, and lurched into his bedroom, passing out on the bed.

Mary Kay looked down. Her blouse and skirt were ripped and covered with smelly, wet liquor stains from the bottle he had gripped the whole time. Her clothes looked like she felt on the inside, dirty and torn. She grabbed a dress from her closet and ran outside as fast as she could toward the barn. A gravel road separated the house and barn; the stones dug into her bare feet. She ducked under the strands of the barbed wire fence.

Instead of following the cow path as she normally did, she angled to the left toward the darker part of the woods. The children did not play here. She ran through the thick underbrush, angrily swiping aside the limbs in front of her. Heart pounding, she was unaware of the brambles that tore at her bare legs. She ran to the creek that meandered through the property. Far away from the house, she pulled off her ruined clothes and scrubbed her skin in the water until she was numb with cold. She pulled the gray and yellow striped dress from the closet over her damp skin. Twisting the discarded skirt and blouse into a small bundle, she looked around. At dusk it was difficult to see in the fading light. Her hands and body shook.

I'm just cold from the water, she assured herself as she moved back into the woods. She would not entertain the notion that the trembling had anything to do with fear. She picked up a firm stick and started digging at the soil by a big oak. She dug with a fury through the damp leaves and soft topsoil. She dug and dug until she could barely reach the bottom of the hole. She sat back.

I could bury a body in this hole, she thought and an image of burying her father there filled her with satisfaction. She grabbed the skirt and blouse. "I wish this was you," she said to the image in her mind as she shoved the clothes into the hole. She would not look as she pushed the dark earth over them.

She stood up and brushed the dirt from her knees, her dress, and her hands. What if Mama asked her about the skirt? When Mary Kay had complained about having to use a flour sack for her sewing, Mama had found some remnants on sale so she could have new material like the other girls. Shame washed over her in waves; she felt her face turning red, and nausea rose in her throat as she moved away from the tree back to the creek. She stared at the water, rushing over the rocks on its way to somewhere. She wanted to be that water and flow far away, to anywhere but here.

She hid in the cool of the woods, burning with hate and shame. She waited until suppertime, when she was sure the others would be back. Then she picked her way through the dark woods. It was true night when she strode across the yard to the back door. The rest of the family had returned and the chatter in the kitchen sounded cheerful; Dad must still be passed out on the bed. As she reached for the door handle, she wondered how life could have changed so little and yet so much.

Just as she had buried her clothes in the woods, she buried the whole day in a deep place in her mind. She had to revive it only once—when Mama asked about the skirt and blouse. Mary Kay muttered something about not liking the results and deciding not to enter the fair after all. Mama looked puzzled, but said nothing.

CHAPTER FOUR

The fainting spells increased in frequency after that horrible day. While before they had lasted only a minute or two, now the periods of unconsciousness grew longer. Mary Kay began to worry about rare diseases. They still had no medical diagnosis, but Dr. Buehler suggested to Grace that her daughter might have juvenile onset epilepsy. Mary Kay overheard him and went to the dictionary at school to look up epilepsy. "Brain wave irregularity." It made her think of monster movies. Was she some kind of freak? Was she turning into a monster? She hoped no one found out; what would her friends say? At times, rage rose inside her like a tide erasing the shore until nothing remains but waves beating against the rocks.

Eventually, Mary Kay was admitted to Latham Sanitarium. Many years earlier it had been a tuberculosis sanitarium, but now it was just a small clinic. Children had their tonsils taken out and women had their babies, but no one stayed more than a few days. Cases that were more serious went to the large hospitals in Jefferson City, more than thirty miles away. Their doctor, knowing the family had no money, arranged for Mary Kay to go to Latham's.

None of the tests explained the fainting spells or the recurring ovarian infections. Latham was not equipped to do the further tests. After a few days she went home, but only briefly. University Hospital in Columbia, Missouri, was sixty miles and a lifetime away from Eldon. Mary Kay was admitted to the pediatrics unit.

She was barely fifteen but older than most of the other children. Many were crippled with far more serious physical problems. She was the only patient there for mental reasons, although no one actually called it a nervous breakdown. Mary Kay felt like a freak. The term stress was not yet a common word, and certainly not used in discussions of children. The doctors still believed there must be an organic cause for her fainting spells. To Mary Kay, any trouble involving the brain or one's mind meant one thing—she was going crazy.

Each day a staff member in a wheelchair came to visit her. He had cerebral palsy and his speech was slightly slurred. They spent their time reading and talking about school. He administered tests and, to her satisfaction, she passed them all. She looked forward to these sessions just as she had always looked forward to school.

In addition to the tests with her wheelchair instructor, she went through a series of medical tests, including an EEG; this was the crucial test. Mary Kay feared it, dreaded it, yet looked forward to it with curiosity. She was certain this would give the answer to her fainting. She lay on a flat gurney with no pillow beneath her head. A white sheet covered her cotton hospital gown.

"You might feel a little pricking as I place these electrodes," explained the nurse as she smeared greasy stuff onto Mary Kay's temples. The nurse moved around, placing copper wires on each temple, above each ear, and on top of her head. "Lie very still and try not to move. You'll be OK."

A long sigh escaped Mary Kay's lips; she did not realize she had been holding her breath. She tried not to think about the scene in *Frankenstein* when the electricity was turned on. Each minute felt like five until nearly a half hour inched by.

"All done," said the nurse suddenly beside her. She removed the wires and wiped away the cream. "You can go back, take a shower, and wash your hair if you'd like. You'll have time before lunch is served." A shower was as unfamiliar a luxury as three full hot meals every day. She felt guilty that her brothers and sisters could not share this with her.

She did not know whether she was relieved or disappointed when the tests came back normal. There was still the question of why she had the fainting spells.

The hospital was a refuge; an escape from Dad where someone listened to the hurt and anger hidden for so long. Each afternoon, after the lunch trays were removed and most of the other children were taking a nap, her doctor came by to visit. He was a psychiatrist and he stayed much longer than the orthopedic doctor who visited the little girl across the hall. They sat in two chairs by the window while the nurse who always accompanied him sat by the door.

After a little casual chitchat, he asked, "Now, where did we leave off?" Mary Kay made a point of remembering his last sentence, and he was initially surprised at this. Soon he began to expect her to remember exactly what had been said the previous day.

"You really do hate him," the psychiatrist commented one day when she paused from one of her fiery condemnations of her father's behavior.

"Yes, I do! With all my heart!"

"And it doesn't bother him a bit," remarked the doctor.

Mary Kay sat in stunned silence for a moment. "You mean he doesn't care that I hate him? The things I say or do don't even make him *uncomfortable?*"

"I doubt it. Most likely, his self-centeredness runs so deep that he is hardly aware of the effect it has on you or anyone else. He simply reacts to what you say or do at the time, but I doubt he even remembers it later."

"But he's always thinking of ways to hurt me!"

She saw the look of skepticism on the doctor's face. "Are you saying he doesn't do those things *on purpose?*" she asked.

"I suspect he doesn't think about them at all, before, during or after. It just happens."

She was stunned by the notion that not only did she not make Dad uncomfortable, but also that he neither noticed nor cared when he was being mean and abusive. She had honestly believed he plotted against her as she did against him. The conviction that her father hated her was awful, but somehow the thought that he did not care one way or another was even worse. Her heart ached as a wave of sorrow began to build. Tears held back far too long threatened to spill. With great effort she pushed them down into their hidden place behind the protective wall she had built.

The doctor sat quietly watching her, and when she seemed controlled again he asked gently, "Have you considered that your anger and resentment toward him might be a way of getting even with him?"

She was not ready to face that question. Her anger seemed more than justified, and at this moment, it was the only feeling she had left. What the doctor said gnawed at her.

"Have I been trying to get even with my father?" she wondered. "Well, of course, I have! Wouldn't anyone? It obviously did not work! Why, he didn't even care when I fainted."

Her words stung her like a slap in the face and seemed to hang in the room as her mind raced. The fainting—had it been another way to get even, to scare her father into showing a hint of concern? She felt a strange mixture of anger, sadness, and relief at this realization. Maybe there wasn't anything wrong with her after all, and she didn't have to be afraid of her fainting spells anymore. In fact, she did not need to faint at all! The relief she felt convinced her it must be true.

A few days later, she told the doctor she had come to the conclusion that her fainting was an unconscious attempt to get back at her dad. She had decided not to do it anymore. The doctor grinned broadly. Perhaps he mistook her lack of emotion for acceptance of her situation but her quick and easy coping was actually building a thicker defensive wall. This doctor apparently did not notice or he just wanted to believe he had cured her. Whatever his thinking, he released her after only a few weeks in the hospital, giving instructions that she was not to return home.

Relieved, she went to Illinois to stay with her older sister Joyce, who was married with four young children. For the rest of the summer, Mary Kay helped her sister, doing housework, and babysitting. As she anticipated, the fainting spells stopped. The normality of this life was both strange and refreshing.

Back home, things were getting worse. Dad stole some dynamite and caps from the rock quarry where he was working. He intended to kill Mama and the kids, but instead he blew fingers off his own hand and was admitted to the hospital. Mama was finally convinced that it was not safe to remain with him any longer. His stay in the hospital gave her the opportunity to leave. Her older children moved her and the younger kids to Iowa to live with her eldest daughter, Jean.

When Dad was released, he filed for divorce in a fit of anger. He never believed Mama would let him go through with the divorce. He wrote to her, telling her his intentions, but she did not answer, so the state granted him the divorce. In Missouri, when one party does not respond, the dependent children become wards of the court.

After the divorce was final, Dad followed them to Iowa. Mama grew fearful that he might take the kids. She told the school, "Don't let him pick up the children."

"You have to have proof of custody before you can prevent a parent from taking his children," the school officials told her.

Jean urged Mama to petition for custody. Still, Mama was hesitant. It ran against everything she believed. She knew God hated divorce; the Bible said so.

"You can't run the risk of his running away with the kids like he did Bill," Jean said, gently but firmly.

Fear filled Mama's eyes. She bowed her head and reached for the papers; her hand shook as she signed them and handed them to her daughter. Jean dropped her eyes and pretended to examine the papers; she could not stand the look of pain, fear, and sorrow in her mother's eyes. Jean filed the papers; with Bud's history, the courts willingly granted Mama full legal custody.

Mama wanted Mary Kay to come back to the family now that Dad was out of the picture. Mary Kay panicked. She was afraid Mama would let Dad come back; she had so many times before. How could she avoid going home? What reason could she give for refusing Mama?

"I'm not going back; I'm not ever going back," she told Jim.[1] They had been seeing each other since Mary Kay moved to Illinois. He was the first boy she had ever dated.

"If you marry me, you won't have to go back." Mary Kay stared at him in disbelief.

"But I don't love you," she blurted out, and then softened her tone at his wounded look. "You're a good man and I'm quite fond of you, but I don't love you the way a woman should love a husband."

"I don't care," he assured her, "I love *you*. That's enough."

Jim did not drink, he had a job, and it seemed like her only escape. Anything

---

[1] Name changed

was better than going home but what about love and living happily ever after?

I guess that is for someone else, she thought, *someone who did not have Bud Petet for a father. That kind of marriage is probably just a fairy tale anyway.* This was one more disappointment and resentment to lock away behind her wall. She did worry about Jim, though. Was it really fair to him? She brought it up again a few days later, just to be sure. His assurances that he loved enough for both of them did not ease her guilt.

Well, at least I am being honest with him. I'll stay with him and be a good wife to him. After all, he's offering me an out, she rationalized, *and maybe he's right, and I will come to love him.*

Each time Mary Kay suspected that what she was doing was wrong, she suppressed the feeling with feeble excuses and justifications. Finally the little voice inside almost faded away. Her ability to block things out had been a blessing. It freed her to enjoy things like school and church activities without the cloud of misery that hung over her home life. Now it became a curse as she blocked out the truth of what she was doing to herself and to Jim. She would not admit she was using this man's affections to achieve her immediate goal.

So at fifteen, she became a bride. Jim was nineteen. Since she was under eighteen, his mother pretended to be Mary Kay's mom and signed the application for the marriage license. After the wedding, they moved in with his parents. She had finished high school before going to Latham. Now she wanted more education, so she enrolled at Moline Public Hospital School of Nursing. Jim found work as a mechanic. Soon they bought a tiny house; it did not even have an indoor toilet, but it was theirs.

"The hospital is looking for night nurses." Mary Kay said one evening trying to sound casual. She had graduated at seventeen, the youngest woman in the state of Illinois to become an RN. This was also the year their first child was born.

"There isn't any reason for you to work." Jim said. "I am supporting this family just fine."

"Oh, I wasn't suggesting that you're not." She knew Jim wanted her to stay at home with their new son. "I was thinking that if I worked nights, I could still be home during the day with the baby."

"Why do you want to go out and work? Folks will think I can't take care of my own."

"But if I don't work, I won't be able to keep my nursing license current. I *want* to work. I like it and it won't take that much time. If I work twelve-hour shifts, I'll only be gone three nights a week."

"That's too much. If I'm going to support the family, then why do you need to keep your license current?"

"But I have *always* wanted a career," Mary Kay protested. "Being a stay-at-home mom was never a goal of mine."

"Well, I guess you should have thought of that when we got married."

"I didn't think when we got married it would be the end of all my dreams. If you would just let me work, everything will be fine. I can take care of the house, the baby, and you, and *still* work. Please let me try."

Jim said he would think about it, but in the end, all they did was fight over it. She had not imagined that in using marriage to get away from Dad she would be nearly as trapped. With every passing year she felt she was suffocating more and more. When she turned twenty, she was in a loveless marriage with a toddler and a new baby girl. The dreams of a career and a stimulating life that she had cherished since childhood were vanishing.

Her lack of love, though acceptable to Jim in the beginning, wore on him. As he sensed her acceptance of him slip away, he became more possessive and frantic to hold on to her. He restricted her activities. She could not have a driver's license, and he would not allow a telephone in the house. He wanted to know where she was at all times, whom she was with, and what she was doing.

In his desperation to hang onto her, his kind and easy-going manner disappeared. She was his wife and she had better do what he said, or else. She knew what "or else" looked like. She had lived with it all her life. So she shut up and obeyed, even as a new root of bitterness began to grow.

Sadly for everyone involved, in an effort to shut out the unhappiness of her life and the pain of her mistakes, Mary Kay's heart hardened. As it did, she discovered she felt little bonding with her children and no compassion for her husband. She was in a prison of her own making. The only emotions left were the two that she had sworn as a child no man would drive her to: anger and fear.

Her anger, as usual, was directed mainly toward her father. Somehow, this too, was his fault. To Mary Kay, it seemed her father was poisoning every area of her life. *If he had been different,* she thought, *I would not be in this mess. I would not have had to get married to get away from him.*

Her husband's continuous insistence that she give up her dreams stirred her old aversion to being controlled. Years earlier she had made a vow: Nobody is going to do to me what Dad did to Mama. *Nobody is going to tell me what to do. I am going to be in charge; I am going to be in control.*

A vow is a dangerous thing; it wraps around the will, hanging on like a python with a death grip. Initially, the person takes the vow, but later the vow takes the person—dictating thoughts, words, and actions that might not have been there but for its hold on the will.

The more Jim resisted her pulling away, the tighter her vow gripped her. They tried marriage counseling but it was too late; she had already decided. She just wanted out. She never gave the counseling a chance. It seemed too hopeless to her; escaping one bad situation did not prove to be reason enough to stay in another.

Jim's patience completely disappeared when he realized she was giving up on the marriage. She would not subject her children to a marriage even remotely like her parents. Once she had fled to Missouri before her daughter was born, but Jim chased her down and forced her to return. She did not want to go through that again. So the next time, she left without the children.

A battle for custody began but quickly lost steam. Her husband would not allow her to take the children. Mary Kay had no job and no plans; she did not know how she would support herself, much less two children. She needed time to get on her feet well enough to provide a decent home for them. She certainly did not want them to grow up in poverty as she had.

Without her around to ignite his temper, Jim seemed to be a good and stable man. Mary Kay considered herself neither stable nor good. She was more convinced than ever that she was completely wicked. Jim was devoted to the children; it truly seemed in their best interest for them to stay with him.

Poverty was not the only issue. She feared that her anger at her father might spill over onto her children. She did not want them to grow up angry and fearful all the time. She was volatile and she knew it. It never occurred to her to deal with her anger and get rid of it; she would not have known how if it had.

Mary Kay found a room in a boarding house and work at a local hospital as a nurse. Jim's parents took care of the children while he worked. They were kind and loving, but when Mary Kay came for her visits, her in-laws always seemed to have the children out of town or busy with activities. Eventually, Mary Kay just spent miserable hours sitting in her car down the street watching her own children play in the yard. If she was seen, the children were whisked into the house.

"Jim, you need to let me see the kids. It's not fair to them or to me."

"You should have thought about that before you left."

"Did you really want to go on the way we were? Do you think it was good for them to see either of us like that?" The phone line was silent. Jim had hung up.

The world and the law were not sympathetic either. In 1965, small-town Illinois judges did not look kindly on women who left their husbands and children for no apparent reason. In December, they were divorced, and Jim received full custody. The door to that pain was not easily shut. When she felt weak or when she was not careful, the door would fly open. There was nothing she could do but keep slamming it shut.

She was still struggling to keep this pain locked away ten months later, when she met Paul Mahaffey.

CHAPTER FIVE

C ome on, Mary Kay. You never go out. All you ever do is work and sleep. Let's go have some fun!"

Patty was leaning against the lockers in the nurse's lounge. She had made this plea before. She was right; Mary Kay's whole life revolved around work, and the off hours were long and dull.

"I guess the only way I'm going to get you off my back is to come with you," replied Mary Kay.

"It's about time! You are so serious. Let's go to that new nightclub downtown."

Going to a nightclub was the last thing Mary Kay wanted to do. She neither drank nor smoked, but she had already agreed and maybe there would be good music. She glanced in the mirror, put on some fresh lipstick, and pulled her keys from her purse. She suspected that Patty's reason for inviting her along was that Mary Kay had her own car.

The nightclub was just what she expected, dark and smoky. Thankfully, the music was good. Patty looked around the room for a moment and then pulled Mary Kay over to a table with a dark-haired, rugged-looking man

"Hello, Tony," she cooed as she slipped into the booth.

I've been set up, thought Mary Kay. *She had a date all along.*

"Come on, Mary Kay," she said pointing to the empty spot on the other side of Tony, "sit down and let's have some fun." Mary Kay hesitated for a moment, but then joined them in the booth. Patty reached for Tony's drink and took a huge gulp. "Mmmm, I needed that." She eyed Mary Kay to see how she would react as she introduced her to the young man.

Mary Kay gave her a swift scowl and smiled weakly at Tony. "It's nice to

41

meet you," she said. As angry as she was, she would not neglect her manners; Mama taught her always to be polite. When the waitress came, she ordered a soda and Patty ordered a cocktail. She finished several drinks before Mary Kay ordered another soda.

"Ah, here he is." Tony stood and reached out his hand to a handsome, blond man. "Mary Kay and Patty, this is Paul Mahaffey. Paul, this is Mary Kay and this is Patty."

Now she *knew* she had been set up, literally; this man was supposed to be her date. She was disappointed, but not surprised when he slipped into the booth next to Patty, who was bubbly and pretty. Mary Kay had never had any illusions about her looks. She always thought of herself as ugly; she assumed everyone else did, too. Whenever someone introduced her and her sisters, they would say, "These are Grace's daughters. Mary Kay is the smart one." She was sure they meant the others were the pretty ones. So it followed that this attractive man would rather not be seen sitting next to her. Still, the letdown burned in her throat like a gulp of hot liquid.

Paul kept looking at her throughout the conversation; she felt like some odd exhibit. She used the only tools she thought she had, her brains and her sharp wit. Though she tried hard to be amusing and clever, she felt defeated from the moment he sat next to Patty, who by now was drunk and silly. The evening was turning out to be worse than she had imagined. Even the boredom and loneliness of her boarding house room was better than this.

If that's what men prefer, thought Mary Kay, watching Patty grin seductively at one man and then the other, *I would rather be alone for the rest of my life.* She had little experience with dating; she had married the first man she had ever dated and there had been no one since her divorce. After a while, Paul picked up his drink, excused himself, and moved to the bar.

Well! He made it clear he didn't like me much, thought Mary Kay. The snub stung dreadfully, and all she wanted was to leave that place. Remembering that she was driving her own car, she said goodbye to Tony and Patty. They did not even seem to notice as she stood to go. As she strode past Paul at the bar she could not resist a sarcastic remark.

"It's not much of a man who can't even be polite to a blind date."

He looked shocked and quickly glanced at the couple left at the table. By now, they were snuggled together in the booth, and it was obvious how their evening would end. Paul jumped off the stool and grabbed her arm, turning her to face him.

"But . . . but . . . I figured Tony must be with you," stammered Paul. "He always goes for the pretty ones."

Mary Kay was not prepared for this response. No one ever said she was pretty. She felt an unfamiliar surge of warmth across her cheeks, melting away all her hurt and anger.

"My behavior *was* rude," he continued. "Please let me make it up to you. May I apologize over a late supper?"

What could she do? He was so courteous and earnest, and his touch on her arm seemed electrified. Just as her throat had tightened with disappointment before, now her heart tightened with excitement and pleasure.

"Well, I guess so," she said, "but I have my own car."

"I came with a friend so I don't have one. Would you mind driving? We could eat at the dining room in my hotel."

At the look of uncertainty that flashed across her face, he quickly added, "Just for dinner. That's all. It would be convenient, but if you are uncomfortable . . ."

"Oh, no," she interrupted, "that's a good idea." His manners impressed her. She felt respected and protected. She was not used to these feelings, but she liked them. They walked to her car, and when he offered to drive she let him. He opened the door for her. This was new also; a flutter of excitement and pleasure ran through her. She thought she might like a lot about this man.

She had never seen anything so grand as the hotel lobby and dining room. The nicest place she had ever gone to was Howard Johnson's on her wedding night. Everything Paul did impressed her, from his smooth manner with the waiter to the expensive, fashionable clothes he wore. The places he talked about sounded glamorous and exciting. She had seen only a few small Midwestern towns and the roads in between.

That's what I need, she thought, *adventure. I need to travel. That is what I am looking for; I live such a boring life.*

43

The peace and contentment she longed for were forever elusive, just around the next corner. Her thoughts revolved around the same theme, endlessly and hopelessly. Her problems were not *her* responsibility; all she needed was to change the people, places, and things in her life.

If I could just go somewhere else, if I could just get out of this town, if I could just change my present situation then I'd be okay, then I'd be happy. If I had enough money or a better job, if I just had this, if I could just get away from that, if . . . . The list never ended, but now, in Paul she had found someone who knew how to live.

"May I take you out again?" he asked, as he walked her to her car.

She hoped he would ask but did not want to appear too excited. "I have to check my work schedule. When were you thinking about?"

"How about tomorrow?" His eagerness sent a surge of delight through her. He continued, "Here's my number, call me and let me know. Next time, we take *my* car." He reached out and opened her car door. She hesitated, but he did not lean in for a kiss.

Good, she thought, *he's not too forward.* Aloud she said, "I think I can get off tomorrow night." She smiled up at him.

My goodness, she thought as she drove away, *that's a first. I believe I just flirted with a man!* It felt strange but good. She decided right then to be available whenever he asked. She knew she could convince other nurses to trade shifts with her; she helped with their schedules often enough. She cashed in many paybacks in the next week; Paul took her out every night.

He obviously had money, and to a young woman who spent her lifetime in utter poverty, that was no small bonus. When a heart is as hard as Mary Kay's had become, it takes a lot to stir it. It takes edge and Paul had edge. He was mysterious and exciting, charming and fun, sexy and sophisticated. She had not even dared to dream of such a man.

Paul overwhelmed her with attention and gifts; she had never felt so loved and special. When she was with him, she hardly felt the pain anymore. Her father, her kids, her failed marriage—all faded into a foggy past. He was a drug and she wanted more.

On the eighth day, he had to leave town on business. He asked her to come along. She was torn up inside at the thought of his leaving. *But I cannot just go off and live with him. It just wouldn't be right*, she thought. *Or would it?*

Mary Kay was losing her grip on what was right and wrong, but in the end, it was Mama's lessons on morality that prevailed. She hemmed and hawed and finally said, "It wouldn't be right and besides, I can't leave my job." She felt better about herself, but it was not much comfort.

Though he promised to come back, she felt hollow, as if her last chance at happiness had left with him. Already she was pinning her hopes on him. He was the man of her dreams, her knight in shining armor, and her ticket to paradise. A cold knot of fear gripped her when she thought she might never see him again.

"I should have gone with him. Who cares about what others think I should or shouldn't do?"

He called her at work three times that day. When she got home, he called again. This time he said, "Why don't we just go ahead and get married?"

Some choices come like the sudden appearance of a cliff around a turn. Mary Kay was not usually impulsive. This time, however, she blindly stepped off the cliff without a thought of the consequences. When one falls so fast and hard, reason seldom comes along. The inner, cautioning voice that she had muffled so many times was now barely a whisper. Instead, she listened to the call to freedom and joy, or at the very least, to an escape from her empty life. She packed her meager belongings, loaded them in her car, and drove off toward an unimaginable future.

PART TWO:

CRIMINAL LIFE

CHAPTER SIX

She drove all night to meet Paul at a truck stop in Marion, Indiana, at five o'clock on a Friday morning. They ate breakfast as they waited for daylight.

Paul asked, "Are you sleepy? Do you need a nap?" Mary Kay shook her head. She was far too keyed up to even think of sleep. What was she doing in this strange place with a man she hardly knew? She was known for being fearless, but this was the riskiest thing she had done in all her twenty-one years. Suddenly an image of Mama flashed across her mind. What will *she* say? Her journey down a river of happiness suddenly hit a snag—fear of Mama's disapproval. She simply pushed away from the obstruction and did not look back as she floated blissfully along.

"What are we going to do, next?" she asked, marveling at how gorgeous his eyes looked in the first light of the most wonderful day of her life.

"To begin with, we'll get you fixed up nice for your wedding day." He put his arm around her and kissed her hair. "I saw a dress shop in town. You'll find a nice outfit there."

She glanced at the casual slacks and blouse she wore. *How could such a good-looking man as Paul give me a second glance?* She turned her face up to him with adoration and awe in her eyes and nodded.

At nine o'clock, they stood at the door of a beauty salon as the manager unlocked it. Paul led her in and said, "We're getting married this afternoon. I want you to make my bride beautiful: hair, makeup, the works."

Paul left after getting a haircut himself. Mary Kay got "The Works": shampoo, cut and style, facial, manicure, pedicure and complete makeup. She wondered how much it would all cost. She was apprehensive when he returned, but he paid the bill without a blink and left a very generous tip besides. She was astonished at his generosity. Why was he so good to her?

Next he led her into a small exclusive boutique. An older, sophisticated-looking woman greeted them immediately. Before Mary Kay could even think of what to say, Paul took charge and gave instructions as he had in the beauty salon. The woman led them to the back of the store, where Paul sat in a comfortable chair. For more than an hour, the clerk brought outfit after outfit for Mary Kay to try on. The clerk directed most of her conversation to Paul, who gave his approval or disapproval each time his bride-to-be emerged from the dressing room.

Mary Kay was relieved he was making the decisions; she had no idea what he wanted to spend or what he thought was appropriate. Each item looked beautiful to her, but sometimes the prices made her gasp with dread. No one she knew ever spent this much money on clothes. What would he do when he learned how expensive they were?

When there were six complete outfits with shoes and accessories set aside, Paul was ready to leave.

"Which one of the six did you decide to keep?" Mary Kay asked.

"All of them. We'll get more later, but we're leaving here early in the morning, so this will have to do for now." Turning to the clerk, he smiled and thanked her for her help while removing bill after bill from his money clip.

Mary Kay stood speechless as the clerk covered each outfit with a plastic garment bag bearing the name of the shop. These six outfits cost more than all the clothes she had ever owned in her whole life! Surely this must be some kind of dream.

"Let's just get a hamburger. Then we can get dressed and go to the courthouse," Paul said.

"Which dress should I wear?" Her voice was soft and timid, quite unlike her. She was not afraid of a man who had beaten her, but now she was unsettled by a man who cherished her.

"It's too early in the day to wear the sequined dress. I like that green one," Paul answered.

After they ate, he took her to his hotel to shower and change. The dress he had chosen for her to wear to their wedding was a knee-length A-line, the color of Paul's eyes. This was not her favorite dress, but she did not dare point this out after his generosity. Mary Kay hid her disappointment at not wearing the dress of her choice to her own wedding. The green one matched well with the sports jacket and tie Paul was wearing, and that consoled her.

The Marion courthouse stood in the middle of the town square. Indiana required no waiting period before marriage; they obtained their license and went directly into the judge's chambers. His secretary stood in as their witness. The ceremony was brief and to the point. When the judge asked about a ring, Mary Kay began to shake her head.

"I have it right here." Paul reached into his pocket and pulled out a small velvet box. The rings were beautiful: an engagement ring with a center diamond surrounded by smaller diamonds that matched the ones on the wedding band.

When had he bought them? They must have cost a fortune! She barely listened as she followed the judge's instructions. As Paul kissed her, she kept thinking, *we're married!* She floated through the rest of the day and evening.

The next day, after a leisurely breakfast, they packed their things and left for the Wisconsin Dells. He decided it would be a good place to spend their honeymoon—he also had business there. She went along with the idea without giving it another thought; she would do anything for her incredible, surprising husband.

The drive would take hours and she followed close behind him in her car until they reached a town crisscrossed with one-way streets. Suddenly, at a traffic light, he was no longer in front of her. Her eyes scanned the streets in front, behind, and on both sides.

Where did he go? How did I miss him? Am I ahead of him or did he pull over? Did he turn? As she sat at the light, a growing sense of dread filled her, until a loud honk startled her. Her heart leaped, *It's him!* But it was only a perturbed driver.

I had better backtrack and look for him. She turned around but after a few miles she lost hope that this was the right solution. *Now, he is getting farther and farther ahead of me. I have driven eight hours to marry him, and twenty-four hours later, I've lost him!*

She turned around again but got lost in the web of one-way streets. When she was finally on the right road again, she drove anxiously until she was nearly in a panic. She knew they had planned to stop in Beaver Dam that day, but she did not know *where* in the town. The only thing she could do was to keep going, sometimes driving fast to see if she might catch him and sometimes slowing down to see if he might catch up with her. The ball of worry in her stomach grew heavier and heavier. She pulled into the town well after midnight. An old hotel stood on the main street; she parked and rushed in. She rang the bell at the desk until the night manager appeared. No, Paul Mahaffey was not registered. She sank into a deep chair in the lobby, too numb and tired to think of what to do next.

Paul, too, was worried when he realized she was not following shortly behind him. He waited on the side of the road for nearly an hour. When she did not arrive, he drove on to Beaver Dam, stopped at an all night café, and went through a stack of coins calling police stations in towns along the way. No accidents reported. Perhaps her car had broken down. He would have to wait until morning to start calling mechanics' shops. He ordered coffee and a sandwich and ate hurriedly at the counter, all the while keeping his eye on the road outside the picture windows. After paying, he got back into his car and drove around the town looking for her car.

Fortunately, it was a small town, and on his third pass through, he spotted her car on the street in front of the historic hotel; a pink 1957 Chevy Bel Air was hard to miss. When he strode into the lobby, she jumped up, threw her arms around him, and clung tightly.

"We're not doing this anymore," he declared. "No more traveling separately." The next day they sold her car. She felt lighter than air; she never wanted to lose him again.

Beaver Dam, Wisconsin, was a beautiful, quaint little town. They stayed for nearly a month before heading on to their next stop. Their life seemed like one long honeymoon. They lived on the road, staying in nice hotels, eating out, visiting museums and historical sites, and going to movies during the day. Sometimes, in the evenings, he left her to go to business meetings. "Men *do* work at night," she reasoned with herself. She hadn't yet asked what he did for a living.

Shopping was a favorite pastime; she marveled at the money he spent. He chose the beautiful and expensive clothes that complemented her coloring and shape—with shoes and accessories to match, of course. He bought her furs and fine jewelry just to watch the amazement on her face. He enjoyed the wonder and delight she showed in discovering each new activity, each new place.

He took her to the beauty salon and chose a new hairstyle for her. When Mary Kay was growing up, the beauty shop was only for very special occasions. Once a year, before they started school, Mama took them to a friend who worked out of her home. All the girls got poodle cuts. Now she went whenever she wanted, sometimes more than once a week. She had pedicures and manicures. She had never even heard of a pedicure before meeting Paul; this unbelievable luxury was now hers.

Paul gave her everything she had given up dreaming of, and things of which she had not even thought to dream. She rode a wave of excited adoration and excessive luxury. They traveled to cities and places that before had been merely names in books. Real life was so much better. She was living her own personal fairy tale, now she knew how Cinderella felt.

One day, in Chicago, he announced suddenly, "We're going to get you a wig. They're all the rage now; how about blond?" While they were at the wig maker, he also ordered a long fall to match her own hair color.

"Now you're going to Elizabeth Arden. They'll teach you how to do makeup to match the different hair colors and how to fix your hair." She was not used to wearing makeup and felt a bit embarrassed; did he think she wasn't beautiful enough? She spent nearly a whole day at the salon as they pampered her; she felt like quite a fine lady when she walked out with a bag full of cosmetics. From that day forward, she was careful to always wear makeup.

Mary Kay especially felt like a fine lady around his friends. He seemed to have them in every town. These men were different from anyone she knew; they smoked, drank, and used profanity. Because she was articulate and had a large vocabulary, she felt that this kind of behavior was beneath her. Paul liked and encouraged this snobbery on her part. He would tell the men, "This is my wife and she doesn't talk that way, so don't talk that way in front of her." His pride and protection made her feel loved.

She was so afraid she would suddenly wake up from this dream; she could not find the courage to ask where all his money came from. Had he inherited it? Had he been a huge success in some business and was now retired? He *was* older than she was by thirteen years. His constant affection and attention lulled her into a sense of security. Occasionally, her curiosity would get the better of her. Though she knew he did not like to talk about himself, she could not help asking questions from time to time.

"Do you have any family?"

"Yes, but I haven't had contact with them in twenty years."

"Why?"

She could only ask about two questions before he became irritable, changed the subject, or busied himself with something. After a long while, she discovered that he had a gambling habit. All the nights when he left her alone to go to business meetings, he actually went to card games. At first, this bothered the tender conscience from her Christian upbringing.

Oh, well, she finally rationalized, *the players are all adults, and if they want to gamble, they can; it's their money. If it's not a problem for Paul or the others, why should it be a problem for me?* Mary Kay did what so many have done: she excused a fault in a loved one that she would never have excused in a stranger. It was just another step in a long habit of making excuses. Besides, it was 1967, a time when "if it feels good, do it" and "whatever's right for you" were the emerging attitudes of the culture.

He seemed to be quite good at cards; he always came back in a good mood and with more money than when he left. Just as Mary Kay always defended herself and blamed others, she now defended Paul and blamed others. *If they aren't as good as him, well that's their fault for playing.*

She understood just how good he was the first time she went to a casino and watched him play. He was at the table for only fifteen minutes when a pit boss came and invited him to leave. They offered to buy him dinner and drinks, but he was no longer welcome to play.

"Why don't they let you play blackjack?"

"I guess because I'm a counter," he replied.

"What's a counter?"

"I can keep track of the cards. I can figure the odds on the cards that are played in my head. I pretty much know by the way other people play and the way they are betting what they have in their hand."

"How did you learn that?"

"I don't know. It just sort of comes naturally for me."

He had a phenomenal mind when it came to card playing, but in any casino they went to in any city, he never played even thirty minutes at the blackjack table. He usually played in private games, often on military bases with the officers. On federal property there was more freedom for gambling; they could gamble on a military base when they couldn't in the city limits.

She thought of it as one of his hobbies and still wondered what he did for a living. Once when she asked, he said something vague about having several different business deals going. When she pressed him for details, he replied irritably, "Don't worry; I'm taking care of you, aren't I?" She feared she had offended him. She did not want to seem ungrateful for the extravagant lifestyle she was living or appear doubtful of him as a provider. She did not ask again.

He often talked on the phone. He never allowed her to listen; he sent her to run errands each time. In the spring, when they had been married over six months, he told her he had arranged for a Bahamian music group to perform at an exclusive country club.

So that's it, she thought. *He's really an entertainment promoter.*

When they arrived in Virginia Beach, they moved into a nice suite in an expensive hotel. What struck Mary Kay as odd was the interest Paul took in the town and its surroundings. He not only learned every street and building, but he also sent her out to gather information. In particular, he sent her to check out the smaller motels, thirty or fifty miles away. Again, his answer was vague when she quizzed him.

"Why don't you just tell me what this is all about?"

"And why don't you just trust me and do what I say?"

"It's not that I don't trust you, and I don't have a problem doing what I'm told. I would just like to understand the reasoning. I don't know why you won't trust *me*."

"What if this is the way I want it?" he said.

"Well, have it your way, but I would probably be much better at gathering information for you if I knew what it is you are looking for."

Paul thought about that for a moment. It made sense to him; that was one of the things he appreciated about her. "All right, we might have to leave this town rather quickly. I've been invited to play at a private card game at the country club on Saturday night."

"So? You often play cards. I don't see why you're being so cautious about this one."

"Some guys will be there that cheated me out of some money. I am going to get it back, but when I do, they will not like it. We'll have to leave town, quickly."

"Then I should probably be packed and ready to go on Saturday afternoon," she said.

"You catch on fast, darling." Impressed, he gave her a hug and kiss. Even after all these months, his touch thrilled her.

"Shouldn't we get as far away as possible?" she asked. "I've only checked motels in the next town."

"One of the guys who stole from me is the police chief. After the game, he will be hot on my tail, and when someone is after you, it is best to get off the roads. They're not going to look for you under their noses."

"I see. He'll be expecting us to go as far as possible and he'll probably make up some excuse to alert the highway patrol." Her eyes grew dark with indignation. "What a jerk! I bet the people of this town don't know they have a dishonest police chief. Do you want me to get moved into another place during the game?"

"Good idea. Then you can come pick me up, and we'll go together."

Her willingness to go along prompted him to explain a little about how he would make sure the money on the table ended up in his pocket. She knew immediately he was going to cheat.

"But it's not like you're stealing," she said. "You're just getting back what is rightfully yours."

He smiled. He needed to find out how far he could trust her. This was small potatoes compared to what else he could tell her.

After his confession, she got caught up in the thrill of the risk. She was more willing to gather information and even offered ideas of her own, which seemed to please him. She was grateful that this escapade seemed to be drawing them closer together.

Mary Kay did not find out until later that their marriage was a calculated move on his part. She made him look more respectable, like an ordinary businessman; she helped him blend in. He knew she could be useful to him in a number of ways. She was compliant and agreeable. What a bonus that she was also intelligent and well read! He enjoyed talking to her. Initially the marriage had served his own well-being and convenience, but he quickly grew genuinely fond of her and proud of himself for making such a good match. It was turning out better than he had hoped.

Late Saturday night, she drove her new Lincoln Continental to the country club. As she sat in the parking lot, Mary Kay could see Paul's Cadillac a few rows back. Since their talk, all the things he did now made sense. He had sent her to Norfolk to buy the Lincoln and told her to put only her name on the title. The Cadillac was registered under an alias and he planned to abandon it after the game. That was amazing enough but she was astounded when he handed her a manila envelope full of cash to purchase the Lincoln. She held her purse tightly to her body all the way in the taxi and until it was time to pay. She did not breathe freely again until she had driven away from the dealership.

Afterward, he did not want them to be seen together. They left and arrived at their hotel at different times and from different directions. They never rode together; he would drive the Caddy and she the Lincoln. She never met any of his business associates. She marveled at his cleverness and attentiveness to details.

She waited outside the country club until he came walking swiftly out of the building. He was not even 5' 8" tall, but he was slim and muscular. In the darkness, she could not see the green eyes she loved or his thinning blond hair, but she could appreciate the cut of his suit; he did like expensive, fashionable clothes.

He opened the driver's side door, and she slid over to let him drive. When they were out of the parking lot and on the highway to their motel, he turned to her and grinned. Out of his coat jacket he pulled a leather wallet fat with cash and handed it to her. She peeked inside and gasped at the size of the bills. He chuckled with pleasure. He had done an outstanding job and his lovely new wife had helped. He felt high and so did she; that night was the most passionate she had ever experienced.

CHAPTER SEVEN

S he now knew Paul's success at poker was not just because he was a counter. He was also a mechanic; he knew how to stack the deck, how to deal from the bottom, and how to perform every other trick to ensure he walked away with the money. He was careful to leave just enough cash so no one would suspect he was cheating. When he was ready to move on, he would "clean the table"; she learned that meant to take all the cash in the final few hands. Then they would quickly relocate to a new hotel in a new town in the middle of the night.

While this lifestyle would have shocked Mary Kay just a few months before, her growing disillusionment with authority made Paul's indiscretion seem small in comparison. He was simply being dishonest with those who were themselves dishonest. She had long ago excused the fact that many of the games were illegal. Most of the games were private, held at hotels, restaurants, country clubs or private homes in cities and counties where gambling was outlawed. Yet all were under the protection of the very authorities expected to be upholding those laws. They were frequently attended or hosted by men in high places—politicians, judges, corporate leaders, policemen, and military officers. So what was the harm in a little cheating if the games were illegal in the first place? He was merely stealing something they were already willing to lose.

She also readily excused Paul's cheating because it added suspense to their life together. The success of the card game in Virginia Beach left Mary Kay with a taste for the daring. She enjoyed the thrill of the risk and the fruit of his winnings. They stayed in the best hotels and drove new, expensive cars. She wore fine jewelry and furs and could buy anything she wanted. Creature comfort became more important than inner comfort. By now she was adept at stuffing any qualms, or thoughts of what Mama would think, behind the formidable wall she had built.

Every so often, after a series of games in which Paul had won a significant amount of money, he would say, "Let's go to the windy city." He rarely played cards in Chicago, so she figured these were pleasure trips: shopping and parties with people in beautiful clothes showing off expensive jewelry. Later she learned that Paul took large sums of money to Chicago to be laundered in case any serial numbers were traceable. He avoided gambling in Chicago because of his connections to organized crime; he did not want to step on toes. But in those early days, Mary Kay assumed their visits to Chicago were just vacations.

The trips elsewhere were a different story. She enjoyed plays in New York while Paul played poker, and she relaxed in spas in Florida while he played contract bridge. In the Bahamas, he played blackjack while she went shopping at the International Straw Market.

When Paul said they were going to Hot Springs, Arkansas, Mary Kay thought, *What could there possibly be in Arkansas?* It was one of several trips they would make to race tracks around the country so Paul could bet on the horses. This interested Mary Kay much more than poker games. She loved horses and often accompanied Paul to the track to watch the races. They sat in the luxury box seats, and Paul concocted some story about who they were and where they lived.

She loved the old historic hotels at The Springs. Mary Kay soaked in the pools of naturally warm water, had pedicures and manicures, and sometimes even a massage. No, it was not at all hard to rationalize her husband's wrongdoings.

Over time, she accepted the risk he was taking, and it did not seem as thrilling as in the beginning. She missed that thrill. She began to wonder, *Would I have the nerve to do what he is doing? What is it like to cheat and get away with it?*

The thought made her heart pound faster. Every time Paul came back, keyed up from his latest exploit, he was throwing sticks on a fire burning within her.

She remembered the excitement of Virginia Beach, and the urge to participate grew stronger. She found herself fingering a scarf or a pair of gloves in a store, and looking around to see if anyone was watching. A surge of excitement ran through her veins as she thought about the risk of stuffing it into her bag and walking out.

One spring morning, she sat in the car fiddling with the diamond bracelet Paul gave her for their first anniversary. She had come downtown to buy—no, steal—a book. She tried not to think of Bible verses about stealing that popped into her mind. She turned her focus to summoning up the courage she needed to be a thief.

Do I have the nerve? she asked herself again. She remembered the day on the fire tower and how she'd overcome her fears. Yes, of course she could do it. She got out of the car and walked briskly down the sidewalk into the bookstore.

"Back again?" The clerk's cheerful voice startled her. Mary Kay had been in the store the day before, checking how many clerks were on duty and the layout of the store. She did not expect anyone to recognize her. Was it a good thing or a bad thing? She decided it was a good thing. Maybe now the clerk wouldn't suspect her, since yesterday she had spent over a hundred dollars. She was still an avid reader; what else did she have to do when Paul was out gambling?

She leafed through a book, slid it under her jacket, and turned toward the door. Prickles of fear ran up her neck and over her scalp. Her heart was in her throat. She tried to look casual, even stopping by the door to glance at the magazine rack. She pushed open the door and stepped into the sunlight. As she turned down the sidewalk toward the parking garage, her pace quickened. She restrained herself to keep from breaking into a full run.

Slow down, she scolded herself. *You don't want to look suspicious.* She was sure the whole world could see the book concealed under her jacket. Though it was a cool day, beads of perspiration dotted her forehead. Only when she reached the garage entrance did she glance behind her to see if she had been followed.

"Thank, God." She breathed a sigh of relief when she saw no one. She felt

61

a pang of guilt at the mention of God, whom she knew did not approve of what she was doing. All her rationalizations and justifications fell flat before the thought of the Almighty. Thoughts of God always made her think of Mama and thinking of Mama at a time like this made her heart heavy. She pushed Mama and God from her mind and concentrated on the euphoria she felt. What would Paul say? What would he think of her daring? She turned the key in the ignition and drove to their hotel.

Paul sat for a moment just looking at Mary Kay. Was he mad? His face looked stern, but she caught a twinkle in his eyes. She let out a sigh of relief; she did not know what she would have done if he had been mad.

"You have to be careful," he scolded. "That's the kind of thing that can land you in jail." When he saw her face fall, he reached over and took her hand.

"Don't feel bad. You weren't caught and that's what matters now. I'm pleased you would do something risky just to impress me. You just need a little training, that's all." He kissed her on the forehead, which always made her feel adored.

"What do you mean, training?"

"Okay, here's how to keep flying under the radar. First, don't heel a joint." At her look of confusion, he explained, "Don't leave without paying; don't walk out of hotels, restaurants, or gas stations without taking care of the bill. Do not get speeding tickets or parking tickets; it's the little things that get you caught. Second, make sure the odds are stacked in your favor."

"Like at your games."

"Exactly. The best way to stack the odds is to have someone watching your back. If you can, get someone on the inside to be part of your deal; especially if they are up the ladder, like a manager or boss or, better yet, the police. That is why my gambling is pretty safe, because of the people involved. A respected pillar of the community does not want his game busted; they do not want their names in the paper. When they protect themselves, they are protecting me, too."

"You mean a cop would help me shoplift?"

"Well," he paused and eyed her for a moment, "I wasn't really thinking about shoplifting."

"So, shoplifting isn't such a good idea?"

"Probably not. Too much risk for too little payoff."

She looked at him with a flush of pleasure. "But, it was so exciting."

He studied her for a moment, started to say something, and then stopped. "What is it?"

He watched her closely, and she knew that once again she was being measured; she just didn't know for what. He stood up and said casually, "Oh, nothing. You probably wouldn't be interested."

"Come on, tell me," she pleaded. "Let me decide if I'm interested."

He walked over to the dresser. "Some other time. Come on, let's get ready and go to dinner. I made plans with some friends."

By now, she knew better than to push him when he was not ready. The anticipation of working with him was exciting enough for the moment. In time, she was sure he would come around to it again. She went to the closet to choose something to wear.

She was not particularly curious about whom they were going to meet; he seemed to have friends in nearly every town. Most of his friends were cut from the same cloth: rather shady, with rough lives and rough language, but she liked most of them. They were colorful and entertaining. They told of daring escapades sprinkled with intriguing details. She learned to take their stories with a grain of salt, but she enjoyed them just the same.

Most of the men had wives. When they were all together, the men drifted to one area while the women talked in another. She usually stayed with Paul. She did not feel comfortable with the women. They weren't rude; they just did not seem to want to include her.

Mary Kay liked being with the men, but she noticed their hesitation when she was around. "Go ahead; you can talk in front of her. We're partners." Paul said. The first time he said it, her heart swelled with pride.

Tonight's friend turned out to be Gene, an associate she had met several times. He was a big man, standing over six feet and weighing nearly three hundred pounds. He loved to eat, and Mary Kay was always amazed at the quantity of food he consumed. Gene's wife, Jeannine, came with him. Mary Kay had never met her, and she was surprised. Not at all the plump matron she expected, Jeannine was a pretty redhead with alabaster skin. Her waist-length hair was pulled back from her face and hung loose over her shoulders.

At first the conversation was awkward, as it was with the other wives. Then Mary Kay asked Jeannine, "Gene said you had a poodle. Do you travel with her?"

"She goes everywhere with me; I would have brought her tonight, but Gene wouldn't let me take her to the theatre." Jeannine smiled. Both women loved dogs, and they talked about the different pets they had owned. A wall between them fell. They talked about books, favorite cities, and clothes, and by the end of the evening, a close friendship was born.

Later Jeannine explained that the other women did not warm up to Mary Kay because she was not a working girl and never had been. Mary Kay could not hide her astonishment. They were prostitutes! Jeannine saw the question in her eyes.

"Yes, me too, before my marriage. Most of the men do not allow their wives to work after they are married. But," she added, "some do. Don't take it personally. The women just aren't comfortable around square Janes."

Now Mary Kay understood. She knew she was different from the others, but she thought it was just because she was well read and didn't drink or smoke or use profanity. The real reason the women were cool to her had never entered her mind.

Paul seemed to like the fact that Mary Kay was different from him or his friends. She could meet anyone with ease and she began to better understand her value to him. She wanted to make herself even more indispensable to him. Her chance soon came.

"I've been thinking about the shoplifting," Paul said casually a few days later, driving back from the movies. She knew he would get back to it, given time. "Would you like to do something a bit . . . more daring . . . with me?"

She remembered Virginia Beach and grinned as a surge of excitement rose in her. "Oh, yes," she replied as though the answer had been on the tip of her tongue for weeks.

"You don't even know what it is yet."

"Darling, if it's with you and it's a little daring, I want to do it, whatever it is." She gave him a sexy, little smile when he turned quickly to look at her. He grinned broadly in return.

"I was thinking you might be able to help me at the games."

"How?"

"Sometimes it's not just poker. They play craps and I thought you might help me out at the table. See, I have some loaded dice . . ."

"What do you mean, loaded?" she interrupted.

"They have metal imbedded in one side, which makes them turn up the number you want whenever a magnet is nearby."

"And I'd have the magnet?"

"Boy, it doesn't take you long! You want to try it?"

"When do I start? Tonight?"

He threw back his head and laughed. "Not so fast! We have some preparing to do. We will get to it soon enough. We start with a plan." He was still outlining his idea for her as they drove up to the hotel. He stopped talking when the valet opened her door. He did not continue until they were alone again in their room. "Well, how about Friday?"

"I'm ready." She knew he was pleased by her eagerness. The thrill was back. The following day, he took her shopping. They visited several stores until they found the right outfit: a floral shirtdress with a wide belt and deep pockets cut at an angle across the front of the skirt. It was just right.

Next they went to the fabric store. While she bought sewing supplies and a piece of coordinating fabric, he crossed the street to the hardware store and bought several large, flat magnets. Back at the hotel, she sewed the magnets inside the pockets and the belt, covering them with pieces of fabric and stitching all around to hide any trace of them. She tried it on to see if the magnets were well hidden.

Sometimes the smallest thing brings the past into sharp focus. Standing before the mirror, she remembered the skirt and blouse she had made in 4-H and what had happened to them. A surge of bitterness welled in her throat and hardened into a rod of steely determination. In an odd way, preparing to steal money from gamblers made her feel better. She felt she was exacting some sort of revenge for the injustices thrust upon her.

She turned and smiled at Paul. "I'm ready now," she said, a strange calm in her voice. He could sense the new strength in her. Any misgivings he had felt about including her disappeared.

She had gone to games with him before and sat to the side watching or drinking a soda at the bar. Now, she stood at the table. At some point, Paul switched the dice. Though she knew he was going to do it, how he was going to do it, and was watching for it, she did not see it happen. *He is good*, she thought.

She watched him closely, waiting for the signal they had arranged earlier. When it came; she leaned against the table and waited breathlessly to see if the plan would work. It did! No one around the table seemed aware of anything except the roll of the dice. The players who bet the wrong way exclaimed in disappointment, but not one of them even glanced at her. She did not understand the rules and strategies yet, but she was soon able to predict when Paul was going to signal. He looked at her and winked. She felt a sense of power at being able to help him, and the adrenaline rush thrilled her. This time not one thought of Mama or twinge of guilt intruded; she was hooked.

CHAPTER EIGHT

Life settled into a pattern. They traveled around the country picking up games along the way. Mary Kay went along whenever there was a craps game. She developed a keen eye for reading people who might be suspicious of Paul. He trusted her instincts and walked away from the table if she gave a sign.

They took winters off and vacationed in southern Alabama, renting an apartment for a few months. Paul loved to fish and often woke before daylight to spend the day at the shore. Sometimes he chartered a boat, and she went with him out into the gulf. She enjoyed the water and even fished a little with the electric rod and reels provided by the captain. Mostly she read books.

Paul enjoyed history, but he did not like the commercial "tourist traps." They went to old graveyards in the countryside to read headstones, or visited obscure museums. Paul enjoyed people, and he and Mary Kay frequently attended parties with his friends. He also liked to spend time alone with her. She learned to read the signs of his restlessness. He would grow quieter and without warning would say, "Come on, let's go for a ride and do something."

Soon they would be on the road again with Mary Kay wondering, "Will we ever have a permanent address, something besides a post office box?"

As they prepared to travel on the road again one spring, Mary Kay noticed Paul packing a black, long-sleeved turtleneck pullover and black pants. This seemed odd because he always bought colorful clothes; he like to accent his blond hair and green eyes. He was a sharp dresser and very particular about his clothes.

"Where did you get that?" she asked.

He frowned, "Why do you ask?"

"Well, I thought you didn't like to wear black."

"Can't a guy try something new?"

"Of course, you can wear whatever you want. I'm just surprised." She put her hand on his arm hoping to smooth things over between them. Why was he so defensive? He relaxed at her touch and looked at her. There it was again, that gaze that made her feel like she was being evaluated. They had been married for nearly three years now. Would he ever fully trust her?

"Paul, sometimes," she hesitated, "like now, I get the sense you're holding something back. What can I do to get you to trust me?"

She really did not expect him to answer. *I don't know why I said that*, she thought, *he always gives me some brush-off answer when I dig too deep.*

She was surprised when he replied, "Okay. I need to be dressed for a job I'm going to do soon." He was cracking open the door of his reserve. She felt encouraged and flooded him with questions—When? Where? What?

When he slipped back into his mysterious mode, she scolded herself for being so pushy. She knew that he would tell her in his own time, but she could not contain her curiosity. Every once in a while she asked him another question.

"What should I do if this happens?" she asked. "Should I leave if that happens?" He must have seen her questions as good planning, because he began to reveal more about where he was going and what she should do if something went wrong. He gave her emergency plans if she had not heard from him by a certain time, and told her whom to call. She knew he was testing her, and little by little, he was learning she could be trusted.

A few weeks later, several hours after Paul had left for the evening, the phone woke her. Paul's voice was low and tense. He gave no explanation for his strange instructions. "Go to the 800 block of Prairie Street, and park halfway between the street lights on the west side of the street. Flash the lights once and then turn them off, but leave the engine running."

Mary Kay dressed quickly; she knew by his tone there was real danger, but she could not imagine what. She followed his instructions carefully and sat in the car peering into the darkness, not knowing which direction to look. Suddenly the car door opened and he slipped into the passenger seat.

"Go!" He said no more and she did not ask. He was wearing the black pants and turtleneck. Back in their hotel room, he looked at her sheepishly. "I suppose you want to know what that was all about."

"Only if you want to tell me." She knew by his remark he intended to tell her, and her response accomplished what she intended. He gave her the broad smile he always did when he was happy with her. Her eyes never left him as he told her what had happened.

All week he had gambled with a dentist who was remarkably successful. Paul suspected he was cheating but was not sure. When he learned the man kept his winnings in his office safe, Paul decided to burglarize the office. The high rise had apartments upstairs and offices downstairs. Unfortunately, the dentist had an alarm system, something new in those days. Paul was not prepared. He was trying to exit and avoid the police when he was trapped. He called her from an empty apartment at the back of the building. The police were on the next street entering the front of the building when she parked between the street lights.

He was angry at himself; Mary Kay was thrilled. She still felt high from the danger of rescuing him. Best of all, he was finally letting her in. She had shown him that he could depend on her when he needed to. Maybe now he would trust her.

She was right. After that night he shared more with her. When she found out later that the dentist was also a card mechanic, he came home and told her about it right away.

"He had connections. He had protection from the outfit. I did not check it out well enough. I should have known that."

"They don't know it was you, do they?" Mary Kay did not quite know who the outfit was, but she guessed he meant organized crime. Something told her it could be very bad for Paul if they knew what he had done.

"No, thank God." Mary Kay winced inwardly. God probably did not have anything to do with it. She brushed aside the guilt feelings that always crept in at the mere thought of God.

"So, you and I are the only ones who know, right?"

His angry expression faded and he smiled at her, "Right. Just you and me."

He took her in his arms. "Thanks for your help. I don't know if I could have gotten out of there without you." She smiled back and snuggled closer; they did not talk about it for the rest of the night.

At first, he just told her about the burglaries. Little by little he shared the details of his life and she adjusted to each revelation, one at a time. When Paul saw that she knew how to "hold her mud," he admitted that he was also robbing banks. He financed his gambling with the money from the robberies. It was not hard for Mary Kay to accept each new detail of his criminal life because each one did not seem much worse than the last thing she had explained away. Besides, she was quite used to the luxury, the exhilaration of danger, the travel, and the loving attention of a handsome, exciting husband. She was not going to do anything to chance losing this life. By the time Mary Kay came to the full realization that her husband was a professional gambler, burglar, bank robber, and safecracker, she did not care.

It was a short step from accepting Paul's trade to practicing it herself. By now Paul trusted her completely and discussed all his plans with her. He was pleased when she asked him to teach her and let her be more involved. She was clever and learned quickly. He gladly accepted her help; it made his job easier. He sent her into banks to draw a diagram of the inside and check out the security system. She went several times, and he quizzed her until she became expert at reading the inside of a bank. During the week, they would watch a bank and learn its routines. In the little state banks, they could get a couple hundred thousand dollars. They hit eight or ten a year.

She developed a complete arsenal of rationalizations to justify their behavior. One excuse was the corruption of officials; in every town they found somebody they could pay off for information or protection: bank officials, politicians, even a governor. Usually someone in the police department helped them. She learned that Paul rarely committed a crime in which the police did not turn their backs and allow him to get away.

Knowing that Paul was meeting with police officers, sheriffs, or chiefs of police, she became completely disillusioned with the law and morality. She knew pillars of the community were taking money under the table; it happened everywhere they went.

Well at least I'm not trying to be something I'm not, like they are, she reasoned. She realized that it was wrong, but everyone else seemed to be doing it, too.

Each rationalization took her farther away from the values her mother had instilled in her. She *had* to excuse her behavior or everything would flood together and overwhelm her. She became so adept at rationalizing that she no longer asked herself if it was right.

But Mary Kay did not have to ask; she knew it was wrong. She simply no longer cared—except when she went home to visit Mama. She did not go home often. She sent postcards and letters and made up stories about what they were doing and shared about the places she was visiting. She told her family Paul was a promoter for a group of Bahamian entertainers. In a way, he was; he set the group up with gigs when it helped him go where he wanted to gamble, like the country club in Virginia Beach or military bases. Her family did not know his real name; they thought his name was Mike. Lies slid off her tongue like butter. When had it become so easy to lie? She never thought to examine it; after all, she only lied for their own good.

She was careful never to stay over on a Sunday. Mama held to her rule that whoever was under her roof on Sunday morning went to church and Mary Kay could not bear that. She knew that in the little country church from her childhood she would realize what was missing in her life. She had more money than she'd ever dreamed of, but it hadn't bought her the "peace that passeth understanding."[2] She had known some happiness, which fluctuated with her situation, but "joy unspeakable and full of glory"[3] always eluded her. She and Paul told each other daily how much they loved each other, but when she remembered a verse memorized as a little girl—"Perfect love casts out fear"[4]—she knew they *lived* in fear, fear of being caught.

Wasn't the whole point of life to grasp the most enjoyment and pleasure she could in her little bit of time on this earth? She was certainly doing that. So why, in the wee hours of the morning or when her mind was caught off guard, did she feel a sinking sensation of emptiness? Those were the times when doubt crept in; where did the Bible fit into all this? Still deeply imbedded in her belief

[2] Philippians 4:7, *King James Version*
[3] 1 Peter 1:8, *KJV*
[4] 1 John 4:18, *KJV*

system was the idea that God existed, the Bible was true, and someday everyone would have to answer for his or her own behavior. She never stopped believing that Jesus had died for her sins, but believing this fact was not enough to keep her from crime. There must be something more to Christianity, but whatever it was, she knew she did not have it. Hadn't she known since childhood that most people were basically good, but that she obviously was not one of them? Oh well, Mary Kay was experienced at ridding herself of uncomfortable feelings. Staying far away from Mama and church helped.

In the crimes they committed, her responsibilities were to gather information, get into buildings, and drive the car. Her social abilities helped her to talk to anyone, anytime. She easily started conversations and asked innocent questions. "What hours are you open? Are you open in the evening? Are you open on Saturday?" During the course of casual conversations she found out crucial information.

She helped Paul and his partners, if he had them, break into buildings by hiding in the ladies room until the business closed and all the employees were gone. Then she let Paul in through a back door. She slipped out the door as he came in, walked several blocks to their car, and drove to the arranged meeting place. A stolen car was left near the bank so Paul could get away quickly. He met her, ditched the stolen car, and jumped in with her. They drove on to their next motel, always less than fifty miles away. They stayed in their room until their police informant told them the search was over. A complete exit plan was prepared for every job, plus several alternatives in case something unforeseen happened. It rarely did; Paul was smart and seemed to cover every base.

When Mary Kay could not hide inside for Paul, he would break into a business another way. He did not use windows or doors; he went in through the ceiling or the basement. If a passing police officer were to shine a spotlight on the building, he would not see anything broken or out of place. Entering this way took more time, so he did it only in buildings where he knew he had all the time he wanted.

Eventually Mary Kay was no longer satisfied to wait on the outside; she wanted to watch him work, to learn to do it herself. Sometimes he said, "No,

I need you to stay outside with the vehicle." Other times, if the location was isolated, he allowed her to stay inside. He showed her everything he did; he took great pride in his skill and his thorough attention to details. She learned how to enter and exit a building secretly. She learned how to disarm nearly every alarm system made. She learned how to watch for the dangers and how to avoid mistakes.

Her favorite job was safecracking. The first thing Paul taught her was to see whether the safe was on day-com, daytime combination. People often did not bother to lock their safes completely from one day to the next. They just turned the dial back a little, so the next day they could simply go to the last number and open the safe. This way, they did not have to go through the whole process, only the last step. If an employee opened the safe for them the next day, they did not have to give the whole combination, just the last number. They went through the whole process of locking the safe thoroughly only on weekends.

So breaking in on a weeknight often made Paul's job easier. He noted which number the dial was set on, and moved the dial one space. If that didn't work, he moved it one space the other direction, then two spaces one way and two numbers the other way. He kept doing that until he heard the tumblers. In this way, he could open the safe without having to break into it.

Mary Kay never did jobs on her own; it took a lot of strength to crack a safe that was not on day-com. Paul preferred to break into safes by "peeling" them. Doors of safes generally have seven layers of metal. He used a heavy hammer and a car jack to peel the layers back, one by one. Then he used a crowbar and, bracing himself against a wall or something stable, he opened a space big enough to squeeze his arm inside to release the lock. Sometimes he used a system of pulleys to apply the strength needed to peel the layers far enough so he could reach inside. A safe could never be used again after it was peeled. Paul always allowed plenty of time for these slow, difficult jobs. He was considered among the best in the field, and Mary Kay was his eager and willing apprentice.

Weeks and months often passed now without a thought of home, or feelings of doubt or guilt. She plunged herself completely into Paul and their career and did not allow herself to think more than a week ahead. She was not going to let a little thing like morality spoil what they had. Better just not to think about it.

One evening they checked the mail in their post office box on the way home. She glanced through it briefly and pulled out an envelope. Nearly a week had passed since they last picked up their mail, and the postmark was five days old. Mama's familiar handwriting drew her attention. The envelope was thin and as she withdrew the single sheet she thought, *Mama must have been in a hurry; she usually writes much more than this.*

Mary Kay scanned the words on the page. She felt a familiar tightening in her chest when she saw the word "Dad". Her eyes moved over the words again, but her brain seemed frozen.

"Dearest Kay, I hope you get this in time to come home. Your Dad died on March 10 and we will have the funeral this week. The Salvation Army in Cincinnati, Ohio contacted me. Connie and Bill went to arrange to bring him home. Please call as soon as you get this. Love, Mom."

She read it three times before she fully grasped what it said. He was dead. Finally, he was dead! She would never have to worry about him again. Glancing at the clock, she saw that it was after nine o'clock; too late to call Mama. She dialed her sister Connie's number instead. Her brother-in-law Larry answered immediately.

"Is Mama OK?" Before he could answer, she asked, "Is he really dead?"

"Yeah, he's really dead and she's okay. Are you coming home for the funeral?"

"No, I can't, but dig that hole deep so he can't climb out." Larry was not surprised. Everyone in the family knew how she hated him. The phone call ended after a few minutes, but she was too edgy to sleep. Whether her eyes were open or closed, she saw only his face. Anger, rage, and bitterness boiled inside her. Nausea welled up and she felt the approach of a familiar headache.

I am glad he's dead, she thought, *so why don't I feel like laughing? Why this sick feeling? It must be because Mama is sad.* She lay quietly, closing her eyes but still sleep evaded her. When light filtered through the blinds, she went to the kitchen and started breakfast.

The day inched slowly by as Mary Kay swept, dusted, washed, and mopped the already clean apartment. Paul, after glancing quickly at the letter, left her alone. When she finished cleaning and had folded the laundry, she took a long, hot bath. She was grateful when sleepiness settled over her. She remembered the sleeping pills Jeannine had given her months earlier, and she searched the medicine cabinet to find the bottle.

Hours later, she awoke with a start, not realizing she had screamed. Paul was shaking her gently, "Kay, honey, wake up. You're having a bad dream."

Heart pounding, she cried out, "Where's Mama? Don't let her see! Don't let her see what I've done."

She looked at Paul with glazed eyes. Her whole body trembled; her skin felt icy though she was perspiring.

She allowed Paul to pull her toward him and cover her. "What was it?" he asked. "Do you want to tell me?"

"I don't remember; I was just running from something."

But she did remember; she remembered every vivid detail. If she had not remembered it that night, she would have at some point; for the next six weeks, the dream was repeated, not every night but often. Mary Kay began to dread bedtime.

During the daylight hours, she wondered if she were losing her mind. Without telling Paul, she made an appointment to see a psychiatrist. She told him the truth about her nightmare.

In the dream, her father was drinking, getting meaner with each glass. She stood between him and her younger brothers and sisters holding a shotgun. When he took a step toward her, cursing, she pulled the trigger. She could feel her finger tighten on the trigger, feel the recoil against her shoulder; she even felt herself stumble backward. Simultaneously, she saw his face explode into blood and bone. The blood spattered over her with a warm stickiness.

"Then I wake up." Mary Kay ended the story as dispassionately as she told it.

"He's dead, but not gone," said the doctor. Mary Kay winced at his words and stared out the window.

"He is gone! I don't ever have to see him again," she finally said. She knew the doctor was right. She dutifully made another appointment, knowing she would never be back.

CHAPTER NINE

A dark gray cloudbank on the horizon growled and rumbled in the distance as they drove east. Above them the bright sun radiated heat ripples onto the highway. Humidity hung in the air. Mary Kay was grateful they did not have far to go today.

She had not felt well for weeks. Old guilt about being sick when she was a child kept her from saying anything to Paul. He had not seemed in the best of moods lately either. Maybe it was the heat, or this last job.

They rarely worked in the daytime, but a bank manager worked out a deal with them. He wanted to be there when Paul did the job. The man had political aspirations and wanted his name and picture in the paper. He had already written his speech. Paul normally would not have agreed, but an unusually large amount of cash was involved. A branch bank in a neighboring town had been damaged by fire, and its money was going to be moved into this one for safekeeping while the other bank was renovated.

They had broken into this bank before; they knew the floor plan and the alarm system. Even so, this job had been thrown together too quickly. They met with the bank manager one last time; he assured them it would go smoothly. The policeman on duty agreed to leave as soon as the doors were locked at the end of the workday.

She parked the stolen car where they had agreed and waited in their own car a few blocks away in the Piggly Wiggly parking lot. When he showed up, much earlier than she expected, he looked grim. She did not even ask; she knew he would tell her when he was ready.

He started the car and turned toward Florida. They had to meet a fence in Miami by the end of the week. She laid her head back on the seat and watched the clouds grow bigger and darker. She must have dozed off, because she jumped when Paul finally spoke.

"The job fell through." She shook her head to come fully awake and looked at him. "The manager failed to tell me that the manager of the bank in Pinedale was coming along with his money. Guess he wanted to make sure it made it safely. Well, it did."

"It was a lot of money," she said wistfully.

"I knew it was too risky from the beginning. I should never have agreed to it."

"I'm glad you didn't do it."

"Why?"

"I didn't feel right about it either."

He suddenly pulled the car over onto the shoulder and swung around to face her. "You what?"

She looked so alarmed that he leaned back against the door and tried to grin, but it looked more like a grimace.

"I'm sorry," he apologized. "Now what did you just say?"

"That I didn't feel comfortable with that job," she offered a bit timidly. She wondered what had upset him so.

His voice was controlled. "In the future, when you have doubts, please voice them. I believe in hunches; they have saved me many times. If I had known you didn't feel good about it either . . ." She knew what he meant. He was very superstitious, and trusted her intuition.

"I'm sorry. I should have told you. I just haven't been feeling well lately."

He gave her a startled look. "What is it?"

"Oh, nothing, probably just a little bug I picked up." He was worried, but she detected something else from him, almost revulsion. With a deepened guilt, she added quickly, "I'm fine, really. Could just be this heat. Do you really think we should be heading *east*? That storm looks powerful." Changing the subject seemed like a good idea at the moment.

She was sick on and off that entire winter in Alabama. She blamed it on the flu, but she knew it was something else. Her periods were messed up; she could normally track them by the waxing and waning of the moon. She developed a familiar appendicitis-like pain.

Paul hated doctors. He never used them, and he did not want her to either. He thought as long as you took care of yourself, over-the-counter medication was enough. She was used to giving Paul his way, but by now, the pain had persisted too long. In the spring, she went to a doctor without telling her husband.

"You have a badly swollen ovary and your womb is tilted," the doctor told her after the exam. "You'll need to go to the hospital for a day for some tests. We need to see what this is. You may have a cyst on your ovary which is causing the pain. If it bursts it can cause serious problems."

The outpatient visit was easily handled; she chose a day when Paul was gone. A few days later, she returned to the doctor to hear the results. "It is a tumor. I am afraid it is cancerous, but it appears to be contained. We need to go in there and remove it."

She drove to the spacious apartment she and Paul were sharing with Gene and Jeannine. She walked straight into their bedroom, opened an overnight case, and began to put a few items in it. Paul followed her.

"What are you doing?"

"I went to the doctor. He says I have a cancerous tumor and he wants to take it out. I'm going to go ahead and check into the hospital this evening." She turned to him and smiled, hoping to reassure him. He stared at her, said nothing, then turned and left the room. She did not realize until later how much it shocked him to hear her talk about cancer in such a matter-of-fact tone. To her, it was simply a case of having a problem and fixing it. She had not attached feelings to problems for years. When she came back into the living room, she was ready to go.

Jeannine asked, "Are you okay?"

"Of course. I'm going to be fine. I just need some surgery."

Paul barely spoke as he drove her to the hospital that night.

"Is something wrong?" she asked.

"I just want to make sure you are going to be all right."

"Of course I will. I'll just be in here three or four days."

The surgery, scheduled early the next morning, left her groggy all day from the anesthesia. When she awoke, Jeannine was there. May Kay asked for Paul.

"He's not here right now."

Mary Kay nodded and fell back asleep. In the evening, she was more alert and again asked Jeannine about Paul.

"He'll come back." Mary Kay took that to mean he had visited while she was sleeping. The next morning the doctor came to visit her. She was alone.

"Well, the surgery went well. The cancer was fully contained and it appears we got it all. There is an interesting development, though." He paused. "When we got in there, we discovered you are pregnant."

Mary Kay thought the medications had impaired her hearing. Did he say she was *pregnant?* That couldn't be. After the birth of her daughter Brenda, the doctor had told her that she would never be able to conceive again. She and Paul had been together nearly five years without her getting pregnant.

"Did you say I'm pregnant? Are you sure?"

"Yes, but I'm afraid that because of the surgery you won't carry the baby to term. I'm sorry. We'll have to keep you in here a few days longer than expected. You will probably miscarry soon."

When the doctor left, Mary Kay called the apartment and asked for Paul. Jeannine told her he was not there. For the first time, she began to feel anxious, wondering where he was and why he had not come to see her.

"Has something happened to him? Was he arrested?"

"No, he hasn't been arrested." Jeannine replied, "Just hold on. I'll be there in a few minutes." When Jeannine arrived she pulled a chair beside the bed. Mary Kay could tell she did not know where Paul was.

"I think he must be checking something out."

Mary Kay knew that meant he was casing a place, but this behavior was unlike him. He never went somewhere without telling a colleague when he would be back; he always left a phone number, someone to contact. He would say something like, "I'm going to be in Memphis. If you don't hear from me in three days, check with this person to make sure I haven't been busted. If I have; come bail me out."

"Did he talk to the doctor at all?"

"Yes, he did, yesterday afternoon." Jeannine's face suddenly clouded. "Why? Didn't the surgery go well? What is it, Kay?"

"Everything went fine." Mary Kay's heart began to sink as forgotten bits of information fell into place and a terrible realization filled her mind. Paul had a nearly phobic fear of illness, and at the top of his list were cancer and epilepsy. Epilepsy ran in his family. His older brother had ten or fifteen grand mal seizures each day and was institutionalized. His sister had petit mal seizures regularly. His mother had had epilepsy. She remembered his relief when she told him she could not have children. He was certain he would have a child like his brother.

Cancer—to Paul—meant that Mary Kay would die a slow and painful death; pregnancy meant they would have a child with severe epilepsy. She now embodied the two things that terrified him most. The cancer had not worried her at all. He probably thought anyone unafraid of dying of cancer must be *really* crazy. His worst fears were coming together at once, and she was the focal point. No wonder he had left. But surely he would come back when he found out she had lost the baby and the cancer was gone.

She did not lose the baby, however, and she was as surprised as anyone. At the end of a week, the doctor released her from the hospital. She was having a perfectly healthy pregnancy. *After all,* she thought, *I am fairly moral . . . I don't smoke or drink or take drugs.* She did rob banks though.

When Paul did not come back, Mary Kay was devastated. They had been married almost five years, and she had never loved anyone so deeply. She was completely emotionally tied to Paul. Before, she had always been able to harden her heart, not allow her emotions to control her, not allow herself to become dependent. But with Paul, she seemed to have no control. Each day that she did not hear from him, she slipped deeper into depression

She never had a chance to speak to Paul; he sent a message through friends that he was not coming back. From April until October, her misery grew with her stomach. Gene went to Chicago to work but her friend Jeannine would not leave her. Mary Kay rarely left the apartment they now shared alone.

On October 20, 1971, Sean Paul Mahaffey was born. Her joy at the wonder of this baby gradually pulled Mary Kay out of her slump. In her darkest moments, she clung to the hope that Paul would come back to her after the baby was born healthy. Weeks passed, but he did not come. Friends mentioned that he sometimes asked about her. Months passed and she began to realize he might never come back. She must think of the future.

After successful jobs, Paul had divided the money among several different hiding places. She found money left for her in those places; it totaled nearly ten thousand dollars. In the early 1970's this was a huge amount, but in the past, they had felt nearly broke if they had only ten thousand. She still needed some way to support herself and Sean. She could not do jobs on her own, so she spread the word among their associates that she needed work and was available to help.

At Christmas, she took Sean home to visit her family, and then they went to visit Jeannine in Granite City, Illinois, a suburb of East St. Louis. Jeannine had a house and they moved in together. They both had connections with organized crime in the city and it seemed like a good place to earn money.

A few sympathetic friends included her on some jobs and shared the take with her. As she had done for Paul, she hid in buildings and stayed to open the doors. Only now she began going in just before closing and holding people at gunpoint. Paul disliked robberies; he preferred burglaries when no one was there. She was no longer depressed; she was *angry*, and her reckless willingness to do robberies was her way of saying, "I'll show you."

Then she did something else Paul would never do. She "stepped on toes." Jeannine's husband, Gene, was connected with crime bosses, and Mary Kay stepped on his toes, hard. It ended with a Mafia contract on her life.

As a hooker, Jeannine had always had a pimp. When she married Gene, he told her she would not have to work anymore. That winter, however, he was gambling heavily and losing, so he made Jeannine go back to work. He put her in a house in another city, and she came home only one week a month. She hated it. She admired Mary Kay because she was no longer tied to a man for her support. She decided she would rather be single, too.

"Come on, Mary Kay. You and I can take care of Sean and make it on our own. We don't need men."

"How can you ever get away from Gene?"

"England. I have always wanted to go to England. Gene has some money stashed away in a lock box. We'll take that and go to England. What do you say?"

Mary Kay knew she was right; Jeannine would have to go very far away, a place where Gene would never find her. She did not particularly want to go to England, but she wanted to help Jeannine. They made their plans.

At that time, travelers to Europe had to show proof of all the common childhood immunizations. Jeannine had been out on her own since she was fourteen; she did not even know if she had had all her shots. Mary Kay knew she had not had a smallpox vaccination so they went together to the County Health Department. However, Mary Kay was still recovering from the Hong Kong flu and they would not give her the shot. Jeannine was ready, but Mary Kay would have to wait.

Jeannine was due back to work in a few days, so they decided she would leave immediately and get settled in England. Mary Kay and Sean would follow when she could get her shots and paperwork in order.

Gene's safety deposit box was across the river in Bellevue. His connections in this town were everywhere. Jeannine knew she would be recognized there but Mary Kay was not as well known. Since she resembled Jeannine slightly, they decided she would retrieve the money from the box.

Mary Kay slammed her right hand in a door until it was obviously bruised and swollen. Then she practiced writing with her left hand until she could make a signature that resembled Jeannine's. With Jeannine's ID and the lockbox key, she drove to the bank. The clerk admitted her without a second look. She emptied the contents of the safety deposit box and drove home. Jeannine gave some of the money to Mary Kay and left town immediately.

When Gene found out, he was furious. Their associates just laughed at him. "That's what you get for messing with women." Louis, the hit man Gene contacted, was insulted that Gene would ask him to "take" Mary Kay; he did not kill women. He found this so repulsive, he not only refused, he also warned her that Gene had put out a contract on her. And he told her that Paul had been arrested in Florida.

CHAPTER TEN

Their friends talked among themselves about what Mary Kay could possibly have done to make Paul leave her. He did not walk out on people this way. It was simply not done; even crooks have a code of honor. She must have done something horrible to have made Paul leave her when she was in a jam.

The rumors kept Mary Kay from getting as many jobs as she needed, and she wanted to vindicate herself. She would show them. Paul was in a jam, arrested and in jail; she would help him. Certainly that would change their minds about her. Solid people stood by a friend when he was arrested. Mary Kay wanted everyone to know she was solid. She took three-month-old Sean to her mother's home in Missouri and drove to Florida. She would not admit to herself whose mind she really wanted to change.

Paul was involved in a confidence racket called "Bait and Switch." He had a few gold coins, and occasionally he made contact with various coin collectors. He showed them the coins, claimed he had inherited them from an uncle, and said there were a lot more. He told them he wanted to sell quickly and quietly; he needed the money right away and did not want to go through probate. If a collector fell for it, they agreed on a price.

Of course, Paul did not have any more coins; that was the scam. At an arranged time and place, the collector traded a case full of cash for an identical case full of rocks. Usually Paul's victims did not go to the police because, a bit shady themselves, they couldn't bear a close scrutiny of their finances. Some of the policemen in Florida knew Paul was running this scam but turned their backs, for a price. It seemed foolproof.

Paul learned of a man in Fort Walton Beach who owned a motel and wanted

85

to buy some coins. Contacts were made, stories were laid, and the amount was agreed upon. Then the man sweetened the pot.

"I have some money in my safe in the motel office I want to get out. I'm about to be audited and I thought . . . if there was a burglary . . ." He looked at Paul and saw that he understood. "If you do this for me, then we can deal on the coins."

Paul agreed; this was not the first time he had received such an offer. It usually meant easy money. He brought in an associate, Bobby, and they planned the job. The motel owner promised he would be the only one on duty at night. The owner's office was in a building away from the front of the motel. The woman working in the office was scheduled to leave early that night since the motel was full. Instead, she decided to take a walk around the grounds and came back in time to see Paul and Bobby breaking into the office. She ran to the owner. He told her he would take care of it; she should go home so she would not get hurt.

The owner grabbed his gun, ran to the motel office, and began firing at Paul and Bobby. He planned to shoot them, take the money, and tell the police he had killed some of the burglars while the others got away with the money. He did not know the desk clerk had already called the police, who arrived in the middle of the shootout. They did not know who was who, so they arrested everybody.

The owner of the motel was released quickly, but the police had found the money on him. The man could not account for such a large amount of cash in his safe. In truth, he had been running an illegal gambling game and was storing the money in the motel safe. Quite a few people in town, including the police, believed Paul's story when he told them the owner had hired him to do the robbery for a split of the profits. Paul might have been released quietly and quickly were it not for the county sheriff. He discovered Paul's long criminal career, his federal prison time, and his wanted status in several states. The sheriff began to boast.

"Paul Mahaffey doesn't know who he's messing with. He is in a jail now that he's not getting out of. He's not going to accuse one of *our* good citizens." After all, it was an election year.

Paul had been in jail a week when Mary Kay arrived and took a hotel room. Raising bail was always plan A. If she could get Paul out on bail, they would simply leave the state and lay low until it all blew over. She notified some key friends about what was going on and contacted the bond company. His bail was fifty thousand dollars. When the sheriff heard they were about to post bond, he added another charge: illegal possession of a firearm. The bail increased to seventy-five thousand. Mary Kay called more friends and raised the money. Another charge was added: discharging a firearm within the city limits. The bail increased again and Mary Kay raised it. Each time when it seemed as if Paul were about to be released, the sheriff added another charge. When the bail reached one hundred sixty-nine thousand dollars, she decided to visit Paul in jail.

"They are not going to open the door; you're going to have to make one." Mary Kay's voice and face were dispassionate. She was not doing this for him; she was doing it to clear her name.

"Get me some blades," he said. She nodded and left.

The next week she returned with single-edge razor blades and a hacksaw taped to her body under her clothes. She did not know how she would avoid the metal detector. She sat near the entrance and watched as visitors passed through the security procedures. Then she saw her opportunity; a reporter entered the receiving room. She moved to the end of the counter near the officer's desk.

"They're mistreating me!" she wailed. "I don't know what's going on and they won't tell me. They're treating me like a criminal." All eyes in the room turned to watch as she sobbed into her sleeve. Her sobs and complaints grew louder until the officer drew her around the desk and sat her in a chair to calm her. They checked her name and found no criminal record. She was making them look bad in front of the reporter, so they let her in to shut her up. Since she was already behind the counter, they did not bother making her go back around to pass through the metal detector.

She was still sniffling softly when she arrived in the visiting room. Paul put his arms around her to comfort her. His touch unnerved her; she resisted the urge to truly embrace him. Untaping the tools, she passed them to him as he held her. He tucked them inside his shirt. Back then, prisoners were not required to go through a metal detector after visitation.

Mary Kay calmed down and they sat at a visitation table. Their conversation was casual. She struggled to keep a poker face; she did not want him to know he was affecting her. After what she considered an appropriate amount of time, she left.

Paul left the visitation area and went right to work in his cell. He cut grooves in the steel bars with the blades and used the hacksaw to finish cutting through each one. He concealed the shine of the freshly cut seam with a mixture of toothpaste and crushed pencil lead. The work was slow; each bar took days, and many days he could not work at all.

Mary Kay traveled back and forth between Florida and Missouri that spring trying to free Paul and visiting Sean. Mary Kay and Paul had strong connections with people who could help. She flew an officer in from the St. Louis police department. He testified in court that Paul could not have been in Florida because he had given him a ticket in Missouri at the time in question. The judge did not buy it. Mary Kay spent almost as much money on lawyers and expenses as she was making on jobs. In spite of her efforts to suppress her feelings for Paul, fantasies of saving their marriage grew stronger.

As she worked on his release from the outside, Paul's friends went to work on the inside. One of them dressed as a bum and was arrested for drunk and disorderly conduct. He was so dirty and smelly that the officers just threw him in the drunk tank without searching him. They never saw the yellow nylon rope wrapped around his body under his clothes. Another friend had the job of cleaning the cells every day, including the drunk tank. The next morning, he retrieved the rope and hid it with his supplies. Later, as he cleaned Paul's cell, he slipped it under the mattress.

Every day the prisoners were visually counted in the day room. If they were not in the day room, an officer came to their cell. Paul began to show up for the day room count irregularly. He told the officer, "If I'm back in my cell, I'm asleep, don't come bother me." Paul paid the officer or gave him cigarettes to leave him alone. If he missed meals, the other inmates said, "He's asleep." The officers soon got out of the habit of checking on him.

The newspapers reported that prison officials did not discover Paul's escape for two days. He broke the bars of his cell, cut his way into a heating duct, and climbed onto the roof. A yellow nylon rope was dangling over the fence at the far end of the jail. They were certain someone was waiting to drive him away. They were right; it was Mary Kay.

The end of June was warm in Florida. They found a motel, where Paul cleaned up and changed into the clothes she had brought. They could not hide in Florida; Paul's picture would be all over the news. They left immediately and headed to North Carolina.

From January until June, while she had worked to free Paul, Mary Kay kept hoping that everything would work out and they would live happily ever after. She knew he must trust her now after all she had done, but there was still Sean and Paul's desertion wedged between them. As the tension grew, they began to argue—something they had not done in the five years before.

Paul was panicked about money. They had less than two thousand dollars and he needed much more to leave the country safely. He managed a few quick burglaries but it was not enough. Their worst fight was about what they were going to do; Mary Kay wanted to go home to get Sean, but Paul would have none of it.

After months of inner turmoil, Mary Kay finally accepted reality. Though he never said so, Paul simply did not want to be saddled with a wife and child. She called a friend in St. Louis, who wired her money for an airline ticket. Two weeks after she picked Paul up at the edge of the prison, Mary Kay left him. She never saw Paul again.

CHAPTER ELEVEN

Mary Kay may have won Paul his freedom, but she lost hers in the process. Her part in his escape made her a wanted criminal. Her friends did not have to warn her; she traded Mary Kay Mahaffey for Sandra Kaye Marshall at the prison wall. In the following weeks, she collected several more aliases, each with a full set of ID. The blond wig from Chicago came out of its box regularly.

Mary Kay left Paul because she wanted to be with Sean, and now she could not go home to get him—Mama's house was being watched by the FBI. They had enough information to know she had family ties with the Petets of Eldon, Missouri, but they were not yet certain who she was. For a while, they thought her sister Connie might have been the one who helped Paul escape. When they eliminated that possibility, they began surveillance of Mama's house from a parked car down the street. Ronnie was a senior in high school. He thought it was funny to hassle the agents.

"How you doin? Want to come in for a cup of coffee?" He asked every day on the way back from school; they never accepted. Ilene did not think it was funny when they pulled her out of class to be questioned in the principal's office. The two agents probably knew they would not be allowed to question her at home. She was not sure it was legal, but she was too scared to protest. The family honestly had nothing to tell the FBI. Over the years, Mary Kay had told them very little about her life, and what she had told them was mostly lies.

Mary Kay called to check on Sean. When Mama told her about the FBI and their questions, Mary Kay claimed it must be a case of mistaken identity. Mama believed her right up until she received a handgun in the mail addressed to Mary Kay. Then there was the matter of the scary looking fellow who knocked on the door and demanded to know where Mary Kay was. He was obviously *not* with the FBI.

Mama had difficulty taking care of Sean. She had a job, and though Ronnie and Ilene were good babysitters, the care of the baby was too much for her. Bill's wife, Kathy, offered to take Sean until Mary Kay returned. No one, including Mary Kay, knew when that would be. She called with one excuse after another, but she was so vague and noncommittal that they began to wonder if the FBI claims were true.

Mary Kay did not stay in one place long. She drifted from state to state, contacting friends and taking whatever jobs they offered. She had cleared her name with her colleagues, but she did not care anymore. She was lonesome for Sean, angry with Paul, and depressed about having to constantly cover her tracks. Soon, nothing seemed to matter; she began to take risks she had never taken before.

Information about a likely robbery opportunity came from a local man named Nick who fenced stolen goods and owned a bar in Northport. Paul had discussed this job with him a few months earlier, and Nick felt obliged to pass the information on to Mary Kay. Mr. Robinson,[5] the owner of a dry goods store in Tuscaloosa, had a large vault in his store, and local cotton farmers, many of them poor, banked their money with him. He advanced them with seed and later, when they ginned their cotton, they paid him back with interest. He had a large amount of cash on hand this time of year.

Mary Kay devised a plan. Late on a sunny, summer afternoon, her car "broke down" right in front of the Robinsons' home. She raised the hood and looked inside. Grabbing a leather briefcase out of her car, she walked to the front door. In a pretty blue and white dress, white gloves, and a hat, she rang the bell and Mr. Robinson opened the door.

"Excuse me, Sir," she said. "My car seems to have just stopped, and I wonder if I might use your phone to call my husband."

Mr. Robinson looked around her to the car at the curb with its hood up. "Of course," he replied and stepped aside to let her in.

The foyer opened onto a living room on the right and a kitchen on the left.

---

[5] Name changed

In the wall by the living room was a tiny alcove where the telephone sat on a shelf. Mrs. Robinson stepped out of the kitchen, wiping her hands on a towel.

"This lady is having car problems and wants to use the phone to call her husband," Mr. Robinson explained.

"Yes, please, help yourself," she said with a smile. She returned to the kitchen while her husband read his newspaper in the living room. Mary Kay quickly dialed a number and spoke into the phone while she set her brief case on a chair and opened it.

"I'm inside. You can come now." She lifted a shotgun from the case and with a loud click, the double barrel fit securely into the stock. She entered the kitchen, pointing the gun at her hostess. Gesturing toward Mr. Robinson, she stated calmly, "Mrs. Robinson, will you please go sit with your husband?"

The woman's face turned white. "Oh no, please don't hurt us!" she pleaded. She hurried into the living room and sat very close to her husband on the couch.

With a forceful voice, Mr. Robinson asked, "What do you want? We don't keep a lot of money here at the house, but you can have whatever you want." With his arm around his wife, he continued, "You don't have to hurt anyone; we'll cooperate." Holding the shotgun loosely, Mary Kay sat in a chair opposite the Robinsons.

"No one will be hurt as long as both of you do what I tell you. Very soon my friends will be here, and I want you to go to your store with them." She lifted the gun and pointed it at the woman. "I'll stay here with your wife. If I don't hear from my friends in thirty minutes, Mrs. Robinson will die."

Mrs. Robinson gave a sharp, fearful cry and clung more tightly to her husband. He patted her hand and replied in a less forceful voice, "It'll be all right. I'll do everything they say, and we'll be back in thirty minutes."

At that moment, the door opened, and Nick and Reed walked into the living room. Nick motioned with his gun for Mr. Robinson to precede him out of the house. As he rose to go with the two men, he said, "The safe at the store is on a time lock, and I can't get it open before morning."

"Then you better remember the override instructions," Nick snapped as they left the house. Mary Kay ordered Mrs. Robinson to go into a bedroom at the back of the house. The guest room twin beds had mattress covers but no sheets.

Bedspreads were folded at the foot of each bed. Whimpering fearfully, Mrs. Robinson lay down as instructed, and Mary Kay taped her ankles together with duct tape. Turning her on her side, Mary Kay taped the woman's wrists behind her back.

"Now you lie there quietly. I won't be so far away that I can't hear you."

Mary Kay searched the house quickly. She found some diamond jewelry, which she put in the brief case. Time seemed to pass very slowly, but less than twenty minutes later, the doorbell rang once and she let the men in. Pushing Mr. Robinson toward the bedroom where his wife lay, Nick growled, "Let's get out of here."

Nick did not look pleased. Mary Kay walked to the bedroom and instructed Mr. Robinson to lie down on the other bed. She taped his hands and feet as she had taped his wife's. Looking out the window, she saw only trees and yard; no houses were nearby. She walked over and opened a window.

"For the next thirty minutes you lie quietly; then you can start calling for your neighbor, but I don't want to hear anything from either of you for thirty minutes." The coupled nodded.

They left the house and drove about three miles to Northport, a suburb of Tuscaloosa, where they ditched both stolen cars on a side street. Mary Kay's car was a block away, and they drove into the country to a house trailer Nick sometimes rented out. The men wanted to return to their homes, but Mary Kay insisted they remain for a couple of hours to let the heat die down.

Nick dumped the money onto the table in the tiny dining area. It totaled only slightly more than thirty thousand dollars; they had been led to believe it would be ten times that amount. Mary Kay combined the jewelry with the cash, but it did not add significantly to the total.

"*What happened?*" she demanded. "You said you had good information from an employee. Where's the rest of it?"

"It *was* good information. It just," he paused, "it wasn't in the safe."

"What do you mean, it wasn't in the safe? Where was it? And why didn't you get it if you knew where it was?"

When she was very angry, her voice became quiet, her words measured and distinct. This calm demeanor earned her the reputation of being dangerous.

Now, as she glared angrily at Nick and Reed, they became visibly nervous.

"Where is the rest of the money?" she repeated slowly, her eyes narrow and unmoving.

"There was this extra drawer in the back of the safe, and that was what Mr. Robinson said was on a time lock; there weren't any keys to it," Nick explained hurriedly.

"That was a keister safe. I told you about that. I also told you if it had a keister, it would take longer to open and to give me a call before the end of the thirty minutes so I would know what was happening."

"It was already getting dark outside and we would have had to turn on lights to see. I didn't want a policeman stopping by to see why we were there."

"So you chickened." She gave them a disgusted look. "Well that's just great; instead of having enough to live on for several months, there's barely enough to get out of town."

She put the jewelry in her pocket and scooped the money into her briefcase. She counted out two stacks of five hundred dollars, and tossed one to each man.

"Since you weren't willing to work a little longer for a larger share, this is all you get." She walked outside to her Ford LTD, ignoring their angry shouts.

The next morning she read in the paper that the Robinsons' neighbors, two old-maid sisters, finally heard them and called the police. They had seen Mary Kay walk to the house, and thought the Robinsons were having a social function and had not invited them. The newspapers called Mary Kay the "Polite Lady Robber" because she said "Sir" and "Ma'am," but Mr. Robinson was also quoted as saying, "The longer I looked at her, the smaller she seemed but the bigger her gun looked!"

In September, Mary Kay worked her way up to Peoria, Illinois, because it was an outfit town: organized crime controlled nearly everything. Peoria was a good place for her to find work; she had friends there. She brought the beginning of a cold with her, and she looked for a place to lie low for a few days until it passed. In the newspaper, she found a room for rent by the week. The small bedroom was in a private home owned by a woman named Pat, who had a little daughter. Mary Kay chose a new name for herself out of the phone book, Susan Snyder, and gave the woman two weeks rent in advance. She slipped a few times when her landlady called her Susan and forgot to answer.

She did not care; her cold was quickly turning into a nasty case of the flu. Plagued by a high fever, she stayed in bed and could not remember ever being so sick. She could not keep anything down, her sides ached from the dry heaves and coughing, and she sneezed until her nose was raw and sore. One day slipped into the next until she had no idea how long she had been ill.

Saturday, September 22, 1972, was a warm, sunny day. Mary Kay was finally feeling better and wandered out of her room in search of food. She wasn't sure when she'd last eaten, and she was *hungry*. For the first time in many days her head didn't reel when she walked across the room. Her landlady had also been sick and was sitting at the table with her daughter when Mary Kay walked into the kitchen.

"Do you have an egg I could scramble?" asked Mary Kay.

Pat looked up with a startled, pale face. "Run to your room," she told her daughter, and stood to face her tenant. "What did you say?"

"I'm feeling a little better and I'm hungry. May I buy an egg or two from you?"

Pat stared at her as though she were speaking a foreign language. "Oh! Well, um," she twisted the dishtowel she held and suddenly pulled a kitchen chair from the table. "Here, sit down, and I'll fix you something."

As Pat moved around the kitchen, preparing breakfast, she watched Mary Kay closely. She kept up a nervous conversation the whole time, telling Mary Kay how she and her daughter had also been sick, though not as sick as Mary Kay. She finally set a dish down and paced a few times across the room.

"Susan, um, would you mind, I mean, do you feel up to doing me a favor? After you eat, of course." The words spilled out in a rush.

Mary Kay's head still pounded, and she did not notice her landlady's nervousness. The food tasted so good, and she began to feel a bit stronger.

"What is it?" She laid the fork down and wadded the napkin on top of the empty plate.

"Well, if you don't mind," Pat glanced at the door, but Mary Kay wasn't watching. "Would you take my car up to my Dad's house for him? He will bring you back. I'd do it myself, but I . . . I . . . my little girl's not feeling well, and I don't want to leave her."

"Okay, no problem. It's the least I can do after you fixed me breakfast." Mary Kay went to find her purse and Pat followed her, giving directions to her father's house. He lived only six blocks away, and it did not occur to Mary Kay that he could have simply walked down for the car. She still was not feeling well. She wanted to get this over with and crawl back in bed.

Mary Kay excused herself at the door to her room, telling Pat she would be right out. She closed the door, went to the dresser drawer, and slipped the .38 caliber silver pistol into her purse. She never went anywhere without it. As a matter of habit, she unzipped an inside pocket in her handbag to see if the ten thousand dollars cash she carried was still there. It was.

When she came out of the room, Pat stood fiddling with the car keys in her hand. Mary Kay took them and walked to the car. Her landlady stood in the kitchen, watching her from behind the screen door. Mary Kay laid the purse on the seat beside her and backed the car from the driveway. Three blocks from the house, just before a traffic light, a car pulled in front of her, out of an alley.

The light was red, but when it turned green the car ahead of her did not move. Mary Kay waited a few seconds and was about to honk the horn when the car door opened. A man stepped out, looked straight at her, and started toward her car. Mary Kay leaned her head out her window. "Stalled? I'll just pull around you."

The man responded in a serious voice, "No, Mahaffey, I don't want you to move."

At this, he held up a badge. For the first time, alarms screamed inside her head; adrenaline surged in her veins and her mind exploded with thoughts. *How does he know who I am? He's a cop! I have to run. My gun! I'll shoot him and drive around. No one will even see me.* Her hands did not move from the wheel of the car, however, and her arms seemed frozen. For a reason that only God knows, she looked away from the man and saw first one and then another officer walking toward the car on her right, guns already drawn.

Her head turned back, as she continued to clutch the wheel. Now a fourth man was walking up beside the first one. He, too, had a drawn gun aimed straight at her. In that split second she realized that if her hands had left the steering wheel she would have been dead before she touched her gun.

PART THREE:

PRISON LIFE

CHAPTER TWELVE

Mary Kay slumped in the back seat of the car, her hands cuffed behind her and her strength drained away. She was mad at herself for not noticing the signals. How could she have missed them? Her landlady must have become suspicious when she did not respond to the name Susan. No wonder she had been so nervous that morning.

And I didn't even notice, Mary Kay berated herself. *How could I be so stupid? I know better than that. I should have left the first time I slipped up. But I was too sick; I'm still sick.* She shifted in the seat and laid her head back, as much to keep her nose from dripping as from exhaustion.

She was not worried, just annoyed about being caught. This was her first offense; they could not have *that* much on her. She probably had enough cash in her purse to cover bail. Her head began to pound harder. *I wonder if they will give me some aspirin when we get there.* They did not. They led her into a room and sat her at a table. They did cuff her hands in front so she could blow her nose with the tissues they gave her.

The FBI's first questions pertained to Paul's whereabouts. She was honest; she had not seen him since early July.

"That was the last time anyone else saw him, too," said the agent. "Do you know Frank Walters[6]?"

She eyed him suspiciously. "Why?"

"Well, about a week after you say you last saw your husband, he was stopped in the mountains of North Carolina for having a taillight out. Walters was with him. A rookie policeman pulled them over and sat in his patrol car while Mahaffey went inside the nearby service station to buy a light

---

[6] Name changed

for the car. After a while, the officer wondered why he had been gone so long and asked Walters, 'Where's the driver?' He didn't know so the officer went into the service station and asked the attendant, 'Where is the guy who came in here to get his light fixed?' The attendant said, 'I haven't seen anybody.' "

The agent continued his story, "Well, they took Walters down and questioned him. He kept telling them, 'I'm just a hitchhiker. He just picked me up off the highway. I don't have any idea who he is.' When they checked his background they discovered he was a parolee out of Louisiana and out of the state illegally. He never did own up to knowing Paul Mahaffey. What do you think of that?"

Mary Kay recognized Frank Walter's name; she knew he was someone Paul had worked with before. She debated whether to tell the agent. She decided it might be in her best interest to tell the truth. Hoping to improve her position, she added that Paul spoke fluent Spanish; she figured he had escaped to Mexico or South America.

The federal agents' interest in her was short-lived; they handed her over to the local authorities when they realized she had nothing else to tell them about Paul. Mary Kay's arrest probably would have received more media attention had it not been for another of the FBI's ten most wanted. That very day, the Illinois Department of Corrections was transporting Richard Speck, murderer of eight Chicago nurses, to the private cell on the top floor of the courthouse in Peoria, Illinois. There he was sentenced to fifty years per victim, to be served consecutively. Numerous death threats and the publicity surrounding the case brought out state, county, and federal policemen all over the city.

Mary Kay did not know this; she had not read a newspaper nor listened to the news for weeks. With no fanfare, she was quietly and efficiently checked into another part of the same jail. Neither the police nor the FBI were sure of her legal name, and she was not about to tell them. It was common for people in her line of work to use various names to make it difficult for police to track their arrest history.

The police do not care which name they use, they just choose one and add a list of AKA[7] names. In addition to her own name, Mary Kay Mahaffey, she

---

[7] Also Known As

had complete sets of identification for three aliases: Sandra Marshall, Susan Snyder and Kay O'Shea. The officer booked her under the name on the ID she was carrying at the time. She would use the name Sandra Marshall for the next six years.

At the processing desk, the officer gave her a property envelope to sign. Less than five dollars was listed. Where was the ten thousand she knew was in her purse? She needed it for bail. When she asked the policeman, he simply shrugged without answering.

Well, she thought bitterly, *I'll be bailed out anyway, perhaps by the end of the day. After all, I have connections.*

When they finally led her to a cell, she was so grateful to lie down she hardly noticed the sparseness of her quarters or the uncomfortable, thin plastic mattress on the bunk. She collapsed into a fitful sleep haunted by body aches and nightmares of huge guns.

She was not bailed out that day or the next. As the warrants arrived and the charges mounted, her hopes of getting released dwindled. There were thirty-five charges in four states, ranging from grand larceny to armed robbery, plus eleven federal indictments. At her arraignment, when Mary Kay explained to the judge that her money had disappeared, he simply looked bored and ruled that she was indigent and eligible for a court-appointed attorney. She was granted fifteen thousand dollars bail, far less than she had raised for Paul in Florida, but no one stepped forward to set up bond. Her friends had deserted her.

An attorney, Tom Penn,[8] was standing at the back of the courtroom at the time, so the judge named him to defend her. She eyed him as he walked toward her; he looked about her age. He introduced himself and gave her a business card.

"I'll come over to the jail in a day or so to talk to you," he said and left. Several days passed. Each day Mary Kay was allowed one phone call, and each day she used her call to leave a message for Attorney Penn. He did not respond. A female officer gave her some paper and an envelope, and she wrote him a letter. Still there was no response. Weeks passed. Then she was called

[8] Name changed

for an extradition hearing. A prosecutor from Alabama asked for her transfer to Tuscaloosa. As she entered the courtroom, she saw Mr. Penn and waved for him to come over.

"Where have you been? I did not know anything about this hearing until the matron brought us to court. Why haven't you been to see me?" Mr. Penn was clearly taken back by her vehemence.

"Yours isn't the only case I have," he muttered. "I can't see you without a female officer, and there weren't any on duty when I came to see you."

"That's a lie! There are women on duty all the time. You never even tried to see me," she accused.

"Yes, I did. The sergeant wouldn't let me come upstairs." The attorney's face was growing red; he was not accustomed to being challenged.

"If you can't even talk your way past a police sergeant, do you think for one moment I'm going to allow you to speak to a judge for me? You must be crazy, and you sure are fired!" The attorney stepped back even though she was handcuffed.

"You can't fire me; I was appointed by the judge," he protested.

"You can either withdraw or I'll fire you in front of the judge and the whole courtroom," her voice filled with venom. She left no doubt that she intended to embarrass him if he failed to withdraw. Penn requested a private consultation with the judge, who reluctantly allowed him to withdraw.

Tom Penn watched amazed as Mary Kay, her face now void of all anger, addressed the judge. "Your Honor, sir, am I allowed to say something?" her voice was now hesitant; she even sounded timid.

"Yes, you may; this is your case," the judge responded.

"Sir, I don't have any money, but I really do need someone to represent me who has practiced law a little longer," her manner was polite and she spoke with quiet dignity. "I understand Peoria has several good attorneys, and perhaps you could appoint one of *these* to represent me."

From her uniform pocket she pulled a piece of paper with three names, each of whom was a well-known criminal attorney. The bailiff passed the paper from her to the judge. Looking at the list briefly, the judge instructed the bailiff, "Call Jack Brunnenmeyer. Tell him I'll postpone the hearing until he sees her, but I want this finished by the end of the week."

A formal Warrant for Extradition was served upon her, and in a hearing on November 17, 1972, she was ordered by the local court to be extradited to Alabama. She was moved to the jail in Tuscaloosa. She was charged with armed robbery, burglary, and grand larceny. Two weeks later they moved her to Birmingham.

The women's jail on the top floor of the Jefferson County Courthouse overlooked a park in the town square. A prisoner could be detained, arraigned, make pretrial appearances and go through an entire trial without stepping into the light of day, until she was either released or sent to prison. Two officers escorted Mary Kay through a locked and guarded door in the basement, into a locked and guarded elevator, up to a locked and guarded floor near the top of the courthouse building. She faced a desk area where all prisoners came to be checked in or out.

Another female prisoner was escorted with her. Her name was Peggy, and she was as tall as Mary Kay was short, and as black as Mary Kay was fair. On the way to the women's jail, the police cruiser had stopped at the city jail where Peggy was put in the back seat next to Mary Kay. Peggy's eyes drooped from a hangover. Immediately after she was placed in the car, Mary Kay leaned forward and spoke to the driver through the mesh screen separating them.

"Good Lord, open the window! This woman smells like a pig sty!"

"Oh, shut up," Peggy snarled. The December wind was blowing and they were only a couple of miles from their destination. The officer ignored the request.

"Are you allergic to soap, or is it water you can't stand?" Mary Kay needled. Peggy shot her an angry look.

Besides arriving at jail at the same time, Peggy and Mary Kay had two other things in common; they were both toughened by life and each hated the other instantly. This seemed to take their minds off what was happening around them. Mary Kay continued to needle Peggy, and finally they fought about it. It didn't help; they still despised each other. They fought so much in the following days that the officers soon despised them as well. It was a lose-lose situation.

The attending officer checked her paperwork, stamped it, filed it, and waved her toward a locked and guarded door. Through the door, she climbed a flight of stairs. At the top they passed through another locked door into the women's quarters. They proceeded past several guard offices, through yet another locked door, and into the area where the cells and the day room were.

A big, brightly decorated Christmas tree filled the corner of the dayroom with gifts piled all around. It was painfully cheerful and reminiscent of home. She had seen nothing like it in the other jails she had been in.

The officers must be having a gift exchange, she thought.

Her escort did not stop at any of the dorm rooms but continued to a narrow hallway that branched off the far left corner of the floor. It was called "O Block." On the right side of this hallway was a short, solid door that Mary Kay would soon discover was the "hole." On the left was a taller, narrow door with a small, barred window. The officer opened this door to reveal a short, tight hallway with four doors, two on each side. Each door opened into a cell large enough for a single bed, a small sink, and a toilet. The officer ushered her into the first cell on the right and locked the door behind her. She heard him close and lock the hallway door. She was utterly alone; the other three cells were empty. Though she was moved to a dormitory room with other women a few weeks later, Mary Kay would return to this cell several times. This was solitary confinement, and she had earned it her first day.

At the top of the back wall of the cell was a tiny, barred window. The bunk was a metal plank connected to the wall by chains at each end. No foam pad softened the bunk. It was early afternoon and Mary Kay had not eaten anything since the biscuit and syrup served more than eight hours earlier in Tuscaloosa. Her stomach growled, but she knew she must wait several more hours. She did what she often did when fear threatened to take over; she sat down, took a deep breath, and had a talk with herself.

They are not going to break me; I will not cry; I will be tougher than anyone here. She clenched her fists. *They may not feed me, but I will not beg.*

She leaned back against the cold cement wall and told herself repeatedly, *I can handle anything they do to me.* Slowly she gained control of her emotions. After nearly an hour, she heard someone opening the hallway door.

A cheerful, friendly voice was speaking, "I'm sorry it took me so long to get up here, but we had several new people come in at the same time." The door to her cell opened. "Oh my, they didn't even give you a mattress!"

The voice matched the smiling face of a tall motherly woman. "Did they bring you a tray; have you eaten anything?"

Mary Kay sat up slowly. She was not sure how to respond to this unexpected friendliness. She glanced at the name tag above the woman's uniform pocket: Nadine Reed.

"No, I don't have a mattress, and I haven't eaten since breakfast," Mary Kay answered, her voice even and flat.

Still smiling, Mrs. Reed stood aside and motioned for her to come, "You can get a mattress out of that last cell. You might want to get two, they're pretty skimpy. I'll order you something from the kitchen," she said as she turned and walked out the narrow door.

Mary Kay stepped into the hallway. The last cell was used for storage; in addition to a stack of thin foam pads, she found some pillows, sheets, and pillowcases. Picking up two of the pads, she dragged them back to her cell and set about making her bed. Mrs. Reed soon returned with a tray of food and set it on the small shelf opposite the bed.

"This is all I could find; lunch has been over for quite a while," she said apologetically. Her kind voice was strange to Mary Kay's ears. She did not care what the food was; she was so hungry, she ate it ravenously. It was the first warm meal she had had in several weeks.

There is definitely something different about this jail, thought Mary Kay as she sat back on her bunk. *The food is warm, the officer is nice, and—it is so clean.*

She found out why at four the next morning when she was awakened, taken into the hall with the other inmates, and given a mop and bucket. Before mid-morning, they had cleaned every inch of the jail.

Christmas was a few days later. Mary Kay was bewildered when Officer Reed led her to the dayroom for a Christmas party with cookies and punch. The gifts under the tree were not for the officers; they were for the inmates. They had been bought and wrapped by local churches. Somewhere in the city were folks who remembered that prisoners are people.

Though she had been there only a few days, Mary Kay received two gifts. The church folk had known that some inmates might come at the last minute and had planned ahead. She was given a comb and brush set and a paint-by-number kit. Would wonders never cease? It was a tiny bright point in a very dark day for Mary Kay.

At first she enjoyed the privacy of her cell, but gradually the solitude wore on her. She looked forward to the early morning work duty because it allowed her a short time of human contact. She also enjoyed the outlet of hard physical labor. On Sundays she was able to sleep a little because instead of cleaning they had church—at seven A.M. Mary Kay was not keen on going to church; it was a painful reminder of Mama and home. She was also reminded of how far off God's path she had wandered. Nevertheless, she went; anything was better than solitary confinement.

She expected that some of the officers would lead the service but was surprised to learn that church folks came from the outside. Who in the world would come all this way at such an early hour to do church in prison?

"They come from a bunch of different churches," Alma said as they walked down the hall. "Some of them are Baptist, some are Holiness Pentecostal, some are Methodist and Presbyterian, and I can't remember the others."

Mary Kay was amazed. She had never heard of different denominations mixing together for church. *This should be interesting,* she thought, *I can't wait to see this.* She was even more amazed when she arrived in the dayroom. There were whites and blacks, men and women of varying ages, and she couldn't tell the Holy Rollers from the Presbyterians; they all were getting along so well. Why would all these folks want to come to jail when they did not have to, especially at seven in the morning?

Mary Kay sat next to a sweet-looking elderly woman who smiled at her. The woman's shy manner seemed to indicate weakness to Mary Kay and this stirred up resentment. She turned to the woman and in her most intimidating voice snapped, "Why do you bother?"

"Well," began the woman meekly, "Jesus loved you enough to go all the way to Calvary. We love you enough to come and tell you about Him."

Her words silenced Mary Kay for the moment but they did not move her heart. The wall she had built was thick and strong; she felt only bitterness. She determined to be just difficult enough to irritate these religious folk but not enough to be banned from going to church altogether. She had to get out of that miserable cell, no matter what.

Another escape from the loneliness of her cell was to attend the weekly Bible study each Tuesday afternoon. A very fine and proper lady named Betty Bostwick led the study. She drove downtown from her beautiful southern home to the Jefferson County Jail every week. She was well to do with many political and social connections—not the kind of visitor ordinarily expected to be found at jail. Her friends did not understand her desire to go into the jail each week.

A few years earlier, Betty had moved back to Birmingham, her hometown, and felt led by God to teach. She waited, but no one at Briarwood Presbyterian Church asked her to teach. Then one day a friend called.

"Betty," she said, "I'm teaching a Bible study in the jail. I have to miss next week. Will you fill in for me?"

Well no other door has opened; I guess I will go to the jail, thought Betty.

It was not long before Betty took over the weekly Bible study. One day she arrived in the courthouse basement, went through the clearance process, and reached the seventh floor as usual. In the room where they held their study, she noticed a new woman.

"The first time I met Mary Kay, she looked like a drowned rat. Her hair was stringy, hanging in her face. She was so bedraggled looking; you could certainly see the effects of the life she had been living." Mary Kay did not think Betty had much to offer her.

I know these stories forward and backward, she thought. *I could tell them everything about Jesus.* However, she came back each week. Betty knew that in spite of all her knowledge of the Bible, Mary Kay did not know Jesus personally. From the day she first met her, Betty prayed for Mary Kay and asked others to pray for her. And there was one woman who had been earnestly praying for her since before she was born—Mama.

The Bible says, "The prayer of a godly person is powerful. It makes things happen.[9]" Soon things began to happen for Mary Kay.

---

[9] James 5:16, *New International Reader's Version*

CHAPTER THIRTEEN

Mary Kay was back in the cell she had occupied on her first day. It was her fifth trip to this cell. *These women are impossible to live with,* she thought. She felt an annoying prick of her conscience and she knew the fault was not in them; it was in her. What is this? she wondered. Her conscience was pricking her more often, particularly with the question, *How did I get into this mess?*

She stood up to stretch and shut out these thoughts. A Gideon Bible peeked from under the flat, plastic pillow on the top bunk where she had stuffed it her first day in the cell. Bibles always brought uncomfortable memories of Mama and home. For the last six years, every hotel she had stayed in had a Gideon Bible to unsettle her. She had not read any of them.

She paced back and forth furiously, trying to escape the crushing load of sorrow and remorse pressing upon her. In desperation, she snatched the Bible and sank down on the lower bunk, hoping to occupy her mind and relieve the anxiety that continued to build. She idly flipped through the pages. Her eyes fastened on a phrase: "a new heart." She was in the book of Ezekiel, chapter 36. She read verses 26 and 27:

> A new heart also will I give you, and a new spirit will I put within you: and I will take away the stony heart out of your flesh, and I will give you a heart of flesh. And I will put my spirit within you, and cause you to walk in my statutes, and you shall keep my judgments, and do them. [10]

A new heart; I could certainly use a new heart, she thought. She knew her heart was stony, knew it was filled with hatred and bitterness. But the truth of those

---

[10] *King James Version*

verses reached deep into a well of sorrow and bitterness and touched a tiny vein of hope. Could she actually have a new heart? She read the verses again and suddenly she was back in the third grade in the little one-room Vernon School where Mrs. Conlon taught her grammar. Little Mary Kay Petet enjoyed diagramming sentences. Now, nearly twenty years later she remembered how grammar helped her understand the meaning of sentences. She began to mentally diagram the verses before her.

God is the one the sentence is about. He's the subject, the one who does the action. The predicate is the action done. The object is the one the action is done to, that's me. God does something to me. He removes my stony heart, He causes me to walk in His ways, and He puts a new heart in me. He does it; it isn't up to me!

It was not up to her! The force of that realization came crashing into her mind. God would make her into the person He wanted her to be. All her life had she worked at developing willpower, and now she understood—*God does it to me. I do not have to do it.* She immediately knew what had gone wrong all those years ago when she had struggled to be a good Christian. She thought salvation was going forward in church, saying the sinner's prayer, and then following the rules. If you believe in your heart and confess with your mouth, get baptized and join the church, you're saved. She had done all that, but she had known deep down she was not saved. She was never able to be good enough.

Now she understood: Salvation had nothing to do with her promises to be good or how good she was able to be through the force of her will. It was not about anything *she* did at all; it was about what *God* did. She did not have to do anything except show up, present herself, say yes and receive. God would empower her to do what He wanted her to do.

A verse memorized years before came to her mind. "For it is God who is at work in you, making you willing and able to perform his good pleasure."[11] How was she so deceived to think it was her job to be good? How arrogant of her to think that she could be good by her own effort! If she could do it herself, then she would not need Jesus; His death would have been a cruel joke.

Relief and gratitude washed over her like a burst of clean rain. *I don't even have to want to, on my own; He makes me willing and able.* She slid off the bunk

---

[11] Philippians 2:13

and knelt on the concrete, not noticing the cold hardness.

"Father, if You mean that verse for me, if You will give me a new heart and make me the kind of person You want me to be, I'll give my life to You. Wherever You want me to go, whatever You want me to do, that's what I will do."

She felt a strange, inner sensation as she pulled herself back up onto the bunk. She recognized it; she had seen it in Mama all those years and longed for it all her life—the peace that passes understanding. Deep gratitude overwhelmed her. She lay down, smiling, a thank-you on her lips, and slept as she hadn't in years.

Long before the piercing morning alarm, she lay awake, thinking. What would God do, now that she had given Him her life? What would it mean to have a change of heart? How long would it take? What would it look like? What would it feel like? She thought about the verses she had read the night before and the word *attitude* came to mind. She had heard this word often; everyone told her she had a *bad* attitude.

For the first time in her life she heard the still, small voice. It was not an audible voice; it was simply a clear, strong thought that said, "Go apologize to Peggy." She knew *that* idea had not come from her! She also knew that if she wanted God to change her heart, she had to do what He asked of her.

"But you don't understand what that means," she argued with God. "Apology means weakness and showing weakness is deadly in a place like this." She had promised to do whatever He asked and already she was not sure she was willing. This task seemed too impossible and fearful to contemplate.

She was still arguing with God when the officer appeared to release her for work duty. She pushed the mop across the floor, mumbling under her breath to God. "What if I start treating Peggy really nice from now on? We will just forget about the fights I had with her and the hateful ugly things I said to her, it is all in the past. From this point on I will be nice and that will count as an apology." This seemed reasonable to her.

She walked into the dayroom and picked up a book. The first word she saw on the page was "apologize." She slammed the book shut and turned on the radio. The song blared, "Will you accept my ah-pol-oh-gee?" She turned it off and went out into the hall to join some women there. They were talking about apologizing.

"Okay! Okay, God, I get the message." Just acting nice would *not* count with

Him; she must go back and ask forgiveness before moving forward. How should she do it? What if she gave Peggy a present? Would that help? She felt in her heart that God would accept that gesture and get off her back. But what could she give her? They had taken everything she owned when she was arrested.

As she walked back to her cell, she remembered the nightgown. A lady in the Sunday school class had discovered she did not have anything to sleep in and had brought her a nightgown. Nightgowns were one of Mary Kay's favorite things but she disliked the high-collared, long-sleeved, yellow flannel one the lady had brought her. Oh no, she liked flowing, silky gown and robe sets.

Just the other day she had received a package from home. In it were letters, some books and cookies, and at the very bottom, wrapped in tissue, was a soft, turquoise nightgown, just the kind she loved. Her baby sister Ilene had bought it with her babysitting money, and it told her, above all, that she was still loved. She cherished that nightgown.

"Well, I have two; I'll give Peggy the flannel one."

Immediately she felt a faint check in her spirit. She knew what it meant, and she knew that if she ignored it, the next time it would be harder to say yes to the movement of the Holy Spirit in her heart. Hadn't she been resisting Him that way for years? She did not like the message she was hearing. Did God really want her to give her beautiful new nightgown to Peggy?

She picked up her Bible and began what would become a lifelong habit—checking "The Book" for answers to her questions, simple or deep. She began where others do when they first study the Bible, in Genesis. Soon she came to the story of Cain and Abel. Before, she had not understood what was wrong with Cain's sacrifice, but now she knew. God was the one who determined what was best, and He would not accept anything less. She had her answer.

The next morning, as the inmates moved into the hall to begin their daily chores, Mary Kay picked up the turquoise nightgown from her bunk, ran to Peggy, and shoved it into her hands.

"Here, Peggy." Her words rushed out. "You can have this. I have two. I'm sorry."

Before Peggy could reply, Mary Kay ran back around the corner, her heart pounding. She looked to see if anyone noticed, but the only person not working was Peggy, who stood in the hall with her mouth open, a nightgown in her hands.

Several days later, Mary Kay and Peggy mopped the floor side by side. Mary Kay's words came in awkward bursts as she explained that God had directed her to give Peggy the nightgown. Peggy looked suspicious but just nodded. She was relieved that Mary Kay was not planting hot goods on her.

The next Sunday, when the group from outside came for Sunday school, Peggy stood in the doorway of the dayroom. Mary Kay motioned her to come and sit with her. She ignored the looks of surprise the other inmates gave each other when Peggy sat beside her.

At first, Mary Kay thought her growth would be easy. After all, she did not use profanity, she did not smoke, and she had never abused alcohol or drugs. In fact, she felt rather smug about how good she had been and was shocked to learn the other women thought she was mean and rude and hateful. Mary Kay wondered what was wrong. God quickly revealed to her how she belittled and made fun of people; even her jokes were unkind and sarcastic.

She was especially bothered when she heard others say she was judgmental. She thought they were wrong, but she asked God to show her what they meant. It didn't take long before it occurred to her that a judge is one who passes sentence on someone. Each time she used words like "ought" or "should" or said, "If it was me, I would have . . ." she was judging someone. She was sure she rarely used these words, but nonetheless, she asked God to help her stop saying them.

Over the following days and weeks she was shocked to hear one of those phrases emerge from her lips in nearly every conversation! When she heard herself speak this way, she stopped in mid-sentence. Others waited for her to continue and looked baffled when she said, "Oh, never mind," and walked away. She never imagined letting God do His work in her would be this hard.

Mary Kay knew she needed to tell the others in Betty's Bible study class about her prayer in solitary. She dreaded it. So many times in the past she had gone forward during church services to rededicate her life to God, but within a day or two the commitment was forgotten. Mary Kay did not want another false start. She determined to tell no one until she was convinced it was real.

One Tuesday, her stomach knotted as she entered the dayroom for Bible study. She could sense God gently prompting her to confess Jesus publicly.

"Not today. I'm not ready," she argued with Him. "How do I know my faith is real?" God's urging was more powerful than her doubts; it had to be today. She sat down in her chair and rubbed her damp palms over her pants. She prayed silently that Betty would not follow her opening prayer by asking if anyone had something to share.

God's answer was no; Betty asked as she always did. Mary Kay prayed more earnestly for someone else to speak first. Once again, God's answer was no. Only the pounding of Mary Kay's heart disturbed the long silence. She was sure everyone else could hear it. She took a deep breath, looked at her hands in her lap, and spoke in a low voice. "The other night when I was on O block, I read a verse in the Bible in Ezekiel that said God would change my heart, so I prayed and asked Him to do that." The words fell over each other in a rush to get out.

"That's why you're different," said one of the women. "I wondered what happened to you!" The others nodded and Mary Kay felt a rush of pure joy.

It worked! God has changed me already, she thought.

Betty was pleased at Mary Kay's confession of faith, but not surprised. She had noticed the change weeks before. Mary Kay had stopped being cynical and sarcastic and became excited by the lessons. She had asked questions before, but now she was curious, not contentious. "After her conversion, she went lickety-split and soaked up everything I could give her. She wanted to learn about issues of fundamental theology; she was really trying to understand what God had for her through His Word. As time went on, I had a hard time keeping up with her. Not only did her attitude change, she had a whole new appearance. There was a glow."

Occasionally, Betty brought a friend to the weekly study in the jail to share her testimony. That is how Mary Kay met Nina Hamilton and Mitzi Hinde, two women who became lifelong friends. Nina and Mitzi grew up together in privileged families, and neither had ever been in a prison. Whatever one did, the other wanted to do as well, so when Betty invited Nina to go to the county jail with her, Mitzi had to try it also. Volunteers who visit prison either love it or hate it. Nina and Mitzi loved it and began to visit regularly. Soon they were corresponding with Mary Kay through letters as well.

Mary Kay made friends with another Christian inmate at Jefferson County Jail. Like Mary Kay, Bertha Barfield grew up attending church and studying the Bible. She had attended Miles College on a music scholarship before coming to jail, and she sang more beautifully than anyone Mary Kay had ever heard. Perhaps this was because gospel songs meant more to her now than before.

One afternoon, Bertha and Mary Kay stood together at the window of the day-room watching the construction of a Sheraton hotel across the park. Mary Kay suddenly turned to her friend, "Bertha, someday we're going to be over there, and you're going to sing and I'm going to share my testimony before a huge crowd."

"You sure are one crazy white girl," laughed Bertha.

In the weeks following her conversion, Mary Kay had time to reflect on her life and to examine the question that haunted her as she read the Gideon Bible in solitary: *How did I get into this mess?* She knew it had not been a single leap from Bible-toting girl to gun-toting robber. Little steps, each so close to the last that it hardly seemed she had moved at all, had eventually brought her to this place. Each lie made the next, bigger one easier. Each selfish choice produced more self-serving motives. Each time she blamed her father for her life, it became harder to see her own responsibility. Lies, no matter how small they seemed at the time, were the stepping-stones that led to breaking the law.

The lying must stop. She knew from bitter experience that if she ignored the still, small voice of the Lord, her heart would become harder and harder until she would not be able to hear His prompting at all. Mary Kay had been avoiding thoughts of her upcoming trial. How would she apply what God was teaching her? To be honest, she must plead guilty. She had done most of what she was charged with and more, much more. The FBI estimated that she had stolen from three to five million dollars. If she pleaded guilty, additional charges might be found against her, which the police did not know about now.

She wondered what she ought to do about the charges in other states. She knew she was going to prison, but she did not want to complete her sentence only to be moved to another state for another trial. She could spend the rest of her life serving sentences in one state and then another.

For days she argued mentally with God, trying to plea bargain with Him. "Lord, I'll plead guilty to the burglary and grand larceny charges, and You get them to drop the armed robbery charge." *That* was a capital offense. No matter how she bargained, it seemed as if God had turned away and was no longer listening.

CHAPTER FOURTEEN

She was returned to the Tuscaloosa jail for trial. The officers were puzzled by the change in her; the last time she had been anything but pleasant. When she asked permission to attend a church service, they were suspicious. She did not complain or threaten when they said it was only for the men. She simply asked if the chaplain could visit her. Instead of cutting remarks and insults, now she talked about Jesus and read her Bible. She was so changed that they wondered if she was trying to trick or coerce them.

One morning, around nine o'clock, she heard the sobbing of a child. It sounded close, and went on and on. Sometimes it subsided to low, exhausted sobbing, and then it would swell into a panicked wail. The cries echoed through the halls of the Tuscaloosa jail, but none of the inmates around her knew what it was about. At lunchtime, a male inmate came around to deliver the meals.

"What is that crying?" Mary Kay asked.

"There's a little boy in the drunk tank."

"Whatever for?"

"They picked up his mother early this morning. She had the delirium tremors and was running through the streets naked. Her neighbors called the police. She had a nine-year-old boy at home. They've put him in there until they decide what to do with him. I guess they are waiting until Social Services comes to pick him up. Officer Murphy[12] keeps threatening him if he doesn't shut up."

How could she be so heartless? When Officer Murphy entered the cellblock a short while later, Mary Kay could hardly contain her disgust.

---

[12] Name changed

119

"Hey, Murphy!" she yelled. "What's that crying?"

"I'll give him something to cry about," replied the woman.

"Isn't it illegal to do that?"

"I'm no baby sitter," she snapped and walked on through the corridor.

Mary Kay sat down on her bunk, fuming. She couldn't let that poor child be treated this way, but what could she do? Suddenly an idea came to her. She lay down on the bunk and began kicking the metal wall. An officer rushed into the corridor and looked in her cell.

"I asked to see my lawyer, and I will continue to do this until he shows up," Mary Kay told him. The officer tried to talk her out of it, but soon every wall, in every cellblock, was reverberating with kicking. The officer left and called Mary Kay's lawyer.

Ralph Burroughs was the public defender and Mary Kay's assigned lawyer. He came quickly when the officer explained the need for his intervention was urgent. Mary Kay told him about the boy. He promised to take care of it immediately and left her cell. Very soon the crying stopped. A cheer went up through the jail. About an hour later Ralph returned to see Mary Kay.

"What did you do?" she asked.

"I told them they were violating this boy's rights, since he wasn't charged with anything, and one of the sheriffs came and took him to his office. I also called Social Services. They were here within thirty minutes."

"What about Officer Murphy? How can she get away with that?"

Ralph shrugged, "Oh, that's just the way she is."

"What do you mean?"

"About twelve years ago, when we put my daughter in kindergarten, she hated it. Every day she whined about having to go. We thought it was just an adjustment period until we found out other parents were saying the same thing about their children. When we quizzed the kids, we found out they were afraid of going to school because of their teacher, Mrs. Murphy. The children told us she often pinched them—hard—and pulled their hair or made them stand up in the front of the room while she made fun of them. Her husband was a deputy sheriff, so the parents got together and decided to let her resign without any charges."

"You allowed her to get away with it?" Mary Kay was incredulous.

"It would have done us no good to push it without the testimony of the other families. They didn't want to traumatize their children any further."

"So you let her get a job as a matron in the county jail, where she works with *juveniles?*"

Ralph looked sheepish and nodded. After he left, Mary Kay seethed for hours. Everyone knew the woman was cruel to children, and yet nothing was done about it. Well, she would do something. She did the only thing she could think to do—she got down on her knees and prayed.

A few weeks later, Ralph Burroughs asked her if she would testify at a grand jury about the event in the jail. She did not hesitate an instant. For the first time in her life, she felt she was able to do something to correct an injustice.

"I'm going to prison for things I have done," Mary Kay told the grand jury, "but I don't understand how the citizens of this county could allow this woman to abuse their own children and then let her hold a position where she has access to other children." In the end, Officer Murphy lost her job.

Many of the officers began to respect Mary Kay; she did what they had not done. Her stay at the Tuscaloosa jail was more pleasant after that. She prayed and read her Bible every day as she waited for her trial to begin. Mama had planted the truth into her that the Bible was the Word of God, and although Mary Kay had strayed far, she never doubted it. She knew the Gospels were four biographies of Jesus; in order to know Him better, she read them over and over, analyzing the different writing styles. During the next two years, she read the Bible from Genesis to Revelation eight times, including reading chapters of Psalms and Proverbs daily. She often stopped to ponder, praying to understand what she was reading. When she did not understand, she assumed any error was in her, not in God's Word.

One day she discovered a disturbing Scripture passage. The opening verses of Leviticus, chapter six, discuss stealing, lying, cheating, and other things she had done. The passage did not merely describe these things, it said she must restore, or pay back, those things she had taken. How could she ever do that? She was not sure how much money she had stolen in the previous five years, or from whom. And how could she repay people for lying to them? This passage raised more questions than answers.

When the trusties delivered the evening meal, she slipped a note to the inmate who slid the tray beneath her door. He gave a slight nod of his head and repeated his usual comment, "Be back in twenty minutes to get the tray."

Her only way to communicate with Glen, the man who led the men's church service, was through the trusties. He was a Gideon who attended First Baptist Church. He occasionally stopped to see Mary Kay after the Sunday service. He was impressed with her questions and more than happy to encourage her. He gave her a Cruden's Concordance of the Bible and showed her how to use it. She loved looking up words and the book soon became worn.

On Sunday morning she watched the clock as the time neared for him to come. She wasn't sure whether he had received her message or if he would be able to come. Shortly after nine, she heard the door at the end of the hallway in front of the cells open.

"Man in the hallway."

The call was a warning to any woman who happened to be using the toilet or shower in her cell, which was in full view from the hall. Mary Kay greeted Glen briefly when he reached the bars of her cell, and she launched directly into the questions nagging her.

"I've been reading a lot in the Old Testament, and in Leviticus it talks about making restitution and I was wondering if that meant I had to pay back everything I stole, and what do you do if you don't remember all of them, and how do you make restitution for lying?"

With raised brows, Glen stepped back from the cell, "Whoa, slow down, I can't answer them all at once. I'm not even sure if I can answer them at all."

Glen told her that God always provides for what He requires; she could repay only what He provided. Since she had no money and no income Glen suggested her responsibility right now was to restore the broken relationships produced by her lies.

"That will only take a couple of decades." Mary Kay was overwhelmed, realizing the number of times she had offended members of her family and the many people who had taken the brunt of her verbal assaults.

Days went by, and she avoided reading in Leviticus. She began to read

Psalm 119:33–40 every morning, praying for the wisdom and understanding that David was writing about. Finally, she knew she needed to return to Leviticus. She was afraid if she disobeyed God, she would not feel His presence as she usually did. What she read there did not just disturb her, it frightened her. She closed the Bible with a shudder.

When he arrived, Glen was usually greeted by Mary Kay's smiling face and cheerful voice, but this time she was obviously troubled. Glen knew that inmates are often slow to trust others with their problems. He waited a few moments before asking, "Is there something you'd like to talk about?"

"No, not really, but I think I need to." She gave a heavy sigh. Glen waited politely until she spoke again, "I know I have a legal right to plead not guilty and make the court prove I'm guilty, but God keeps bugging me to plead guilty. I don't mind doing that, I *am* guilty, but if I plead guilty I'm afraid that I'll have to tell on some other people. I am not sure I can or should confess someone else's sins. I have been in Leviticus again. It says if I know about a sin and do not do anything to stop it, then I am as guilty as the one who does it. Does that mean I have to plead guilty *and* testify against others?"

Glen was at a loss. "That's a deep question. I am not really sure what a Christian should do in that situation, but I can talk to my pastor. Dr. Randall is a real scholar and he might know."

Disappointed that she would have to wait, and doubtful that the pastor would visit her in the jail, she asked, "Do you think he would write me a letter if I sent him my questions?"

"I'll tell him you have some questions about the Bible and perhaps he'll give us some help." Glen was hesitant to commit his pastor. He had never told Mary Kay that the victims of her crime in Tuscaloosa, the couple she held at gunpoint in their home, were prominent members of First Baptist. He was afraid they might feel betrayed if their pastor visited her.

He prayed with her and assured her before leaving, "God will give you an answer. James 1:5 says, 'If any of you lacks wisdom, let him ask of God, who gives to all liberally and without reproach, and it will be given to him.' "[13]

A few days later, an officer announced that she had a visitor. Mary Kay

---

[13] *New King James Version*

could take nothing with her. She was put in handcuffs and escorted from her cell to the visiting room reserved for attorney/client visits. Mary Kay was surprised to see a stranger when she entered the small room. The man was no taller than she, stout and nearly bald. He was dressed in a light gray suit; she could see that it had definitely *not* been purchased at Sears. He stood on the opposite side of a table that separated them and waited until she was seated before introducing himself.

"I'm C.C. Randall from First Baptist Church. Glen told me a great deal about you. I'm not sure I can answer your questions, but I must say I was interested in how you came to ask them."

The next hour seemed like minutes to Mary Kay as she and Dr. Randall talked. She told him the story of her childhood—about growing up in church and about hating her father. She related the story of surrendering her life to Jesus Christ and how much she was learning as she read the Bible. "I knew some of these stories so well when I was little, but when I read them now, it seems I understand so much more than I did before."

Dr. Randall smiled and nodded encouragement as she spoke. When she was done, he said, "I understand you're having some questions about your guilt."

"Oh, no, I don't have any question about that," she exclaimed. "I'm guilty all right. I intend to confess, but how much should I tell when it involves other people? I am also wondering if I should write letters to the other states and confess my crimes there? I was reading in Leviticus—oh, I wish I had my Bible."

Dr. Randall pulled a small, slim Bible from inside his coat. "Oh good," Mary Kay said. She reached for it and turned to the book of Leviticus. Another hour passed before a deputy opened the door.

"Sorry, sir, your time is up."

"It looks like I'll just have to come again so we can finish this conversation," Dr. Randall said with a smile. Turning to the officer, he said, "I'll be with you in just a moment, as soon as we pray." The deputy nodded, backed out of the room, and closed the door. The pastor said a short prayer. Then he promised to check his calendar and return as soon as he could.

Pastor Randall was as good as his word and returned two or three more times before her trial date. Their conversations gave her much food for thought. Yet his encouragement and acceptance ministered to her more than any particular answers he provided.

Several years later Mary Kay learned the price he had paid for befriending her. Several members of the church were angry with him because he had visited the despised criminal. Less than a year after she went to prison, he left First Baptist Church and accepted a position teaching at a seminary in New Orleans.

As Mary Kay searched her Bible she came upon 2 Timothy 1:12. ". . . nevertheless I am not ashamed: for I know whom I have believed, and am persuaded that he is able to keep that which I have committed unto him against that day."[14]

Do I trust God? Do I really trust Him? she wondered. She pulled out a piece of paper and wrote the verse down. Over the next several days, she added it to a growing collection of verses she had memorized. This verse, in particular, settled the question of whether she should initiate contact with other states or wait to see what they would do about the other charges. Reading in 2 Timothy she decided to wait, trust the Lord, and tell the truth when the time came.

Her attorney told her that one of her accomplices in the armed robbery charge was not cooperating with his attorney. Reed was a novice, it was his first charge, and Mary Kay knew he did not want to betray her in any way. However, he was hurting himself by not cooperating. She remembered that the passage in Leviticus said that if she knew about a wrong, she was supposed to do what she could to correct it.

Mary Kay asked her attorney if she could meet with Reed and his attorney. Reed was free on bail so they visited her. She told them that she was going to plead guilty no matter what Reed did, so he should do what his attorney advised: blame her and request probation. She would back up his story; she really had influenced him to commit the crime. If he cooperated, they would give him probation since this was his first offense. For the first time in years, she felt good about something she had done—not only was it not illegal, she was helping someone else.

---

[14] *The King James Version*

Perhaps no one was more surprised than her attorney, Ralph Burroughs, when she told him to change her plea to guilty. "Tell them we'll accept a ten-year sentence," Mary Kay instructed him with a touch of her old bravado.

His face grew somber. "They're not offering ten. The prosecutor is asking thirty to life."

She nodded, but her heart sank. A sentence of more than ten years meant mandatory prison time; she would not be eligible for simple probation. With the number of charges against her, she did not really expect probation, but since this was her first conviction, she hoped for leniency. Mary Kay reached into her pocket and felt the scrap of paper with the verse in second Timothy.

The morning of her court date dawned sunny and warm. June was beautiful in Alabama, but Mary Kay would not have noticed even if she had been able to see it from her jail cell. Immediately after breakfast, Sandra Baker, her lawyer's secretary, arrived. Mrs. Baker had been her primary contact with the attorney and she was always pleasant and kind. She did not act as though Mary Kay were someone to be afraid of, as others did. She brought a dress, modest and understated, just what lawyers want their female clients to wear to lend an aura of virtue in the courtroom.

The effect was spoiled when the officer came in to accessorize it with hand-cuffs and leg irons. A chain encircled her waist and was attached to the cuffs in front. At the back, another chain went from her waist to a short chain that stretched between the leg irons. Movement was slow and painful as the chains hit against her ankles.

The deputy led her downstairs from her cell, but instead of walking across the alley to the courthouse, she steered Mary Kay into an elevator. Beneath the jail was an underground hallway that led into the basement of the court-house. It was rarely used, except to avoid media coverage or for security pur-poses. The door opened, and several deputies, armed with shotguns, stood waiting. She turned to look at them as she was guided along the corridor. She was startled to see they were following her. With a puzzled look she turned to the female officer leading her.

"Guess you didn't hear," the officer said. "Rumor has it that if you go to trial, you'll be shot before you can testify. I also heard that the prosecutor got some death threats." The woman's face looked grim. Mary Kay's fears about testifying against others were confirmed.

No one spoke again as they walked through several halls and into another elevator that took them up to the third-floor courtroom. The leg irons slowed their progress. Ralph waited for them when they stepped from the elevator. One of the deputies pulled open the tall, heavy doors to the courtroom.

Usually all inmates with hearings or trials on any given day are taken to the courtroom together. A deputy stands and watches them while lawyers, prosecutors, witnesses, and observers mill around, talking until the judge enters. However, except for the bailiff and the prosecutor, the only other people present in the courtroom on this day were two additional armed officers and two men in business suits sitting in the back row. She did not recognize either one of them and they did not look at her as she passed.

Mary Kay sat at the defendant's table with Ralph and his secretary. Everyone stood when the bailiff announced the arrival of Judge Joseph Colquitt. In his mid-thirties, he was the youngest sitting District Court judge in Alabama at the time. To Mary Kay, he looked more like a college student than a judge. Although he was only a few years older than she was, she felt much older than him.

Her lawyer joined prosecutor Louis Lackey in front of the judge. They spoke briefly in low voices, but Mary Kay's thoughts were so restless she did not even try to hear what they were saying. She was worried about the two men in the back.

"The defendant will approach the bench," the bailiff cried. Mary Kay shuffled to the front, stood between the lawyers, and looked at the judge.

"You are Sandra Marshall?" he asked. It was not illegal to use an alias. Mary Kay had decided to keep this name to protect her family, especially Sean.

"Yes, Your Honor."

"Do I understand correctly that you wish to change your plea from not guilty to guilty?"

"Yes, sir, that's correct."

"Are you fully aware of the nature of the charges against you?"

"Yes, sir, I am."

"Did you make this decision under duress?"

"No, sir."

"Have you been offered a plea agreement or any other inducement? Have you been threatened or coerced?" She began to respond, but his questions came too fast. The judge was simply rattling the questions off as if from rote memory. His voice droned on in a flat tone. Finally, he was saying, "In accordance with the Statues of the State of Alabama . . . for the crimes of armed robbery and grand larceny, this court sentences you to serve twenty-one years . . ."

His voice trailed off, and from the corner of her eye she saw the prosecutor, shaking his head vigorously and mouthing quietly, "No, no, Your Honor, thirty years." Judge Colquitt hesitated and looked at Ralph Burroughs. Before her lawyer could enter a verbal objection, the judge looked at the papers in front of him and muttered, "Oh, well, twenty-one years and a day will do it."

Then he directed his gaze at her and continued his sentence, "At Julia Tutwiler Prison for Women in Wetumpka, Alabama."

What had just happened? Mary Kay was dazed, but Ralph seemed thrilled as he led her back to the table. Sandra hugged her and whispered, "The judge had agreed with the prosecutor to give you thirty years, but God apparently had something else in mind."

As she turned, Mary Kay saw the two men at the back rise and leave the courtroom. Three deputies came forward to escort her back to her cell. "I'll come by tomorrow to see you," said Ralph as he flashed a big grin. She was still bewildered; everyone seemed to think it was so great that the judge had given her only twenty-one years. To her it seemed no less a lifetime than thirty. She was only twenty-eight years old. "Twenty-one years and a day. Twenty-one years and a day." The phrase ran continuously through her mind; she did not even remember the journey back to her cell.

CHAPTER FIFTEEN

The building could have been a factory or a dairy or a school but for the fence. Tall, chain-linked steel with razor wire corkscrewing across the top, it was meant to be good at keeping people out, or keeping them in. On a hot, humid July day, the police cruiser arrived from Tuscaloosa County Jail. Mary Kay looked out the car window at the words carved into the building above the door: JULIA TUTWILER PRISON FOR WOMEN. This was the one place she had not wanted to go and the very place God seemed to want her to be. The summer sun blinded the three inmates as they emerged stiffly from the back seat. Each woman wore a waist chain, handcuffs, and ankle cuffs. They shuffled toward the building, hampered by a common chain looped from waist to waist.

With an officer in front and one behind, the threesome mounted the steps to a large barred door. The officer ahead of them pushed a buzzer. In a few minutes a woman emerged to admit them into the small entryway. The door clanged shut behind them, sending a shudder through Mary Kay. Ten months of clanging doors had not accustomed her to that sound. The door in front of them opened, and they stepped into a large waiting room with no furniture. The second door sounded as final and harsh as the first as it closed behind them.

The walls were lined with pictures of state officials and lists of visitation rules. To the left were restrooms, and to the right was the door to the warden's office. Straight ahead was the front desk and to the side a long hall led to the prisoners' living quarters.

The three chained women stood silently, careful not to look at each other lest they expose their fear and dread. The officers approached the desk clerk's window to exchange papers and came back to remove the cuffs and chains. They turned and left without saying a word. The woman who opened the door remained. She appeared to be in her early fifties with snow-white hair and fair skin. She wore a blue uniform.

"My name is Mrs. Faust, and I am the one who handles your mail every day." Her face was pleasant as she spoke. "You will be spending the next several days in the infirmary for orientation. Turn your possessions over to me. I will go through them, and they will be returned to you in a few days when you are assigned to a dorm. The officers are having lunch right now, but when one is available to escort you, you will follow her down the hallway. Meanwhile you must wait here. You may use the bathroom if you choose, but you need to understand that the windows are locked and it will not benefit you to try anything."

They saw women in lighter blue, shapeless dresses gathering in the long hallway, looking in their direction. At the end of the hallway double doors opened to a large dining room. Two barred gates separated the new arrivals from the dining room, and at each gate stood an inmate with a key in her hand. These "gate girls" opened the gates when an officer approached, but unless an inmate had a pass, she was not allowed through. Along each side of the hallway were closed doors, and at the far end a huge fan hummed. No windows or air conditioning gave relief from the summer heat; the only breeze came from the fan. It did not reach their end of the hallway.

A long thirty minutes passed before two officers joined Mrs. Faust. The female officer looked about the same age as Mrs. Faust but their ages and their uniforms were their only similarities. Arlene Holley was six feet tall, looked like a football player, and sounded like a Marine drill sergeant. The male officer was as tall as Mrs. Holley but was lean and lanky and smoking a pipe. Mr. Bell nodded toward the inmates without speaking.

"All right, ladies," barked Mrs. Holley, "we are going down the hall; single file. You will not stop and visit with anyone. You will not accept anything anyone tries to hand you, nor will you give anything to them. Mr. Bell will lead the way, and I will be watching from behind." Mrs. Holley sounded like she was giving orders to an entire platoon instead of speaking to three women who stood less than five feet from her.

The gate girl opened the gate and stood aside as they passed through. As if on signal, every door in the hallway opened, revealing inmates crowded together watching them. The arrival of new inmates was not announced by loudspeaker, but news spread rapidly through the dorms. Inmates gathered in the central hallway to watch as the "new fish," usually dressed in "free-world" clothes, walked in scared and bewildered.

As they were led down the hall toward the infirmary, Mary Kay's two companions walked closer to each other and kept their eyes down. Voices spoke from the growing crowd. "Oooh, baby, you sure are fine." "You can come to my house. I'll take care of you." Taunts followed them as they walked between the lines of women. "Oooh, is the baby afraid?" Mary Kay felt like a bug under a microscope; it was unsettling but she carefully kept her face emotionless. She walked evenly, keeping pace with Mr. Bell's long strides, her eyes forward so she would not appear intimidated.

"She thinks she's tough doesn't she? Look at that." She knew this last comment was about her. Mary Kay turned to look an inmate straight in the eye. "Get back to work," an officer snapped, but the inmates merely took a few steps backwards. As the little group approached the dining room, Mr. Bell turned left.

"Sandra!" A familiar voice called from somewhere to her right, and Mary Kay tried to locate its owner. Glancing quickly around, she saw a sea of faces, some white and some black, but she did not see who was calling her name. It had to be someone from jail, no one else would have called her by that name. Mrs. Holley's voice bellowed, "No loitering, ladies; keep moving."

When orientation was complete a few days later, Mary Kay discovered the familiar voice was Peggy's. She had arrived several weeks before, and she helped Mary Kay adjust to this new environment. The relationship begun in anger and violence months before continued to grow into a devoted friendship. Inmates who had been in jail with them were amazed. Although housed in different cellblocks, they met together daily to read the Bible. Peggy did not read well so Mary Kay read passages to her and then they discussed them. After several months, Bertha arrived from the Jefferson County Jail and joined them.

Mary Kay waited for the other states and the federal government to act on the remaining charges against her. In her Bible she still carried the slip of paper with the verse from 2 Timothy 1:2 that she had carried in the court-room. When she was tempted to worry about the charges, she would repeat the verse, remembering that she had given the matter to God. His answer came after she had been at Tutwiler less than a month. She was called to the warden's office.

"Your lawyer called me this morning," said Mrs. Wood. "He asked me to tell you that all the charges from the other states have been dropped, as well as all the federal charges."

Mary Kay sat in amazement. She had not expected such mercy and grace from God. Her revulsion toward her earthly father had kept her from being able to see God as Father, but that day it changed. She began to see Him as the father she had always wanted, one who loved and protected her.

One day, Mary Kay sat in the dayroom talking to several women about the Bible. "Those stories are just fables," one remarked. "Why, there are a lot of stories they tell in church that aren't even in the Bible, like the Legend of the Dogwood Tree and Jonah and the Whale."

"Jonah is in the Bible" Mary Kay replied. "In fact, there's a whole book about him."

"But it's not about a whale," the inmate argued.

"Actually, it is."

Quickly the women began to take sides, and Mary Kay said, "I'll prove it; I'll be right back". She saw Bertha in the dorm and invited her to join the conversation. Bertha was not inclined to argue, but she followed Mary Kay back to the recreation room where the others were waiting.

Later that night, Bertha, who had simply agreed with Mary Kay's reading of Jonah, spoke of the earlier conversation. "Lots of my people don't really know much about the Bible even if they went to church. Most of them think that white men wrote the Bible, so they're not sure if it's true."

"But the women liked hearing about Jonah," said Mary Kay, "and they believed it when we read it to them. What if we have a Bible study and just read stories like Jonah and Daniel in the lion's den, and the wall of Jericho? Do you think some inmates would come?"

Thus, the first Bible study at Tutwiler Prison was led by Bertha and Mary Kay and centered on stories that they had first learned and believed when they were children. Many of the women had acquired a mixture of superstition, myth, and legend, unrelated to what the Bible actually taught. The group spurred lively debate and many surprises, and eventually more than twenty women joined. Later, Bertha continued teaching that group while Mary Kay led another group of believers who were already familiar with the Bible and were interested in growing spiritually. They chose a specific topic or a book of the Bible to study together in more depth.

Mary Kay struggled to live life God's way in prison. One temptation she fought was the urge to escape. Her calculating mind realized how easy it would be to bypass the lax security. Breaking out of a place shouldn't be much different from breaking in, and she was good at that.

"God, I don't want to do anything to dishonor You, but I don't know how strong I can be. I need help; this place is more than I can endure." Immediately, the thought came to her: *Tell someone.*

At first, she was reluctant and embarrassed, but she knew there was wisdom in talking to others. Secrets have a mighty hold; when they are revealed, they lose their power. She forced herself to push past her reluctance and was surprised to learn that others were suffering from the burden of imprisonment and wanted to honor God. She did not feel so alone, and the urge to escape faded as she grew close to her friends.

She learned an important lesson—most of her Christian growth happened in relationships. Many loners in prison tried to do it on their own but kept slipping back into sin. She did *not* want to go back where she had been, so she fought the urge for do-it-yourself Christianity. How grateful she was to God for putting loving, sincere Christian sisters in her life!

The urge to escape was strong, but it was nothing compared with her battle with anger. The bitter taste of indignation often welled in the back of her throat. It had been happening as long as she could remember. She was easily offended and her sharp tongue and rebellious attitude still caused her trouble, even though she had been a Christian for nearly a year now. She knew she must quit nursing hurts, old and new, but how? This habit would be hard to overcome, and she was not sure how to go about it. She prayed constantly and asked others to pray for her.

One day, she read this verse: "We take captive every thought to make it obedient to Christ."[15] Was the problem in her thinking and not in her emotions?

"I cannot do two opposite things at the same time," she reasoned. "I cannot sit down and stand up at the same time. So what can I do to take my angry thoughts captive? What's the opposite of anger?" Immediately the answer came—praise. That was it. She could not be angry and sing praise hymns at the same time. Besides, she loved to sing, so whenever something irritated her, instead of brooding on it, she started singing. She knew it made sense; even so, she was surprised when, after several stanzas of a hymn, the hurt and anger drained away.

The new technique came in handy every time she had to cross "the line." It was one of several things that annoyed her about prison. The long hallway ran the length of the main prison building with shorter hallways branching off it. From this center hall, the kitchen and dining room, the infirmary, and supply rooms opened to the east. Across the hall the chapel, library, offices, and lobby branched to the west. Prior to the 1964 civil rights law, black women were housed in dormitories in the south hall and white women in dormitories in the north hall. They were not supposed to be in each other's areas, but they often had to walk through them to get somewhere. An officer stood in the center between the north and south halls; that was "the line." When a white inmate approached to go out to the recreation area on the south side of the building, she had to ask the officer, "May I cross?"

"Where are you going?"

"I'm going to the yard."

"Yes, you may."

When a black inmate approached the officer to go to the chapel or some other destination on the north end, she, too, had to request permission.

"May I cross?"

"Where are you going?"

"I'm going to the infirmary."

---

[15] 2 Corinthians 10:5

"Yes, you may."

Even though the women were now integrated in the dorms, the old custom of requesting permission to cross the line had not died out.

We are all adults, Mary Kay thought, *and we have to play Mother-May-I to go out into the yard?* This is wrong. Resentment rose up again, until she remembered her new technique for breaking the anger habit.

"On a hill far away, stood an old rugged cross . . ." She sang loudly and walked past the puzzled officer with a smile.

For a while, it seemed she was singing all the time. Then one day a friend asked, "Are you okay?"

"Why?"

"You don't sing as much as you used to."

"Praise God! It's working!" Mary Kay laughed when her friend looked bewildered.

In the fall, Peggy and Mary Kay decided it was time to be baptized. Peggy had never been baptized, and Mary Kay felt her childhood baptism was simply a ritual with no real meaning. They went to the chaplain to ask about it. His main concern was whether they were going to escape. He did not seem to care at all what they believed about Jesus Christ; he did not ask about their salvation experience. As they talked, he suggested they did not have to be baptized in water; it could be anything. He claimed Phillip had baptized an Ethiopian eunuch in sand.

"What?" Mary Kay was appalled. She was sure the passage said, "They came to some water."[16] But she knew it would not do to argue.

"I don't really want to be baptized in sand; it's so hard to get out of your eyes." The chaplain did not even catch the sarcasm in her voice.

Later, in the dining hall, she told Peggy, "I don't think I want to be baptized by him."

"Me either," Peggy agreed, "but what are we going to do? Oh, Lord, save our chaplain or send us a new one!"

They prayed that prayer together every day. They were delighted to discover they had an ally in the warden. She was a Baptist and believed in baptism by

---

[16] Acts 8:37

immersion, just as Peggy and Mary Kay did. Mrs. Woods arranged with the pastor of a small, nearby church to use their baptistery. There was a young couple who led a Bible study at the prison on Saturday mornings; Mary Kay and Peggy asked the husband if he would baptize them.

The women wanted to invite some of their outside friends, but they did not know when the baptism would be. On Wednesday morning, November 13, 1973, they were told to dress in the white uniforms they wore whenever they left the prison. They had fifteen minutes to dress before being escorted, in leg irons and handcuffs, into a prison van.

The pastor was more than happy to fill the baptismal for the occasion. One of Mary Kay's favorite officers, Arlene Holley, who had led her down the hallway on her first day in prison, was a committed Christian. She was their female escort along with a male officer. Also present was the young couple from the Saturday morning Bible study and the pastor of the church. Mrs. Holley took their leg irons off, but Mary Kay and Peggy went into the water in handcuffs. The church was kind enough to lend them robes to cover "Department of Corrections" stenciled on the back of their shirts and down a pant leg in big, black letters.

By January, their prayers were answered; a new chaplain arrived. The former chaplain did not just leave Tutwiler, he left the system altogether. It spooked Mary Kay a bit. *Is it right to pray against someone?* She was still trying to understand what it meant to live for Jesus. She knew this journey takes a lifetime and beyond, but she never dreamed the lessons would become harder. And she was about to learn what God meant by the instruction, "Be doers of the word, and not hearers only".[17]

The inmates lined the hallway, watching the new batch of arrivals. Word of their arrival spread before they left the front lobby. "It's the blonde; she's the baby killer." Ginger was a natural blonde with tight, frizzy hair, and she stood alone while the other new arrivals huddled together. "You can always tell by the hair when a person has black blood." This last remark came from a group of white inmates.

As Mary Kay had done, the new arrivals remained in the infirmary for the

---

[17] James 1:22, *New King James Version*

first several days. A week later, Mary Kay walked into her cell and saw the empty bed across the aisle was now occupied. Ginger was unpacking her meager belongings into her locker box—a small chest with a drawer and two padlocked doors that opened into a cupboard with a single shelf. All the chests in the room were old, with chipped, white paint. Mary Kay watched as Ginger laid a Bible on top. The cover and edges were worn. Next to it she placed a photograph of a man, a woman and three children—a girl about ten, a boy about six, and a toddler with hair like Ginger's.

The prison grapevine supplied Mary Kay with the details of Ginger's conviction. She was charged with first-degree murder in the death of the ten-year-old girl in the photograph, her stepdaughter. The prosecution claimed she had hit her with a baseball bat.

Ginger was assigned one of the worst jobs in their dormitory—cleaning the bathroom and mopping the floor. The other residents continually let her know how they felt about her. Just after she had cleaned, they added spills to get her in trouble. They often accused her of stealing. An inmate walking by would kick over the mop bucket and then cuss her for leaving it in the way as she cleaned.

Ginger's rigid poker face was betrayed by her red eyes. Mary Kay watched how often she read the Bible on her locker. She spent hours seeking comfort in its pages. She attended the weekly worship services conducted in the chapel, sitting alone in the back. Frequently one of the inmates approached her and snarled, "You've got my seat. Move out of here, baby killer." Ginger quietly complied.

Mary Kay grew uncomfortable with the abuse Ginger suffered, but she wondered if she might deserve it. About three months after her arrival, Ginger discovered that the photo on her locker box was missing. She searched, and found it under the bed. The glass was broken, the frame bent, the photo torn; it was no accident. Her restraint dissolved into tears; prisoners never cried in front of others, but Ginger was defeated.

Mary Kay was watching from her bunk and a wave of shame came over her. *I didn't do it,* she thought, *so why do I feel guilty?* Looking around the cell, Mary Kay saw several inmates who might have destroyed Ginger's picture. Even women who had not destroyed it would not have stopped the one who did.

She shuddered as she realized her own silence also gave unspoken approval to their behavior. Suddenly Mary Kay sensed God telling her, *That's your sister.* The next thought was, *Go to dinner with her.*

Everything in Mary Kay immediately rejected the idea. To befriend an accused child abuser was unacceptable in prison culture. What would it do to her reputation? Since she had arrived, Mary Kay's witness among the inmates was the strong, consistent testimony of a committed Christian. No one, not even a Christian, associated with a child abuser. Surely God wasn't asking her to destroy her witness before the others, even the Christians. The thought persisted. *She's your sister.*

Mary Kay stood and walked to the bathroom hoping to quiet the nagging idea, but there was no hiding from the Hound of Heaven. The supper bell rang, and Mary Kay tried to suppress the thought of walking into the dining room with Ginger. It did not work; she was losing her ability to rationalize and compartmentalize. She walked to her bed to leave her towel and pick up her cup before going to the dining room. Almost as if she were guided by something outside herself, Mary Kay crossed the aisle to Ginger's bed.

"Are you going to supper?" she asked quietly.

Ginger was startled as much by the kind words as the question. She raised her head. "Who me?"

"Yes, you. Are you ready for supper? They rang the bell."

Ginger sat up on the bed and wiped her eyes. "Yes, I'm going." But she did not move.

Mary Kay thought, *What in the world am I doing?* Out loud she said, "I notice you read the Bible a lot. Anything in particular?"

Ginger slowly stood, and as the two walked side by side out of the cellblock into the hallway, Ginger murmured, "I read the Psalms a lot. But I like the New Testament, too."

Walking through the double doorway, Mary Kay heard the expected rush of whispers ripple around the room. "Look who's with the blonde." "What's she doing?" "Why are *they* together?"

She and Ginger moved to the food line. One of the black girls who attended Bible study with Mary Kay walked by and mumbled. "What are you *doing?*" Mary

Kay did not respond. Taking her tray, she waited while Ginger got hers and then led the way to the table where she usually sat with her friends. When she placed her tray on the table, the other women immediately stood, picked up their trays, and walked away without speaking. No one joined Ginger and Mary Kay.

Conversation was difficult; Mary Kay could not keep her focus off all the people around them. How would this affect her other relationships? Well, it was in God's hands now. She picked at her meal and tried to engage in a casual conversation with Ginger. When they had finished eating, Mary Kay excused herself at the door of the dining hall, "I need to go to the library. See you later."

Mary Kay entered the library, which was also a classroom. She sat at a desk at the back of the room and sorted through her confused thoughts and emotions. She reached for one of the Bibles on a nearby shelf and flipped through its pages. Her eyes rested on a passage. "The Son of Man must suffer many things and be rejected by the elders, chief priests and teachers of the law and he must be killed and on the third day be raised to life . . . If any one is ashamed of me . . . I will be ashamed of him."[18]

Once again, God answered her questions in His Word. If she was ashamed of one of His children, it was the same as being ashamed of Him. If she was to love the Lord with all her heart, Mary Kay had to love her neighbor, even if she suffered rejection in the process. Ginger was her neighbor.

---

[18] Luke 9:22-26

CHAPTER SIXTEEN

Many inmates claim innocence in prison, but as Mary Kay got to know Ginger and heard her story, she realized that she *was* innocent. Her stepdaughter's older sister had actually been the one who hit her with the baseball bat. The family of her husband's late wife had never liked Ginger so they hired a special prosecutor and coached the girl into accusing her stepmother.

Ginger and her lawyer requested that she and the girl be given sodium pentothal, the truth serum. When the young girl admitted what she had done under the medication, the prosecutor blocked Ginger from taking the test. They did not want anything else to damage their case. On the witness stand, the girl reverted to the testimony she had been taught. Some jury members were not convinced but eventually were persuaded to convict Ginger of the lesser charge of manslaughter since she was the only adult present when the girl died.

Every week, Ginger's mother came to visit her, and since Mary Kay had no family nearby, they usually invited her to join them. Her mother always brought treats that reminded them of freedom. One day she laid a bag of toasted coconut marshmallows on the table as she settled into her seat. Mary Kay froze as the sharp edges of a distant memory cut into her.

Dad was driving up to the house after work. Ronnie and Ilene ran out, not to greet him but to grab his lunch box. They raced back into the kitchen and opened it on the little metal table, searching for leftovers. Dad often had toasted coconut marshmallows inside; they were his favorite treat. Sure enough, there was half a bag. By the time Dad walked in, Tom had joined them, and something about the way Tom was dividing the marshmallows bothered Dad. He grabbed a handful of the spongy puffs and shoved them in front of Tom's face. "Eat them!" he ordered. Tom took the marshmallows and stuffed them into his mouth.

Mary Kay leaped across the kitchen, took hold of her father's arm, and pulled as hard as she could. He whirled around, grabbed her hair and swung a balled fist toward her face. The toasty, sweetness of coconut filled her nostrils in the moment before his fist made contact with her nose. It would be a long while before she smelled anything again. Blood gushed from her broken nose but it did not stop him; before he was finished he had cracked three of her ribs.

Mary Kay felt the sting of hot tears as the scene flashed through her mind. She jumped up. Ginger and her mother watched in surprise as she rushed out of the courtyard and into the dorm. She threw herself onto the bed, releasing years of tears into the pillow. In a few moments she felt Ginger settle quietly beside her and felt gentle strokes on her back. Long minutes passed before she could choke out the story. When she finished, Ginger gave her a consoling hug and went to the bathroom for toilet paper to wipe their eyes.

"Now put it in the notebook," Ginger suggested gently when they finished blowing their noses. Months before, each one had started a journal of her spiritual struggles and victories. Mary Kay nodded, opened the cupboard of her locker box, and pulled out the red spiral notebook. Her life was beginning to fill its lined pages. On a page labeled "Debts" she wrote carefully at the end of an already long list. When she was finished she bowed her head.

"Father God, that's another thing I choose to forgive my Dad for," she whispered. "With Your help, I'm not going to hold it against him anymore. I cancel the debt."

"Amen!" said Ginger.

As she had done with each item on the list, Mary Kay crossed it out then drew a cross next to it, a reminder that all sins, including her own sin of unforgiveness, were nailed to the cross of Jesus. She felt tender and raw, as though her heart had been scrubbed with steel wool. Months of prayer and singing passed before the pain healed. A year later, she could finally eat a toasted coconut marshmallow.

God was continually working in Mary Kay's heart; she was sure she was a difficult project. He drew her thoughts back to the first verses in Leviticus 6 concerning restitution, the ones that had troubled her so in the Tuscaloosa jail. Now He moved them forward from the back burner where they had been simmering for some time. She knew He wanted her to do something—she must begin to make restitution.

In the preceding months she had learned that as soon as she asked Him to help her to do what He required, He did just that. However, Mary Kay was not really sure she wanted to do what she needed to do. She also knew that it was dangerous to be ruled by feelings, rather than by His truth. She did not have to want, or feel like, doing something in order to be obedient. God would help her feelings conform to her decision eventually.

With a deep sigh of resignation, she leaned back on her bunk and imagined she was leaning on her Friend, "Okay, Lord, I know I need to start making restitution for some things, but I don't know where to begin or even how to repay anyone. Lord, I believe I am willing, but help me in my unbelief and make me willing and able to perform Your good purpose.[19] Thank you for your mercy, Amen."

Almost before she finished this prayer, she was reminded of something. As a teenager she had gossiped about one older sister to the other. This caused conflicts between them. When they confronted her about what she had said, she claimed innocence. How did they feel about her now?

As the Holy Spirit convicted her about the damage she had done to their relationship, she knew she must confess and ask forgiveness. It did not matter that years had passed and their relationship had survived and moved forward. Reluctantly she reached for her tablet of paper and began to write. At the end of a long and chatty letter, she wrote: "I may have offended you by my attitude when I was a teenager and if so, I hope you will forgive me."

She looked at the weak apology and did not need to pray; she knew God was not satisfied with her obvious attempt to blame her behavior on her age. She tore the pages off the tablet and began again, but by the time she had written the second page, she knew the letter was again too long. She tore the pages from the

---

[19] Paraphrase, Philippians 2:13

tablet and tossed them after the others into the small wastebasket by her bed.

"Lord, help me to say the right thing so it will really sound sincere." This time her pen seemed to move quickly over the page.

> Dear Jean and Joyce,
>
> Remember that remark I made about the way you two "lived out of each other's pockets"? I lied about that to both of you. I was the cause of your anger because of the deceitful way I communicated, and I was very wrong. Will you please forgive me? Since giving my life to Jesus Christ in jail, I'm trying to live the way He instructs us to in the Bible.
>
> I am grateful for His mercy and pray for you both to be well and happy. Love, Kay

The letter was short and sweet, and the moment she signed her name she felt a huge sense of relief, as if a tremendous weight had been lifted from her heart. This wasn't so bad after all! If confession and repentance made her feel this clean, why was she reluctant? She had taken the first step toward restitution, and it felt good.

She resolved to do what she believed God was telling her to do. She wrote many more letters of apology, and in each one she kept to a simple outline: 1. What she had said or done. 2. That she was wrong in doing it. 3. Would the person forgive her? 4. That she was now a Christian and trying to live according to God's Word. She didn't include anything else. If God wanted her to make financial restitution, He'd provide a way. For now, the letters would have to do.

Conversation among the inmates often centered on children; mothers loved to talk about their kids. Mary Kay never told anyone she had children of her own. The less that others knew of her personal life, the better. Besides, wouldn't it be better for the children if no one knew? She told herself these were the reasons for her silence, but deep inside she knew that shame kept her from mentioning her children; only a very bad woman gave her kids away. She knew she could not explain her actions to anyone; she could not explain them to herself. Rather than face the hostility of the other women, she simply did not tell until the day a registered letter arrived.

She was called from the dining hall into the warden's office to sign for the letter. She stared at the thick manila envelope; the return address bore the name of a legal firm near her hometown in Missouri. Her sense of dread made it hard to breath; this can't be good news. Alone, she might have put off opening the letter, but Mrs. Wood's presence pressed her to tear open the envelope. She pulled out a stack of papers and read the letter on top. Her brother Bill and his wife, Kathy, were petitioning the court to adopt Sean.

"Is everything okay?"

Mary Kay sank into the chair and glanced across the desk into the warden's concerned eyes, but quickly turned to look out the window. A lump in her throat kept her from speaking. She laid the cover letter on the desk and pushed it across. Mrs. Wood quietly read it. She slid it back to Mary Kay and waited.

"You are the only person here who knows I have a child." Her voice sounded small and far away. The ticking of the clock seemed to fill the room. "Actually I have three children. My first two live with their father and his second wife. I send cards and letters, but they never write back."

"I'm so sorry."

"Giving up custody of my children to their father was a selfish thing to do; I know that now. I was more concerned about my happiness than I was about them. It was easier for me to give up my custody rights than to fight it out. And Sean—well, once I left him with my Mom, I never got a chance to go back. Every time I pray, I mention my three kids."

"You did a lot of wrong things, but you are a new person now that you belong to Jesus."

The smile Mary Kay tried to generate never made it past a slight twitch in the corners of her mouth. She knew Mrs. Wood was trying to be kind, but her insides felt like broken glass.

"Do you think giving up my baby would be selfish?" She did not wait for an answer but kept speaking, more to herself than to the woman across the desk. "I haven't seen him in nearly two years. I suppose it *would* be better for him; he could be a teenager before I get out of here. I certainly can't do anything to help him from here." Her voice trailed off; her lips were saying what her heart did not want to hear.

"Perhaps you should pray about it before you make a final decision." Mary Kay nodded and put the packet of papers back into the envelope.

"Would you keep this for me?" She did not want anyone else to see it. Mrs. Wood nodded and slipped the envelope into the front of a file drawer next to her desk. As Mary Kay walked out of the room she heard Mrs. Wood say, "I'll be praying for your decision."

She had known the right thing to do from the moment she opened the letter, yet she resisted making the final decision. Praying only strengthened her conviction that giving Sean to Bill and Kathy was the right thing to do. But the closer she came to walking into the warden's office and signing the paper, the more tattered her heart felt. She consoled herself with the knowledge that he would be raised in a loving, Christian home and he would still be family; only now he would be her nephew.

This turmoil over Sean stirred up grief for her other two children. How could she have been so selfish? Her pain was magnified by the knowledge of the pain she caused them. When she had asked Jesus to live in her heart, she hadn't expected Him to fling open locked rooms. Now she could not force this one closed again; He must have His foot in the door. Memories and regrets poured out.

Mary Kay found it impossible to stay in the room when the women discussed their children. Visitation days were especially difficult. She often worked in the visitation room on weekends since her family lived too far to come. She kept busy making change for the soda or candy machines, fetching items for the inmates since they were not allowed to go back and forth between to their dorm rooms and the visitation room while they had visitors, and following instructions from the officer on duty.

Watching mothers with their children was painful enough—and now Christmas was coming. This was her first year to celebrate Christmas as a Christian, and it should be joyous except it would also be her first at Tutwiler. Holidays only magnify the loneliness and loss that inmates already feel. A gloom settled over the whole population, intensifying Mary Kay's own misery. She signed all the required pages of the lawyer's packet for Sean's adoption and asked the warden to mail them. She felt peace in doing God's will, but it did not lessen the intensity of her pain.

At Christmastime various groups came to the prison to spread holiday cheer. They began to come after Thanksgiving, sometimes several groups a day. Each program followed nearly the same pattern: carols, a talk or a skit, refreshments, and presents. Few inmates felt uplifted by what seemed to them to be timid or holier-than-thou folks going through their paces with their eyes on the clock. The inmates sensed that the visitors longed to be done with their charitable act, knowing they would not have to come again until next Christmas, and hoping someone else might volunteer next year.

The inmates joked about these folks getting their good deeds in before the end of the year, but they showed up for the presents and cookies. The gifts were anything but exciting, just small toiletries—shampoo, soap, toothpaste—samples mostly. Nevertheless, the women eagerly collected the items and stored them in their locker boxes. Just before Christmas they laid them on their beds in little piles and started trading with each other until they were satisfied with each pile.

"I'll give a comb for some lotion."

"Hey, Judy, you want some toothpaste? I need more shampoo."

"Anyone have some of those little soaps shaped like seashells they'd be willing to trade?"

They wrapped the items in tissue paper, the Sunday comics or some other part of the newspaper and carefully locked them back in their cupboards. Mary Kay watched from her bunk in bewilderment. Then it made sense—the number of piles on each woman's bed matched the number of children she had.

They're going to give those to their kids for Christmas! Oh no, there is sure to be lots of wailing in the visitor room that day. What child would be thrilled to get a bar of soap or a toothbrush for a present? Her heart ached for the women as she imagined their children's disappointment.

On Christmas day, she watched uneasily as the mothers gave the children their gifts. Without exception the children tore open their packages, barely glanced at the items, and threw their arms around their mothers. "Oh, Mama, thank you! I love you."

Mary Kay watched in wonder—the children didn't care what they received, only that it came from Mom. She remembered her own Mama scrimping, saving, and going without a winter coat to give each of her children some simple gift; she recalled the joy she felt when she opened hers. Just like these children, she knew how much love came with the gift. That love was all that mattered. She had such a wonderful mother; why hadn't she been a mother like her? Mary Kay's new heart ached for her lost children. How could she ever forgive herself?

"Forgive *yourself?*" asked Bertha as she and Mary Kay sat at a picnic table in the yard. Mary Kay had decided it was time to confess what she had done to her children. Her motivations were both spiritual and selfish; she wanted relief from this pain. "Why do you need to forgive yourself? Hasn't God forgiven you?"

"Of course, God has forgiven me, but, I thought, well . . ." Mary Kay struggled to explain why it seemed important to forgive herself. "I just don't think I'll be free until I can forgive myself."

"So you are setting yourself above God?"

Mary Kay was appalled. "I'm not setting myself above God," she protested.

"You are if you think that God's forgiveness isn't enough to set you free, that you gotta have your own forgiveness to really feel free. Then who's work is it, yours or His?"

Mary Kay looked confused.

"Look at it this way," continued Bertha. "Let's say that you do need to forgive yourself. Can you forgive yourself before God forgives you?"

Mary Kay thought about it for a minute. "No, I guess not because then you wouldn't feel a need for God's forgiveness if you felt forgiven already."

"Right. And after you have received God's forgiveness, are you completely forgiven? Do you need to add anything to it?"

The sense of what Bertha was saying began to dawn on Mary Kay. "No, His forgiveness is complete and utterly sufficient." She thought for a few minutes. "I was struggling to do what was never intended to be done. No wonder I couldn't accomplish it. All I have to do is keep reminding myself that God has forgiven me, keep receiving His mercy and grace, and quit judging myself—

which is also not my responsibility. "

Bertha smiled. " 'And the truth will set you free.' "[20]

" 'If the Son sets you free, you will be free indeed.' "[21] Mary Kay smiled back, but then her face became serious again. "Grace is sometimes just too easy, isn't it?"

"What do you mean?"

"Well, if we beat ourselves up enough, we think maybe we can somehow do penance and really feel cleansed. But that is all about us; it completely devalues what Jesus did. It's as if we would feel better if we did it ourselves rather than simply accept God's grace. You are right, Bertha, I *was* trying to add something to what Jesus has already done. Oh, Lord, forgive me."

"He already has." Bertha smiled. "The devil's tricks *almost* make sense. I guess one clue that something is a lie is if it turns our attention from Jesus and onto ourselves. That stinking rat!"

Mary Kay laughed; a weight was lifting from her shoulders. In the days and weeks that followed, Mary Kay reminded herself of her conversation with Bertha whenever she felt tempted to berate herself.

I can feel sad for the pain my children suffer because of this, she thought. *But, thank You, Jesus; I do not have to accept the shame any longer. You have forgiven me.* While she could not be with them as a mother, she could take them before God as a mother, in her prayers, just as her mother had done for her.

---

[20] John 8:32
[21] John 8:36

CHAPTER SEVENTEEN

In the spring, Gideons began coming to the prison on the third Friday of each month. The Gideons divide regionally into groups called camps. Each month a different camp came to Tutwiler for two hours. They held group devotions, sang songs, and spent at least an hour visiting with the inmates individually. Scattered at the tables in the dining room, these groups of two or three talked, prayed, and sometimes cried with each other. Their simple acts of love had a deep impact on the women.

A young Gideon, Jimmy Dean Brown, and his wife, Ann, met one month with Mary Kay. She shared with them about reading a Gideon Bible when she was saved. They were excited and immediately decided Mary Kay must share her testimony at the next Gideon convention.

As they left that day, they went straight to the warden's office to ask permission. Mrs. Wood told them that only the commissioner, L. B. Sullivan, had the authority to grant their request. The following week, they called his office, but he was hesitant to agree because of racial tensions. He said he could not allow a white girl to go without also letting a black girl go.

"No, problem," replied Mary Kay when the Browns reported back to her. "Tell them you want Bertha to go too. She can sing and I'll speak."

Several Gideons wrote the commissioner requesting he allow Mary Kay and Bertha to attend and offering to pay for guards to escort them. The convention was in November of 1974. By then Mary Kay had a medium-security clearance so the commissioner decided that if the chaplain accompanied them, it would be sufficient security. They had to be back in prison that same night. The chaplain and his wife agreed to take them. The Gideons reimbursed them for mileage.

Mary Kay and Bertha arrived in Birmingham wearing starched, white shirt-dresses, their dressy prison uniforms. The chaplain drove them downtown to the Sheraton hotel, across from the Jefferson County Jail.

"Look, Bertha! Look where we are. I told you we would make it! We're here, we really are here, and we're going to do just what I said."

They grinned at each other, remembering the day they had watched the hotel being built from a window in the jail. Mary Kay's impulsive prediction now proved prophetic.

"You said we would but I didn't believe you," marveled Bertha.

In the ballroom, were over a thousand people—Gideons from all over Alabama, along with representatives from the national headquarters and several hundred pastors and their wives. Since no one knew until the last minute whether Mary Kay and Bertha would be able to come, their names were not on the schedule.

Bertha nearly ran back to the car when she saw the crowd. Mary Kay was so busy bolstering her friend's confidence that she did not even think about her own presentation. As Bertha's beautiful voice rose over the crowd in song, Mary Kay's heart swelled with pride and love for her friend. Then it was Mary Kay's turn. She stood before the microphone. A sudden calmness possessed her.

"I told my friend we would make it big some day. Bertha said, 'Yeah, all the way to the big house.' "

The laughter from the crowd lifted her; she felt at home. Now she knew what God wanted her to do—speak to people, sharing the messages He gave her.

After Bertha and Mary Kay's appearance at the convention, many Gideons who were not previously involved in prison ministry began to go to prisons around the state. Alabama inmates were matched with Gideons and their wives from their own hometown areas. When they were released, a godly couple was already waiting at home to disciple them. This became an ongoing project of the Gideon's women's auxiliary.

The Gideons taught simple and practical lessons. From them Mary Kay learned the importance of apologizing and the appropriate way to do it. One lesson that greatly influenced her was called "Being Women of a Separated

Walk " She learned that as God's child, she was not a woman of the world; her calling and standing were different. Everything about her, the way she talked and dressed and acted, should reflect her relationship with Jesus. She remembered what she learned the day she was saved—that God would empower her to do His will; she simply had to let Him. As she practiced saying "yes" to God, she saw her old ways slipping away. Great joy and strength filled her, knowing she was in His hands.

As a result of the convention, Mary Kay began receiving other invitations to speak. Gideons or churches wrote to the commissioner for permission and paid honorariums to the chaplain and his wife for escorting her. Mary Kay remembered how she and Peggy had prayed for a new chaplain. God must have prompted those prayers; she could not imagine the old chaplain going along with all this.

The next few times, the commissioner still required Bertha to accompany her. After a while, Mary Kay was allowed to go alone. Bertha was relieved; she did not like being in front of people the way Mary Kay did. Initially the invitations came only once in a while, then monthly, and finally almost weekly. At first she wore a prison uniform until eventually Betty Bostwick bought her some pretty dresses, which the warden kept in her office.

Gideons are a punctual group; they start on time and finish on time. They taught her how to reduce her speech to only the most important parts. She did not always know how much time she would have, it might be eight or thirteen or thirty minutes. She would pray and the Lord would show her what to leave out. She discovered she had an inner clock. This was one reason she became such a popular speaker; she knew how to keep within her time limit. Knowing how to shut up and sit down is sometimes as important as what is said.

Mary Kay knew nothing about the Gideon ministry before prison, except for seeing their Bibles, first in hotel rooms and then in jail. She was impressed when she learned that members pay an association fee to cover administrative costs, and they pay all their personal expenses out of their own pockets. This allows them to put one hundred percent of the donations they receive toward placing Bibles.

One day Debbie, an inmate serving life without the possibility of parole, came to Mary Kay crying. She had received a phone call from home telling her that her mother had died of a heart attack. She could not go home to the little town of Homa, Louisiana, for the funeral, because of her sentence. Mary Kay called the Gideons there and told them about Debbie's dilemma. A man and his wife went that day to the funeral home, explained why they were there, and told her family that Debbie sent her love. Later the man's wife went back and ministered to some of the family members, who became Christians. From then on, Mary Kay's fondness for the Gideons was fixed.

When Mary Kay arrived at Tutwiler, the inmates hoped that a college program for them would begin soon. The men's prison nearby already had one. The number of men in prison was so much greater than the number of women (ninety-five percent to five percent) that programs and resources took a long time before filtering down to the women.

However, it was the early 1970s and Women's Lib was affecting even the prisons. Several federal lawsuits erupted, protesting the unequal treatment of women. One difficulty was money. Many of the men had served in the military and were eligible for military-funded educational programs. No such resource was available for women.

An Educational Council was formed to explore the feasibility of a college program for the women. Tutwiler would choose an Inmate Representative to send to the council. Mary Kay wanted to go to college, and she wanted to be that representative.

However, she did not meet the criteria for serving on the Educational Council. The rules stated that the inmate must have minimum-security clearance, have been at Tutwiler at least six months, have a GED or high school diploma, have passed the college entrance exams, and be elected by her peers. Even if she had minimum-security clearance, which she did not, Mary Kay had no chance to be elected because she was unknown and white. Two-thirds of the population was black. A popular black woman was elected.

Jean was a quiet, reserved person. Mary Kay talked with her about representing the inmates. Jean was not excited about it; she disliked being in the spotlight, and she hated controversy. Mary Kay was afraid she would agree with whatever the council decided. If a college program were to succeed at

Tutwiler, the inmates needed someone unafraid to challenge the status quo—someone like Mary Kay.

The Alabama State Prison Commissioner, L. B. Sullivan, had a suggestion box at the prison. Once a month he opened the box and read the suggestions. He met with each inmate to discuss the comment. If an inmate made a complaint about a guard or fellow inmate, she had better be ready for a face-to-face meeting with them. Mary Kay's comment explained that she would be a much better inmate representative than Jean and asked to talk to him about it.

When she walked into the warden's office, he said, "So you're Mahaffey. They tell me you're as mean as a rattlesnake." He knew some of the people she had known on the street. "You know you're not eligible to be the representative."

"Yes, I know that and I'm willing to go out in handcuffs so you don't have to violate security issues. I have already told Jean I am going to take her job away from her, and she doesn't care. Jean won't stir up anything. She won't accurately represent the inmates. I will. I'm not intimidated by other people."

"So I see. Well, I'll have to think about it." A council meeting was scheduled a few weeks later at Draper Men's Prison, about ten miles from Tutwiler. The morning of the meeting, Jean was told to be ready to leave at nine o'clock. A gate girl came with a message for Mary Kay. "The warden wants you to be ready to go also."

Inside the prison, inmates wore blue chambray shirts and jeans. Outside, they wore their white uniforms. Minimum-security inmates were allowed to wear free-world clothes unless they could not afford them. Mary Kay went in her white uniform and handcuffs; Jean wore free-world clothes. The council consisted of the dean of students from Alexander City State Junior College, the director of in-prison programs, the wardens or their deputies, and representatives from each prison. Jean was introduced as the elected representative from Tutwiler and Mary Kay was introduced as the alternate representative. Only Jean would be allowed to vote.

They discussed college classes at Tutwiler. The state stipulated that only academic classes could be offered and there could be no labs. When it was time to vote, Mary Kay turned to Jean, told her how to vote, and Jean voted.

The next meeting was at Tutwiler, and once again Mary Kay told Jean how to vote. At the third meeting, Mary Kay attended as the only representative, and it remained that way. Jean's absence was never discussed.

The prison officials favored having college classes but claimed there was no money in the budget. Dr. Paul Blackwell, the dean of students, pointed out that no federal rules excluded inmates from applying for Pell grants. In fact, school administrators would gladly come to help the women fill out the application forms. So money concerns were solved for the other inmates, but not for Mary Kay.

After all her work on the council, Mary Kay discovered she was not eligible; Pell grants were for undergraduate work only, and she already had a nursing degree. She had no money for tuition and books. Did this mean God did not want her to go to school? The thought saddened her, but she began praying, "Lord, if You really want me to go to school, I need to have the money." She hoped someone would decide that she was eligible after all, since her nursing degree was a three-year diploma program focused solely on nursing and had not included any of the academics required for a bachelor's degree. This proved to be wishful thinking.

Just before school began, she got a letter from Pastor Bob Curlee, of Centercrest Baptist Church in Birmingham. Months before, she had written him asking for a daily Bible reading publication she had seen with the church address printed on it. He sent it to her and began discipling her through letters. At the bottom of his latest letter he wrote: "P.S. I feel impressed that you have a need. How much and what for?" She wrote back immediately about the college program.

A few days later she was called to the warden's office. Pastor Bob had sent a check, with instructions to use it for her education only. He asked the warden to tell Mary Kay to write and let him know when tuition was due again. She did not know until much later that he had brought her need before his congregation. They decided to pay for her schooling. He would announce on a Sunday morning, "I've received a letter from Mary Kay, and her tuition is due. We're going to take up an offering at tonight's service." The congregation at Centercrest paid for her books and tuition for two years.

CHAPTER EIGHTEEN

Mary Kay completed the junior college program. The state of Alabama required inmates to serve at least one third of their sentences before they were eligible for parole. She had five years left, more if her parole application were denied. Now what could she do to keep busy?

Some of the males who had been through the educational program were being allowed to attend Auburn University at Montgomery to pursue a four-year degree. Of course, Mary Kay wanted to do this, too. The demand for equal opportunity for women was becoming a problem for the state; Mary Kay did all she could to contribute. First, they claimed she wasn't eligible because her sentence was too long. She replied that some of the men in the college program had longer sentences than she. They argued that inmates had to be within two years of their parole date to participate in the study program. Mary Kay pointed out men in the program who did not meet that condition. The council continued to give excuses, and she quickly punched holes in each one. Still, they refused to consider her for the program.

Mary Kay discussed this with Mrs. Wood, who gave her the name of a state representative. Marilyn Quarles was serving on a special committee appointed by Governor George Wallace to bring equity to women in the state of Alabama. Mary Kay wrote to tell her of the inequity of her situation. Mary Kay shared that she made better grades than the men, that her prison record was not significantly worse than theirs, and in some cases was better. Obviously the issue preventing her fair treatment must be her gender.

God doesn't pay much attention to people's rules. He has His own rules, and His timing is perfect. At that time, Governor Wallace was under considerable pressure nationally concerning equal rights; this produced the formation of the Women's Equity Committee. To keep the governor and his committee happy, Mary Kay was reclassified for the study program and moved to the women's work release center in Wetumpka in August 1975.

Mary Kay couldn't avoid the requirement to go through work release before being eligible for education release, but she was thrilled to be out of Tutwiler. The release center was only a half-mile down the road from the prison, but it was a world apart. It was a collection of three small, wood-framed homes that had originally housed corrections officers. One house contained the administration offices, the kitchen, and the dining room. The other buildings had three or four bedrooms each, with double bunks, two bathrooms, and a sitting area.

Mary Kay was grateful for her nursing degree because she was assigned to work in one of the nursing homes in Wetumpka. This job was nicer than the other women's; many of them worked hard hours in the textile mills. The prison van took her to and from work every day. She was not allowed to go anywhere except the nursing home grounds or the release center. In addition to working full time, each inmate had to work ten hours each week around the center doing cleaning, mowing, cooking, or laundry. Whenever she asked about college, she was told they did not have transportation for her to go to Montgomery or that she did not have enough money.

She was paid a small amount for the work she was doing, and she felt God wanted her to continue the restitution process. This time she began to repay what she had stolen, but she couldn't imagine how she could ever pay it all back. What was it the FBI had estimated . . . three to five *million*?

One of the smaller amounts she owed was a telephone bill of more than a hundred dollars that the telephone company had charged to Mama's phone. In 1971, this was a sizable sum, especially on Mama's meager income. Mary Kay had used a stolen telephone credit card and made the calls from Mama's house; after she went to prison the Lord reminded her that she still owed her that money. The phone company had long since collected the money. Mary Kay figured that another family member had probably paid it for Mama but she sent the money to her anyway.

Inmates who graduated from the two-year junior college program had nothing on their transcripts indicating they were prisoners. Mary Kay graduated with a 3.98 grade point average so a local private school, Huntingdon College, contacted her and offered her a scholarship. The head of the psychology department there was a member of the corrections board and knew that Mary Kay was an inmate. He did not think *his* college would want a prisoner mixing with wealthy private-school students.

He spoke to Dr. Alan Shields, a sociology professor at Auburn University, about the possibility of inmates going there. Auburn was over sixty miles away, too far for a daily commute; the Department of Corrections would not provide transportation. Female inmates could access a program there only by moving to Auburn. Five women at the work release center had graduated from the in-prison program and had the grades and ability to finish a four-year program.

Dr. Shields visited Mary Kay and the other four eligible prisoners at the release center. He had been a teacher in the college program at Tutwiler and wanted to open a women's halfway house in Auburn. Mary Kay wanted to be a part of it.

Commissioner Sullivan encouraged Dr. Shield's dream, but he was retiring, and his replacement, Commissioner Richard Baker[22], disliked Mary Kay intensely. He thought Mrs. Wood and Mr. Sullivan coddled her. "You are a master manipulator," he told her. "You're going to do some hard time now."

He decided she would not go to Auburn, and she would not be a part of the peer counseling program Mr. Sullivan had started and for which he had recommended Mary Kay. Mr. Baker decided she would only work until she finished serving her time. Mary Kay could not prove it, but she suspected he had arranged for drugs to be placed in her locker so she would be sent back to Tutwiler. This happened twice, and both times God protected her—she was working a double shift at the nursing home. The release center officers, Mrs. Brown and Mr. Crenshaw, testified on her behalf: "She couldn't have done it. She wasn't here."

Mary Kay thought being at the release center would be better than

---

[22] Name changed

Tutwiler, but it turned out to be one of the worst periods of her sentence. The new commissioner denied all speaking requests for her that came across his desk. He also required that she do twenty hours of volunteer work rather than the ten the other prisoners had to do. Months passed without any hope of relief. She was sure that she would spend the next five years at the release center just working or that someone would find a way to send her back to Tutwiler.

"Please, Lord," she prayed, "if it's Your will, make something happen." She could not bear the thought of stagnating for five years.

She did not know that Dr. Shields was still working on his halfway house. He founded a nonprofit organization, bought a house and renovated it, received permission from university officials, and proceeded with the plan as though it were already approved—in spite of Mr. Baker's refusal. God would not allow the commissioner to prevent His plan from being fulfilled and once again His timing was perfect; it was an election year. Governor Wallace was preparing to run for his fourth term and he needed something to gain the women's votes. Dr. Shield's project was just the thing. Governor Wallace overrode Commissioner Baker's denial and approved the plan. Mary Kay moved to Auburn in August of 1976.

Based on her good grades, she received a scholarship conditional on her maintaining her high marks. She enrolled under her real name, Mary Kay Mahaffey. At first it was awkward—she had used Sandra Marshall for over five years.

The women were told not to reveal to anyone that they were inmates. They could go to church, to class, and shopping with the housemother or someone she approved. Mary Kay was even allowed to go to an on-campus Bible study. The other members of the study thought she lived with a group of students. When they asked her to go out with them afterwards, she always gave some excuse, like homework.

Her first class, on the first day, was Psychology of the Criminal Justice System. She walked in and saw two uniformed police officers.

Are they going to have an officer in the room with me all the time? Mary Kay thought. For three weeks she wondered if they were watching her in other classes as well and why they were being so nice to her. Finally she realized, *They don't know I'm an inmate! They are just taking this class like anyone else.* All the time, she had felt like "Convict" was stamped across her forehead.

One assignment in that class was to write a paper about some aspect of the criminal justice system. She wrote about the sentencing process, using the example of a woman who had been in Jefferson County Jail and at Tutwiler with her. Bertha Colston[23] and her husband had a habit of drinking and fighting. In one of their fights, he was fatally stabbed and she was arrested for his murder. Her court-appointed attorney told her she could plead guilty to second-degree murder and get a life sentence or go to trial and risk the death sentence. She took his advice, pleaded guilty to second-degree murder, and received a life sentence. Her lawyer never told her about her other options. She could have pleaded self-defense and might have had the charges dropped to manslaughter, or several other alternatives. The police report had said that she was taken to the hospital with a broken arm and that the house was a wreck. All the signs indicated self-defense, yet her attorney picked up his paycheck without even bothering to try to defend her. Bertha was black and semi-illiterate. On the finished paper, Mary Kay's professor wrote, "Very well done. Almost as if you were there."

For Mary Kay, the happiest time of her life thus far was attending college. She was living in a comfortable home, she was growing spiritually, and she was doing what she loved best—learning. It would not last. Jennifer,[24] one of the inmates in the house, was serving time for helping with a murder for hire and was having an affair with the officer who was the liaison between the prison and the school. He signed a pad of passes and gave them to her. One day she told the housemother someone in her family had died and she was going to Texas. When the housemother objected, Jennifer said, "Just keep your mouth shut, I have a pass. Nothing's going to happen."

The next day, the women came back from school to find the house crawling with officers. Jennifer's brother had called the department to ask if she had permission to travel to Texas. All the women were accused of aiding and

---

[23] Not the same Bertha who sang at the Sheraton
[24] Name changed

abetting an escape.

Mr. Baker seemed angry and pleased at the same time; now he had the grounds he needed to shut the halfway house.

"If you want to know what happened to Jennifer, talk to Officer Tidwell,[25]" said Mary Kay. "He's the one who gave her a pad of passes."

"Shut up and get your stuff. You're going back to Tutwiler."

Mary Kay had a job in the financial aid office at the college. "Can I call my boss first? I'm supposed to be at work."

Mr. Baker let her make the call and told an officer to listen to the conversation. Her boss was one of the few people on campus who knew she was a prison inmate. "Mr. Roberts, I can't come to work. Ginger, Leah, Bobbie, and I are going to have to go back to Tutwiler. Jennifer has left."

"I'll be right there," he said and hung up.

The officers went upstairs to watch them pack. They stalled, packing slowly and stopping to ask questions. Charles Roberts soon arrived and shook his finger in Mr. Baker's face. "This is wrong, and you know it's wrong. If I have to mortgage my house and hire the best civil rights attorney in the state, I am not going to stand by and let you do this."

Mr. Baker would listen to no one; he had decided these convicts were going back to Tutwiler and that was it. Once at the prison, they were separated and put in solitary confinement. State investigators questioned them each then questioned the house mother; all the stories were the same. One of the investigators quit when he realized it did not matter what he said; Mr. Baker would do what he wanted and charge them anyway.

The inmates who brought their meals told them the rumor going around Tutwiler: that they had all escaped and Mary Kay and Leah were picked up in New York. "We're not guilty," said Mary Kay. "You'll see. It will be proved that we're not guilty, and within a week we will be back in Auburn." She had nothing to base this boast on, but she felt in her heart that the Lord was taking care of it.

She had no idea how well the Lord was taking care of it. A few days later, Mr. Roberts visited her. He said he had seen Katherine Cater, the dean of

---

[25] Name changed

women, immediately after Mary Kay's phone call to ask if she knew anyone in the system who could help.

"No, not anyone off hand, except Lillian," she replied. Her former bridge partner was none other than Lillian Carter, the mother of then President Jimmy Carter. While Charles Roberts was shaking his finger at Mr. Baker, Miss Cater was calling her friend Lillian.

When Jimmy Carter was governor of Georgia, a prison inmate was his daughter Amy's nanny. When he became president, the inmate was paroled and went to Washington with them. Miss Lillian believed Miss Cater when she said Mary Kay was reliable. Miss Lillian called Governor Wallace.

"George, don't you have enough guilty people over there?" she asked. "Do you have to start locking up innocent people?" Wallace knew nothing about the matter. The mother of the president had called him, and he did not know what she was talking about. He was *not* happy, and he let Mr. Baker know it.

Meanwhile, Jennifer came back, unaware of the turmoil she had caused. As soon as she entered the house, she was taken into custody and transferred back to Tutwiler, where she served an additional five years for escape. Mary Kay and the others were returned to Auburn. As she left, Mary Kay said to the inmate who brought her meals, "I told you we were not guilty and that we were going back. So you pass the word around. When you trust in the Lord with all your heart, He will take care of you."

Life changed at the halfway house, however. Mr. Baker still wanted to eliminate the program. They were no longer allowed unlimited phone calls, and passes were rarely given.

These changes did not diminish the joy Mary Kay felt about being there. Once again, it was short-lived. A month later, on a Saturday morning, she received a call to come downstairs. As soon as she entered the housemother's office and saw the look on Martha's face, her heart dropped into her stomach. She knew the news was bad. She was not mistaken; the day before, her youngest brother, Ronnie, had been found murdered in a Nevada desert.

CHAPTER NINETEEN

The mind blocks what the heart cannot yet hold. Her first thought was mechanical and practical: *I need prayer to help me through this.* She called her friend, Mitzi.

"I want to go home," Mary Kay said. "I know it's impossible. I just want to be with my family."

They prayed together over the phone, then Mitzi said, "Let me see what I can do." Her husband, Jack, was a Gideon. He called his fellow Gideons and asked them to pray; they all knew and loved Mary Kay. Then he called a friend who was a lawyer, Cleve Redding, and asked him what could be done to get Mary Kay out of Alabama. He was surprised by Cleve's reply.

"Jack, I'm your man. I happen to be George Wallace's extradition officer; I'll just go ask him." A month before, the governor had heard about Mary Kay from the president's mother, and now his own extradition officer was asking for permission for her to leave the state. Wallace thought for a moment then said, "First we'll have to ask Warren Hearnes, the Governor of Missouri." The day before, Mary Kay's brother Bill had contacted Mr. Hearnes's office to request permission for her to travel to Missouri. Now the governor of Alabama was asking the same thing. Governor Hearnes reasoned that saying yes might be a good idea.

Mr. Redding called Jack back. "Governor Wallace and Governor Hearnes just gave verbal permission for Mary Kay to go to Missouri for her brother's funeral. However, since she is on study release, this will be under Mr. Baker's jurisdiction." Jack knew what Richard Baker thought of Mary Kay. He looked forward to their conversation.

"Absolutely not!" Mr. Baker shouted when Jack called to ask him to arrange the paperwork. Jack had expected such a reaction. He smiled though he knew the commissioner could not see him. He wished he could see Baker's face as he told him that two governors had already approved her travel. After a long silence, Baker replied in a tight voice, "She can pick up the papers at Tutwiler. She will have to arrange her own escort."

Mitzi called Mary Kay's family in Eldon to ask about an escort. Chuck Arnold, a police officer Mama knew, volunteered to fly to Alabama and escort her. Pat Bunn, an Alabama Gideon, offered to put the plane tickets on his American Express card until payment could be made. Several of the Gideons were taking special offerings in their churches. When all the collection money was counted, it covered all the airfares plus five dollars. Jack and Mitzi arranged the flights, three round-trip tickets—two for Chuck and one for Mary Kay. Betty Thomas, her Bible study leader, bought her an outfit and drove her to Tutwiler to get the papers.

On Monday morning, she was taken to the Birmingham airport where she met Chuck; he was kind enough not to wear his uniform. Commissioner Baker had directed him to keep her in handcuffs the entire time she was gone. She was grateful when he removed them as soon as the prison officials left; she was certain he did it out of respect for Mama.

On the flight home, Mary Kay's heart was filled with grief and fear. Mama had visited her in prison three times, but she had not seen the rest of her family since before her arrest. What would their reactions be? She wanted them to see that she had given her *whole* life to the Lord. How could she show them that she was completely changed and that she would not return to the person she was before?

Her greatest concern was how she would react when she saw Sean. She must be careful not to say anything that might offend Bill and Kathy. Mary Kay wanted them to be confident that she would not create problems for them, ever. She knew she had forfeited any rights to Sean when she signed the papers. Would they always be concerned around her, worrying about what she might say or do?

The plane flew to St. Louis, where they changed planes for the flight to Columbia, sixty miles from Eldon. As they waited to board the next plane, a casket was loaded into the luggage compartment. The sight suddenly made Ronnie's death real to Mary Kay. Until then, she was certain that there had been some mistake and that as soon as she got home it would be explained. He could not be dead; Ronnie was only twenty-three. She hadn't seen him in five years.

Ilene, Bill, and Kathy were waiting at the airport with Mama, who hugged Mary Kay tightly. As they stood greeting each other, a hearse from Eldon drove across the tarmac to the plane, and the coffin rolled slowly down the ramp. Mary Kay realized then that it was Ronnie.

The family welcomed her, but Mary Kay still felt like an outsider. She feared they might associate her with Chuck Adams, Ronnie's murderer, instead of seeing her as a family member. She was taken aback by her older brother Don's grief; he was completely distraught. Ronnie had been staying with him in Las Vegas when he was murdered. It was the third death in the family in a year. They had lost Jean's husband, Joyce's grandchild, and now Ronnie.

Mary Kay was overwhelmed with emotion when she saw Sean. He was now a slight six-year-old and looked just like Paul. She tried to be casual.

"Hello, Sean. I'm your Aunt Kay." Kathy and Bill had told Sean that he was adopted but decided he was still too young to know the truth about his birth mother.

"I know," he said with a smile. "Why did you go to prison?"

"I took things that weren't mine. When you do that, the police put you in prison."

"Okay."

As she watched him run to play with his cousins, she knew she would not only grieve the loss of her brother; she would also mourn the loss of her son, again. Later, Sean asked if he could spend the night with Mary Kay and Mama. He was very close to his grandmother, and he liked to be around company. Mary Kay told him to ask his parents first. She was surprised when they agreed; perhaps they *did* see that she had changed.

Since Ronnie grew up in Eldon, news of his death filled the airways. They unplugged the TV and radio to shield Mama. They were stunned by a few people who called asking rude, horrible questions such as, "Is it true they cut Ronnie's body up in little pieces?"

"Don't let Mama answer the phone," cautioned Connie. Mama sat in her rocking chair, hardly speaking. It was a dreadful time for all of them. Like individual islands of grief, they floated through the next two days, occasionally coming together and then moving away. Mary Kay could not cry until the day after the funeral, on the flight home. She knew Ronnie had been murdered, but she did not know how. When Officer Arnold said he had been stabbed between thirty and forty times, she broke down and sobbed.

Later, Mary Kay marveled that her first reaction to Ronnie's death had not been anger or bitterness. She knew now that God really had given her a new heart. In the hours while she had waited to hear whether she could go home, she turned to the Bible. She expected God to comfort her and was surprised that the verse that struck her most was Hebrews 12:15 "See to it that no one misses the grace of God and that no bitter root grows up to cause trouble and defile many."

What comfort was that? She knew what the Lord was telling her. If ever a root of bitterness could form within her, this would be the time. God was gently warning her not to let go of what He had given her. Against every natural inclination, she began to pray for Chuck Adams, the man arrested for killing Ronnie.

She wasn't the only one praying for Chuck. The day after Ronnie died, Mama called her pastor and asked him to send someone to the jail to witness to Chuck. "There must be something terribly wrong with that young man for him to do something like that to our Ronnie," Mama told him.

"It's not as noble as people think," Mama explained years later. "I had to do something so bitterness and anger wouldn't set in, and that was the only thing I could think to do. It's one thing to have a child taken from you by illness or accident, but when one of your children is brutally murdered it is very difficult to not ask God why."

Week after week, Mary Kay and Mama continued to pray for Chuck. God gradually filled Mary Kay's heart with compassion for him. She knew she could not love that man on her own; Jesus was working in her heart. After

Chuck was convicted and sent to prison, Mary Kay wrote him a letter:

"Dear Chuck, I forgive you for killing Ronnie, but that won't do you any good. Not if Mama, our whole family and everyone who knew and loved Ronnie forgave you. Only if you receive the forgiveness of Jesus Christ, will you ever have any real peace in your life. Chuck, Jesus goes to jail; I know, because that's where I met Him." Years later, she received a reply. He wrote to tell her Jesus was now his Lord and Savior too.

Chuck took my brother, thought Mary Kay, *but now he is my brother in Christ.* She did not understand how it took the death of her brother to bring Chuck to the point where he could receive Jesus, but then, she also did not understand how God could give His own Son to die for someone like her.

Some folks assumed she must be highly connected because of the powerful people involved in the recent events of her life. She knew God had done it all. Her feelings of rejection were steadily being healed by God's personal intervention on her behalf. She had not actively sought for God to prove Himself or to heal her. The difficult circumstances that kept coming into her life seemed as if they should damage her more, but in spite of those trials—even because of those trials—God helped her. Every time God intervened in her life in an individual and personal way, she understood a little more how much He loved her. She was learning to see Him as her Father; the perfect Father she had always wanted.

At the university, Mary Kay was in a dual objectives program working on both a Bachelor of Science in psychology and a Bachelor of Arts in education. One year remained before graduation. She had served just over five years of her sentence; two and half more years were left to serve if the board approved her first appeal for parole. She planned to graduate with her master's in psychology at about the same time she was paroled.

Mary Kay knew all the details of the parole process. When the time came, she would receive a letter informing her that in three months she was scheduled to meet the parole board. Before that meeting she must develop a home plan, specifying a job and a place to stay, and submit it to a parole officer for verification and approval. The parole board would interview her to determine what she had learned from her incarceration and how she expected her behavior be different when she was released. They would decide if her home plan was acceptable. If they opted to release her, they would notify the prosecuting attorney, the sentencing judges, and her victims. A thirty-day period would then begin, during which any of those could protest her release. Another letter would tell her their final verdict. She had made all her mental preparations for this process, but God had a different plan.

On Monday, March 6, 1978, the housemother called Mary Kay at work. "You got a phone call from the Office of the Board of Pardons and Paroles in Montgomery. They want you to call back as soon as you can." Mary Kay was puzzled. She had never heard of the Parole Board calling an inmate on the phone. She dialed the number and told the secretary who she was.

"What time do you get back to the halfway house?" the woman on the phone asked.

"I get off work at four-forty-five and I'm back by five o'clock P.M."

"That's too late."

Mary Kay thought, *How can it be too late? I have permission to be out until five thirty.*

The secretary continued, "The parole board meets at two o'clock."

"What does that have to do with me?"

"Oh well, don't worry, that's okay. Thank you for calling me back." The woman hung up. Mary Kay stood and stared at the receiver in her hand. "She's a fruitcake. I don't meet the board for twenty-two months. What does she think I'd be late for?"

On Wednesday, the housemother met Mary Kay at the door. "There's an officer here to see you."

Oh, no, thought Mary Kay, *it must be an officer from another state. I have been locked up over five years, and now they are going to put another charge on me.*

As she stepped into the entry, she recognized one of the corrections officers from Tutwiler. A rush of relief washed over her; if she had faced arrest, a deputy sheriff would be standing there.

"I've got your papers," he said. Mary Kay was puzzled. The only papers a corrections officer would bring personally were furlough papers. She had not requested a pass or a furlough.

"What papers are you talking about?"

"Your parole papers. Sign here."

Mary Kay stared at him. "You must have made a mistake. I haven't even met the board."

"Are you Sandra Marshall, 107979?"

"Yes, I am."

"Then sign here and let me go home. It's five o'clock and I'm off duty."

She looked down at the paper. There was the name, Sandra Marshall, and the gold seal of the state of Alabama. She took the pen he offered and obediently signed where he pointed. She barely listened as he spoke. "You have twenty-four hours to report to your parole officer, Jim Benson[26]. His office is in the Lee County Courthouse." She was still staring at the paper in her hand when he said, "Good evening," and left.

---

[26] Name changed

PHOTOGRAPHS

The family in 1947:
(back) Dad, Joyce, Mama, Bill, Jean;
(front) Mary Kay and Don.

Mama with Don and Mary Kay when
she was two years old.

The house on the hill. Tom is in the lower left corner holding a hula hoop.

Connie, Ilene and Mary Kay in 1960.

Paul and Mary Kay, 1970.   Sean at 19 months.

The entrance to Julia Tutwiler Prison for Women, Wetumpka, Alabama.

Mary Kay's mug shot taken during her processing into Tutwiler prison.

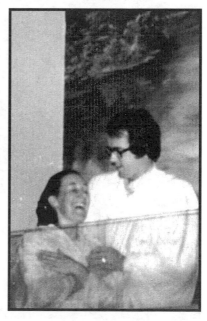

Mary Kay's baptism, November 11, 1973

The family before Ronnie's funeral in 1977: (left to right) Ilene, Connie, Bill, Mary Kay, Mama, Don, Joyce, Tom and Jean.

Jack and Mitzi Hinde with Nina and Hank Hamilton, 1979.

Mary Kay and her daughter in 1981
when Brenda was 16.

The second year of Angel Tree
in 1983 with an unidentified
volunteer in the mall.

Chuck Colson in Montgomery with a young Angel Tree
child wiping away her brother's tear.

The Shepherd's Fold house.

Mary Kay and Don on the porch of her first house, 2003.

The family in 2002 at Mama's last Christmas: (from left to right) Ilene, Mary Kay, Tom, Don, Joyce, Mama (in bed), Bill, Connie and Jean.

Mary Kay's square on Mama's quilt.
It reads, "Grace Made the Difference."

Mary Kay, Chuck Colson, and the author, Jodi Werhanowicz.

Mary Kay and Don
in front of their house with
their dog, Cellblock, 2003.

Mary Kay as Maudie Mae.

PART FOUR:

FREE LIFE

CHAPTER TWENTY

Mary Kay stared at the paper. "How did this happen? I never even met with the parole board. I didn't make a home plan."

Her mind raced through possibilities but nothing made sense. She looked up at the housemother. "I don't have any place to go. Can I stay here tonight?"

"Of course, you can," replied Martha.

Mary Kay lay awake most of the night, puzzling over her astonishing new freedom. The next afternoon, after classes, she met with her parole officer. She sat, nervously watching him shuffle through a stack of papers. When he finished the pile on his desk, he turned and removed folder after folder from a file cabinet behind him. She watched as he carefully leafed through each one and returned it to the file. Finally, he closed the drawer and turned back to her.

"I can't find any papers on you. Are you sure you've been paroled?"

She clutched her parole paper tightly and held it out for him to see. He took hold of it, but she did not loosen her grip.

"Well, those are parole papers all right. You're released, and it says here that I'm your parole officer, but I sure don't have any paperwork on you." She waited, wondering what he would do.

"I guess you'd better come in every month to see me. As long as you're in school you won't be required to have a job. Do you have a place to live?" She shook her head, and he continued, "Well, let me know the address when you get one. Don't leave the county without letting me know, and if you ever want to leave the state, we'll have to get written permission. Any questions?"

Mary Kay shook her head again. She was not about to ask her biggest question—how she happened to be paroled; she did not want them to discover it was a mistake. She thanked him and walked out of the office. She could plan and carry out a bank heist, but she did not know what to do now that she was free. Back at the halfway house, she called one of the local Gideons to ask if she could come to their prayer breakfast. She needed advice . . . godly advice.

"I don't have any ideas on a place to live," she explained to the group on Saturday morning. "I have very little income and no furniture. Do you think I should rent a room in someone's home? I think I'm a bit old for the college dormitory."

"I know a woman who might have a place. I can check it out today." Marvin Waller was retired from his home repairs and remodeling business. Now he visited the widows in his church, doing odd jobs around the house for them. On Sunday morning, he called Mary Kay at the halfway house.

"The lady I mentioned says she might let you live in her chicken house." This did not sound promising, but there weren't any other options. She agreed to go with him to meet the lady.

Anna Lou was an elderly woman who lived on a corner lot only two miles from the college campus. At one time, her property had been part of a large dairy farm. She kept the largest lot when the farm was broken up into smaller lots and sold. A young couple and their two sons lived in the big brick house that was the original farmhouse. Behind it were two smaller houses; Anna Lou lived in the larger of the two; previously the milk processing barn. The smallest house had been the chicken house but was converted long ago into a little apartment.

Marvin introduced Mary Kay and asked her to share her testimony. When she was done, Anna Lou's smile was warm. "I don't think there is much of anything in there, but you are welcome to rent it."

They walked across the lawn and through the door. The studio apartment had a concrete floor, a small stove, a built-in drop leaf table, and a tiny bathroom. The rent was manageable. She took it.

Marvin offered her a carpet remnant; it was a nearly perfect fit. Mary Kay asked Dr. Shields if she could have her bed from the halfway house. He agreed, and several Gideons came by to help her move in. They brought a wicker rocking chair, a set of dishes, and some linens with them.

Boards stacked on bricks served as a bookcase and divided the room into separate sleeping and sitting areas. Her first piece of furniture was an old desk she bought for ten dollars. She was more excited about that apartment than about any other home since her childhood house on the hill. And there was a bonus: Sometimes Anna Lou made a tuna casserole and brought half to Mary Kay.

Now she needed a car. Riding the bus was fine for school, and friends took her to run errands, but she was receiving invitations to speak out of town. Not wanting to impose on others for those trips, she began to pray for a car. She was used to Lincolns and Cadillacs, but she told God a small car with standard transmission and good gas mileage would be fine.

One day, the Gideon who loaned her the airfare to go to Ronnie's funeral, Pat Bunn, called. He owned a used car lot.

"I have a car for you. It's about six years old, a Toyota Corolla." Mary Kay took the bus to Birmingham to see the car. It was a reasonable price though it did not have air conditioning—she forgot to pray for that. There was another problem; she did not have money for it at any price.

"Take the car anyway," said Pat, "and then try to find financing."

"That's very nice of you, but there is a bit of a problem. As a requirement for parole, I cannot be in debt—no credit cards or loans. I have to maintain a small savings account and checking account which my parole officer monitors."

"Take it." He pressed the keys into her hand. "The Lord will work out something; I'm sure of it."

Not wanting to offend him, she took the keys and thanked him. As she drove the car back to Auburn, Mary Kay wished she felt some of his confidence. She was sure she would be making another trip to Birmingham next week to return the car.

Her first stop was to see her parole officer and inform him of her acquisition. She did not want to raise any suspicions as to why she was in the possession of an unreported car.

"Oh, you can have a loan; you just need my permission and I certainly don't have a problem with it. The real question is whether you can find anyone who will give you a loan."

Mary Kay shook her head in amazement as she walked out of the office. Could Pat be right after all? On the drive back to Auburn she had been so skeptical she didn't even bother to pray. Now she began to pray earnestly, confessing her lack of faith and talking to God about the loan. She worked barely twenty hours a week because of her course load, and all the money she earned went to living expenses.

I guess I'll go and talk to my bank, she thought, *but I'm going to have to tell them my history. They will never loan me the money when they find out I am an ex-con.* On her way, she drove by a bank and she sensed God was telling her to stop there.

"But, Lord," she protested, "that isn't my bank. Mine is farther down the road." She kept heading toward her own bank but the impression remained strong that God was saying, "No I want you go in that bank back there."

"I don't know anybody there," she argued, "I don't have an account there. They surely will not loan me any money because they don't know who I am. They know me at my bank; I have an account and just maybe, they will loan me the money."

She went on to her bank, filled out a loan application, and spoke to the loan officer. She knew it was just a formality, that the answer was no before she walked in. She was right. When she reached her car she sensed God telling her to go back to the other bank.

"Is that You, Lord? You know I don't want the rejection again," she prayed but she drove to the bank anyway. She circled around the block, once, and twice, until the urging became so strong she finally parked.

"I'll go up there and I'll show You they won't give me any money." The woman at the desk looked up when Mary Kay approached.

"Who do I need to speak to about a car loan?"

"That would be Mr. Whitaker[27], the branch manager. Have a seat and I'll tell him you want to see him."

Mary Kay did not sit long before a tall, middle-aged man with a disarming

---

[27] Name changed

smile came striding up to her. He reached for her hand and took it in both of his.

"Why, Mary Kay, it's good to see you again." She studied his face, trying to remember who he was and how she knew him. He saw her bewilderment. "You spoke at my church a couple of weeks ago. I was very moved by your testimony." He led her into his office and offered her a seat.

"What can I do for you?"

"Well, sir, I have this little car that I need to finance." She knew she was talking too fast but pressed on anyway. "I'm not employed, I'm going to school full time, but I have a little income once in a while from honorariums when I speak. I guess you know my background; I really need a loan for the car, something that will allow me to pay whenever I have some money, which I'll do, I promise." She stopped to catch her breath.

"I think we can work out something." He laughed at her look of relief and amazement. "We will give you an 'on demand' note; we won't set up a payment schedule; you just pay what you can, when you can. We can renew it every six months, as long as you pay something—anything—on it during that period."

She walked out of the bank amazed and a little sheepish. With nothing but her signature she had the money for the car. "I guess that *was* You, Lord. Forgive me for doubting."

Whenever she had a little extra money, she went to the bank and made a car payment. Sometimes it was only twenty-five dollars. When a church was very generous, she could make a four or five hundred dollar payment. Weeks might pass between payments, but after only eighteen months the loan was paid off. Now her credit was reestablished, a major accomplishment for a parolee. She often marveled at how unusual and improbable that loan was; few ex-cons get such a chance, even after years of clean living.

Since a verse in Ezekiel was the vehicle of her salvation and the car was the vehicle carrying her to share that testimony, she named the car Ezekiel. Even her license plate said "Ezekiel," providing several opportunities to share her testimony.

A few months after buying the car, she was invited to speak at a Gideon banquet on a Saturday night. The hotel was nearly two hundred miles away. Mary

Kay had enough gas to drive there but not enough to return. She was broke, so she decided to borrow twenty dollars from some friends at the banquet.

After the banquet, she and her friends walked toward their hotel room. They passed a man sitting alone in a lounge chair by the pool. Mary Kay felt compelled to ask her friend Bill to approach the man and talk to him about Jesus. Bill agreed, and his wife, Nancy, and Mary Kay went to the room to pray for them. The man had come to the hotel to commit suicide, but Bill led him to the Lord that evening instead.

In their excitement, Mary Kay forgot to ask them for gas money; about thirty miles out of town she remembered. She did not want to turn back so she began to pray, "Father, You know I have to speak in Birmingham in the morning. Please get me all the way there." Nearly a hundred miles stretched between her and her next stop, but she made it. The next morning when she got into her car, there was not even enough gas to start the engine. She bought gas at a station next door, and poured the gas into the carburetor to make it start.

When she was not going to school, Mary Kay spent most of her time traveling and speaking. She graduated summa cum laude in June 1979 and immediately applied for graduate school. She was only one of thirty students accepted into the Master's in Counseling Education program and began school again in September at Auburn.

In January, a group in Atlanta invited her to speak and offered to buy a plane ticket so she would not have to drive. Mary Kay received permission from her parole officer, and on a Saturday morning she boarded the plane and took her seat. She had brought the last few days worth of mail with her to open and read during the trip. As she flipped through the stack she saw a letter postmarked "Alabama Board of Pardons and Paroles."

Oh no, her heart sank. *They've found out they made a mistake in paroling me early. Will they send me back to the halfway house? Surely they won't send me back to Tutwiler? Or will they?*

Mary Kay stared at the envelope for a long time before she summoned the courage to face what was surely bad news. As she opened the paper inside, she saw another certificate with the gold seal of the state of Alabama. Another parole paper? No, it was a full pardon—with restoration of all civil, legal, and voting rights!

Mary Kay was no less stunned than when the officer served her parole papers. She sat still in her seat trying to absorb what the paper meant and how it might have happened. She thought of the state representative for Lee County she had met when speaking at a Rotary Club meeting. She had asked him about the possibility of getting off parole early. In Alabama, parole lasts for the duration of the offender's full sentence, and there is a mandatory three years before one can even petition for a pardon. The petitioner must have letters from employers, references stating he or she is a good citizen, and a stack of paperwork showing not even a parking ticket associated with his or her name. Ordinarily the parole board grants only restoration of rights, not full pardons. She asked the representative if, when the time came, he might write a letter of recommendation to the board.

She called him when she returned on Monday. She reminded him of their talk and her request for a letter.

"Oh, do you want me to do that now?"

"You didn't already write one?" Mary Kay was quiet for a moment. "I thought you had because I got a letter this weekend releasing me from parole and granting me a full pardon."

"Well, congratulations! I'm sure I can expect your vote even though I didn't write the letter for you," he laughed.

Just as with her parole, Mary Kay never found out how her pardon came about. She knew one thing—she had a good Friend in high places.

CHAPTER TWENTY-ONE

When the phone rang, she had only to take a large step from anywhere in the tiny apartment to reach it. This time, a man's voice spoke on the other end.

"Hello, Mary Kay, this is Jim."

Jim? Jim who? A list of Jims went through her mind: a classmate, her mechanic, a few Gideons?

"We've been having some problems here. Do you . . . would you . . ." he paused, and Mary Kay went back through her list of Jims; who was this? "Can Brenda come and stay with you for a few months?"

Jim! Her first husband—the father of two of her children! Had it been so long she didn't even recognize his voice? A wave of shame rolled over her; how hard her heart must have been.

"Brenda has been giving us some problems. No one in the family wanted me to call you, but if you don't come get her, she is probably going to be put in a juvenile detention center or something. She's your daughter, too."

Mary Kay's mind and heart were swirling. Excitement mingled with fear at the thought of seeing her daughter again—of actually living with her. Is she really a juvenile delinquent? Mary Kay wondered. What have I done to my daughter?

Remorse and dread filled her as she formed an apology in her mind for her years of selfishness. Regardless of his part in the divorce, she had hurt Jim. Did he know she had been in prison? If he did not know when he called, he definitely knew when he hung up. Her prison time did not seem to matter to him. Brenda needed her, and Mary Kay wanted her, desperately. She told Jim she would make arrangements and call him back. She sat for a long time after he had hung up.

191

She remembered the tiny towhead as she last saw her, playing in the front yard of Jim's parents' house, out of reach of her mother's arms. What was she like at fifteen? Could they make up for all the lost years? Would Brenda accept her, could she even learn to love her a little? How would she feel about an ex-con for a mother? The what-ifs were too difficult to contemplate; Mary Kay forced them from her mind and focused on the practicalities.

Let's see, we'll need a bigger place; this one is too small for two people. Mary Kay had planned to move to Birmingham anyway when the spring semester ended. Her friends Nina and Mitzi, as well as other friends, lived there and there was a big airport for all the travel she was doing. Next fall she would begin the final year of her master's program, and she could take two night courses on Tuesday and Thursday and commute the hour and a half between Auburn and Birmingham. Yes, it was a good time to move. A warm feeling of mothering welled up; she whispered a prayer of gratitude. God was giving her a second chance.

Mary Kay was in the midst of finals when Jim had called. She planned to take the summer off from school to travel and speak, to pay for tuition in the fall. As soon as exams were over she was scheduled to go to Nova Scotia.

"I can't cancel this speaking engagement and I can't afford to take Brenda with me to Nova Scotia. What can I do? I am certainly not going to pass up the opportunity to get to know my daughter."

Mary Kay called her brother Tom and his wife, Maureen, who lived in a town near Jim. They graciously agreed to drive to get Brenda and allow her to stay with them until Mary Kay returned from Canada. After her visit to Nova Scotia, Mary Kay flew to Illinois. As the plane approached the runway, she grew more excited and nervous. Would Brenda be a sullen, difficult teenager? Would she be able to adapt to Mary Kay's hectic lifestyle?

As she walked down the ramp into the terminal, her eyes scanned the people waiting at the gate. Mary Kay recognized Brenda instantly—it was like looking at herself in a mirror. Mary Kay was excited, but she did not want to overwhelm her daughter. When Mary Kay walked up to the group, she gave her a brief and awkward hug.

"Hello," said Brenda, "Uncle Tom has shown me pictures, and you look just like them."

"You look just like them, too." Everyone laughed and the tension broke. "How has your visit been?"

"Oh, we've had fun." Brenda proceeded to tell her what she had been doing. Mary Kay was relieved to find Brenda easygoing and friendly. This might not be as difficult as she had feared.

Before leaving the state, Mary Kay met with the local probation officers. She could not resist asking why they were so willing to allow this teenager to go to another state with a virtual stranger. They told her that Brenda was not a delinquent at all; she was an "A" student who never caused problems and was well liked at her school. Without going into detail, the officers assured her they believed this was best for Brenda. Mary Kay had to trust that God had arranged this in His generous way.

Mary Kay wanted to see Charlie, her son. Though he was only three years older than his sister, he was already a husband and father. He refused to speak to her over the phone. His rejection hurt deeply but she could hardly blame him. Brenda convinced Charlie's wife to meet them at the airport. She brought along two-year-old Nathan. He ran to his Aunt Brenda, his favorite baby-sitter. She picked him up and turned to Mary Kay.

"This is your grandma. Can you say Grandma?" Brenda asked. Nathan just grinned. He quickly warmed up to Mary Kay and soon was hugging her and sitting in her lap. For Mary Kay, it was a bittersweet moment. He looked so much like Charlie as a toddler. Mary Kay was thrilled to meet her first grandchild, but it did not ease the sorrow of not seeing his father.

Brenda tried to hide her tears when they said goodbye to Nathan and his mother. The excitement of flying quickly distracted her as they walked onto the ramp; she had never been on an airplane before, and Mary Kay was pleased to be the one to take her on her first plane ride. Nashville was their first destination, where Mary Kay was scheduled to speak at several churches. These were new experiences for Brenda; except for weddings and funerals, church was an unfamiliar place for her.

Brenda was a delightfully funny, warm-hearted, and vivacious girl. She got along well with everyone they met, both young and old. Mary Kay continually prayed, "Lord, help me to be a good mother. Help me to say the things that need to be said, but to do it gently and with love. Help me to be sensitive to this teenager whose life has just been turned upside down. Help me, Lord Jesus."

Back in Alabama, Brenda stayed in Birmingham with Mitzi and her husband, Jack, while Mary Kay returned to Auburn for the third quarter. Everyone agreed it would be easier for Brenda to start at the school she would attend the next fall instead of having to change again. Brenda was very adaptable and agreeable.

Mitzi's home looked like a mansion to Brenda. She had never known a lifestyle like this; she had a lovely room, and Mitzi and Nina took her shopping and bought her all the clothes a teenager could want or need. She enrolled at a high school less than three miles away, and Mitzi or Jack took her to school every day.

Mary Kay finished her third quarter in Auburn, driving to Birmingham on weekends. When she drove to speaking engagements, Brenda went with her. At the end of the quarter, Mary Kay moved to Birmingham, and she and Brenda went apartment hunting. They found one they liked in the same district as Brenda's school. When Nina came to see their new place, she exclaimed, "This is where I used to live!" Just a few years earlier she had occupied the same apartment.

That summer Brenda traveled with Mary Kay as she spoke across the South. In the evening, they often lay on the bed together and talked. Mary Kay would cradle Brenda's head in her lap as she brushed her hair and told her stories. Brenda loved to hear about her own birth and early childhood. She often quizzed Mary Kay on various family members and family history.

Mary Kay was surprised to discover that Brenda had never been to a sleepover before. Mary Kay encouraged her to bring her friends to the house. When she finally did, Brenda kept coming in and asking if they were being too noisy.

"Honey, that's what teenagers do. I don't mind. I'm enjoying it, aren't you?"

"Oh, yes!"

Mary Kay had no salaried job, and Brenda seemed nervous about "living by faith." Mary Kay explained how God had supplied all her needs for the last four years. An old cigar box covered with bright yellow wrapping paper sat on the shelf. On the top Mary Kay had pasted a card on which she wrote "GOD'S BILLS" and beneath that Matthew 6:33 and Philippians 4:19. When she received a bill, she put it in the box. Every month—sometimes before she needed it, sometimes at the last minute—God supplied payment. He was never late.

One month, even after the bills were paid and groceries purchased, sixty dollars remained in the checking account. As Mary Kay considered ways to use the money, a phone call came from Brenda's school.

"Hello, are you Brenda's mother?"

"Yes, I am," Mary Kay replied proudly. Then concern crept in. "Is something wrong; is Brenda all right?"

"Oh yes, Brenda is fine, but she really needs to have appropriate shoes for PE class. We have sent two letters home, and she still does not have the shoes. I'm afraid she will get an F in this class if she doesn't have the proper shoes."

When Brenda came home from school, Mary Kay asked about the gym shoes, and the girl's gaze dropped to the floor. "I didn't give you the letters because we didn't have enough money; I looked at your checkbook."

"How much do they cost?"

"I think they're about forty dollars."

"Brenda, we do have the money for those shoes."

"But what about the bills?"

"Honey, the bills are God's job; that's why I put them in the box. When you need something, you tell me. We'll put it in the box, and He will take care of it. If another bill comes, He will provide the money to cover it, too."

As soon as supper was over, they went to the mall to buy shoes. Over the months, Brenda saw many examples of God's provision, yet she remained worried about their financial security. Mary Kay wondered if she should find a full-time salaried position. In March she would graduate with her master's degree, but she didn't want to launch too quickly into a career without prayer and advice from her friends, Mitzi and Nina.

From the first time they had met in the Jefferson County Jail, these two friends had taken Mary Kay on as their private project. They did this sort of thing well, maneuvering and arranging until their good intentions became good deeds or at least, sincere apologies when things did not work out the way they intended. They saw from the beginning that Mary Kay was being used by God, and they liked to be where God was working.

Mitzi's brother-in-law, Jess Miller, had recently formed a Care Committee with a few other men to explore the possibility of a prison ministry in Alabama. They were in touch with an organization started by Charles Colson. Mr. Colson had been a member of President Nixon's inner circle and had gone to prison as a result of the 1972 Watergate scandal. While incarcerated he was moved by the deep need of prisoners for spiritual guidance, and he founded Prison Fellowship upon his release. Nina and Mitzi decided not only that Mary Kay should be involved, but also that she should run Prison Fellowship in Alabama.

"Hey, Mary Kay," Mitzi's cheerful voice was instantly recognizable over the phone. "You need to get the job of director of that new prison ministry that Jess, Molton, and Drayton are starting."

Nina yelled in the background, "Oh, yes, Mary Kay, do. Mitzi will be the bookkeeper and I will be the secretary, and the three of us will run the office. So you go on up to Washington, D.C. and get this job." Neither of them knew what being state director meant, and the fact that Prison Fellowship had never had a female director certainly did not deter them. They were on a quest. Mary Kay loved public speaking, but the idea of helping inmates, some of them her own dear friends, drew her into their plan. It wouldn't hurt to check it out.

She talked with the Care Committee. They liked her and sent her to Washington to be interviewed at the national offices, but there was more opposition to her than anyone had anticipated. No one was bothered by the fact that she had been a crook or was an ex-convict, but some were bothered by the idea of a *female* director. Not Chuck Colson, though; he and Mary Kay took to each other right away. However, she had to prove to the others that she had the support and backing of the community. For nearly six months she volunteered and did many of the things a director would do, while she finished her master's degree.

In April 1982, after six months of interviews and various meetings with Prison Fellowship staff, Mary Kay became the first director of Prison Fellowship in Alabama as well as the first female state director PF USA had ever had. And just as they had planned, Nina became the secretary and Mitzi, the bookkeeper.

One of Mary Kay's first duties was to conduct an in-prison seminar. As a ministry Prison Fellowship was still young, and no printed material was available; each group did what its members thought best.

"We're going to do a seminar in a new prison called West Jefferson," Mary Kay said one morning.

"Who is going to be the Bible teacher?" asked Mitzi. They discussed various options until Nina had an idea.

"I know. Hank can do it."

Hank was Nina's husband, and Mary Kay knew he was a good teacher, so she agreed. Nina would tell him. He was out of town on business, so they went ahead with their plans without finding out first if he would like to do it. Nina made up flyers, got Hank's clearance at the prison, and set up a three-day seminar with the officials. They had no title for the seminar, so they simply advertised it as a seminar by Bible teacher, Hank Hamilton.

Nina met him at the airport on Thursday before the weekend seminar. She still had not told him that on the next day he would need enough material to teach for three days—in prison. On the way home, Nina approached the topic carefully.

"Hank, have you ever thought about teaching in a prison?"

"No, Nina, I never thought about that." They had not been married long, and he had not learned to read her yet.

"Wouldn't it be interesting to teach men in prison, and they would come to know Jesus, grow up in Christ, and become great people?"

"I have never been interested in prisoners, and I would never go into a prison. If a prison was the last place I could go, I still wouldn't go there."

Nina thought, *Oh no, this is bad; this is going downhill faster than I expected.*

"Well, you know," she ventured, "the Bible says to be instant in season and out of season and to be ready to give an answer for the hope that is within you. So, if someone asked you to give just one Bible lesson in a prison, would you be ready and willing to do it? Like if God was asking you to do it?"

"No, I wouldn't."

By now they had reached their home. Hank pulled into the garage, turned off the car, and turned to face Nina. "Just tell me. What is it? What are we talking about here?"

By this time she didn't have the nerve to bring up a three-day seminar, so she said, "Well, it's only one Bible lesson in this new prison that's just opened."

"Oh, well, okay, I might be interested. When is it?"

"Tomorrow night."

"That gives me a lot of time to prepare!"

"You teach all the time. Just use something you've already done." Nina was deeply relieved; it might be well to wait until after his first night to bring up the fact that the seminar was also supposed to be all day Saturday and Sunday. When they arrived at the prison the next night, a banner stretched across the meeting room wall: "Three Day Seminar with Hank Hamilton." Hank stopped dead in his tracks, staring at the banner. Then he whirled to face Nina. "*Three* days?"

Nina gave him a sheepish grin as the chaplain interrupted and greeted them; she was safe—for the moment. Before the night was over a tall Ethiopian man was gloriously saved, and Hank's heart was knit to working with inmates.

A special kind of joy and fulfillment is given to people who sacrifice to serve passionately those whom society scorns. Hank served in prison ministry for the next eighteen years until he died.

CHAPTER TWENTY-TWO

During the school year, Brenda often stayed at Mitzi's house when Mary Kay flew out of town for speaking engagements. Late one Sunday evening she arrived to pick Brenda up. Her daughter and Mitzi were grinning from ear to ear as they led Mary Kay up the stairs to Brenda's room. Crepe paper streamers and balloons decorated the door, and a sign in the middle read: "AND THE ANGLES REJOICED."

"Angles?" Mary Kay asked, puzzled. "Don't you mean *angels?*" Mitzi and Brenda laughed at their error, and slowly Mary Kay began to understand—Brenda had invited Christ into her heart! Mary Kay began crying and laughing, and they all hugged. For a moment, Mary Kay felt envious that Mitzi had the honor of leading her daughter to the Lord, but she was too relieved and delighted to hold onto the feeling.

Soon afterward, Mary Kay saw an example of Brenda's simple faith and immediate obedience to God's direction. In the evening, Brenda often stayed in the living room until Mary Kay quit working at her desk and went to bed. Eventually, Mary Kay realized Brenda was afraid of being in her room alone. They discussed her fears.

"What are you thinking of when you're afraid?" asked Mary Kay.

"I've watched a lot of scary movies, and sometimes I can't get the images and sounds out of my mind."

"Satan works through those movies," Mary Kay explained. "That's why Psalm 101:3 says not to allow 'any evil before my eyes.' "

They prayed about it together. In church the next Sunday, the pastor asked if anyone needed prayer. To Mary Kay's amazement, Brenda went forward and confessed to the entire church that she had watched horror movies and other

199

things she shouldn't have. She said she "didn't want to give Satan an open door" and asked Pastor Jack to pray for her. Mary Kay was deeply touched and very proud.

In addition to in-prison seminars and Bible studies, Mary Kay was instructed to do a Christmas project. She remembered all the Christmas projects from her days in prison and thought those ideas were boring. Every church, club, school, ministry, and organization did the same thing. Most of them came just once a year. Where were they the rest of the year?

If she had learned one thing in prison, it was obedience to authority. So she dutifully set about trying to think of something, to comply with this request. It would not be just another Christmas project; she was not about to do what everybody else was doing. What could they do that was different and better?

She was still searching for a fresh idea weeks later when Mitzi asked her to share her testimony at the Christian Business and Professional Women's Club luncheon. As usual, Nina went along. Afterwards, a woman in her late twenties approached Mary Kay. She could see the lines of anger and bitterness in the woman's face.

"As far as I'm concerned," she snapped, "regarding convicts, you can lock those people up and throw away the key."

Mary Kay was taken aback. This was not the usual response to her story. The woman knew she was one of "those people," yet her words were full of venom. Mary Kay was unsure how to respond.

"Well, you're not the only one who feels that way," she finally managed to say.

The woman proceeded to tell how her father went to prison when she was young and how their family had suffered. She was certain her brother's delinquency was their father's fault. She did not seem aware that her brother was making his own choices.

"What about the inmates' kids?" she demanded. "*They* are the real victims. If you ever want to do anything for the kids, let me know." She turned on her heel and marched out of the room.

That's it! thought Mary Kay, *The inmates' kids—we don't have to do anything for the inmates; we can do something for their children.*

Mary Kay's thoughts flashed to her first Christmas at Tutwiler and the piles of soap and toothpaste the women carefully wrapped in toilet paper to give their children. Every year the women repeated that same routine. The same groups came and gave the women the same things. The mothers gave their children the same meager gifts, and every year the children's reaction was the same.

I still can't believe those kids were so excited, she thought. *Just think how they'd feel if they got real gifts.* "Oh, thank You, Lord! What a wonderful idea! We'll give real Christmas presents to the inmates' kids."

Mary Kay could hardly wait to get to work. On the way back in the car she shared her idea with Nina and Mitzi, "I believe the Lord has given us our Christmas project."

"Oh, wonderful!" exclaimed Nina, who had the faith of a child. If Mary Kay said the Lord had decided it, then it was decided. "What is it going to be?"

"Remember my telling you about how the women in prison would give their children toiletries for Christmas?" They nodded. "Well, this year we are going to give their kids *real* gifts."

"What kind of gifts?" asked Nina. "Not pitiful charity gifts, little pencils, shoes that nobody wants. There are plenty of groups that already give that stuff to underprivileged children. We don't want to give *those* kinds of things."

"We'll give them exactly what they want," said Mitzi, catching Mary Kay's vision. "Every child wants more than one present. We'll give them two gifts, things they really want with no price limit."

"I think one gift should be clothes," Mary Kay said, "and the other can be whatever they want. We'll have them ask for four gifts, two of each kind, and that way we can give them at least two."

Nina asked, "How are we going to find out what they want? Who's going to do all that shopping?"

"The inmates know me; I think they'll give me the names of who is taking care of their children and where the kids live. We can call the children's caretakers and ask them what they want. Then we'll get people from the community to buy the gifts. But we want the inmates to get the credit; the children have to know that the gifts are from their parent in prison."

"How are we going to get people to buy the gifts?"

"Oh, that won't be hard," declared Mitzi. "We can find people; we'll call all our friends. We can call the newspapers and radio stations."

"We could also put a sign on the door of our office," Nina suggested, "with a Christmas tree in the window. We'll get a lot of exposure from people passing by." The Prison Fellowship offices occupied the first floor of the Brown Marx building in downtown Birmingham, courtesy of Molton Williams, who had a real estate office there.

"We can put little ornaments on the tree for each child."

"Or paper angels with their names and what they want written on them." said Mary Kay. "It will be our angel tree."

The more they talked, the more ideas popped up. "Wait a minute. I can't remember all this," Mary Kay said. "Y'all are just going to have to go to the Care Committee meeting with me Monday morning."

"At seven in the morning?" gasped Nina. "You expect me to be up and dressed by seven in the morning?" They all laughed. Mitzi and Nina had long since been fired by Mary Kay as bookkeeper and secretary for taking *very* long lunches or not coming in at all. They were always volunteering for a new need; if there was a ministry to do they just did it. They were dear friends and tireless servants of God, but committing to a regular job was neither woman's strong point.

On Monday morning, the Care Committee immediately embraced the project. Ideas bounced around the room and each member took on some task. Someone suggested setting up the project in a mall; the merchants would surely agree because people would shop in their stores after choosing an angel from the tree. Drayton offered to contact the owners of Brookwood Mall. Jess Miller volunteered to contact the *Birmingham News*. Drayton offered to loan his secretary, Marjorie, along with his office space.

Mary Kay, Nina, and Mitzi were joined by Marjorie and several other friends. Someone designed the angel for the tree, and they cut each of them out by hand. They made signs for the store registers saying "We are an Angel Tree supporter." Many merchants agreed to offer a ten percent discount if shoppers presented their angels and purchased the gifts in their store.

In August Mary Kay contacted the chaplain at Tutwiler and went to talk to the women there. Nina had designed an application form for them to fill out, asking for the names and ages of their children along with the addresses and phone numbers of the caregivers. Just as Mary Kay had expected, the prisoners were quite willing to give her the information, but they were skeptical that anyone would want to buy their children presents. She did the same in one of the men's prisons nearby.

Volunteers used the phones in Drayton's offices after five o'clock to call the children's caregivers. They could hear each other making calls at the various desks around the room.

"Hello, my name is Nina Hamilton with Prison Fellowship and we're calling about your children's Christmas."

"How did you get my name?"

"From your husband.

"He's not my husband. We're not married."

"Well, then, the children's father made an application to get gifts for your children, and we are calling to see what they would like to get for Christmas."

"What do I have to pay?"

"You don't have to pay anything. We're providing gifts for his children."

"Why would you want to do that?" or "What does he want?" or "I don't know anyone by that name." Nothing like this had been offered before; some were very suspicious and refused to participate. Some of these called back later and said they had changed their mind.

Whenever possible the volunteers spoke to the children directly to find out what they wanted.

"Oh, old loafers, or a pair of socks." They were used to castoffs; they could not imagine anyone would get them something new, or a toy.

"No, we want to know what you really, really want."

"I always wanted a Cabbage Patch doll."

"Do you think I could have a real football?"

Some even admitted to wanting a bicycle or Nintendo or a doll house. "We can't promise that you're going to get these gifts, but we're going to put them on the list," the volunteer would reply. They decided to let the child list four items, two clothing and two toys, in the hopes that they would get one of each.

On each paper angel they printed the child's first name, age, and all the gifts the child wanted; about a hundred angels were completed. Their plan was to scratch each item off the list on the angel when someone brought it back with a gift, and then put the angel back on the tree. Each angel had a number which corresponded to the application that a parent in prison had filled out.

They chose the day after Thanksgiving to erect the angel tree since it was the busiest shopping day of the year. They placed the tree at the top of the escalator in Brookwood Mall. It would remain at the mall until the tenth of December; by then they hoped to have received at least two gifts per child. They expected moderate success.

"Well, I'm telling you, it went berserk," recalls Nina. "They overwhelmed us with gifts. One man's three-month-old daughter had died the year before. He looked over the tree and got a three-month-old girl and went and got a whole layette set. We told them they could buy what the child wanted but they could also buy whatever else they wanted, that it didn't matter what they bought. Another man was divorced and couldn't see his eight-year-old son. He found an eight-year-old boy on one angel and bought everything you can imagine."

Gifts poured in. Some, like bicycles and Big Wheels, needed to be assembled. At the end of the first day, they realized they had no plan for storing the gifts. Molton came to the rescue, offering a whole floor of his building. The huge task of transporting all the gifts from the mall to the office building began.

They had never imagined the response they would receive; they ran through all one hundred angels that first weekend. On Monday, Mary Kay called more prison chaplains and drove all over the state dropping off and picking up applications. Volunteers made phone calls, filled in paper angels, and rushed them to the mall all week. By the cut-off date, gifts for five hundred and fifty-six children were in storage. Not only were all four gifts on each angel provided, but some people also bought more than was requested.

None of the volunteers had had more than a few hours of sleep each night for weeks, and the work was far from over. They now had to organize and distribute more than twenty-three hundred gifts, making sure that the right gifts reached the right child.

They put five hundred fifty-six numbers on the floor and piled each child's gifts on his number. Every night, the core volunteer group, Mary Kay, Nina and Hank Hamilton, Drayton and his secretary Marjorie, Mitzi, Molton, and Nancy, spent the evening sorting, wrapping, and assembling toys. This was a tired and silly bunch, riding the skateboards up and down the hallways of the office building at two in the morning.

They called the families and set up times for them to come collect their gifts. The families who had no transportation into Birmingham or who lived too far away had the gifts delivered to them. Gideons throughout the state of Alabama were mobilized. The Birmingham newspaper agreed to transport gifts to the outlying towns with the morning papers. In the wee morning hours, Gideons met the trucks loaded with gifts which they then delivered to the families. Coordinating it all was a nightmare.

On Christmas Eve, Mary Kay, Nina, and Mitzi were still delivering the last of the gifts. By the time it was all over, they were so exhausted they could barely enjoy their own Christmas. Mitzi was hospitalized, and Nina swore she would never speak to Mary Kay again.

CHAPTER TWENTY-THREE

By January, everyone was rested and speaking to each other again, but they all agreed—they never wanted to do another Angel Tree Christmas. Prison Fellowship had fifteen to twenty Bible studies going on each week in prisons and jails all over Alabama. Before Christmas, the attendance at the studies averaged five to ten inmates, but in January volunteers began calling the office.

"Mary Kay, I need more Bible study books. We've got a bunch more people." Or, "Send us some more books. We don't have enough."

What is going on? Mary Kay thought, *we have never ordered this many study books before.*

Inmates whose children had received Angel Tree gifts were flooding into the studies. They had received letters from their families telling them what had happened. Some brought pictures of their children, holding their gifts, to the Bible studies.

"Is this the group that bought presents for my kids?"

"I can't believe anyone would get gifts this nice for my children."

"My kid got a really nice jacket." Or a bike . . . or a doll.

"I didn't think there were folks out there who cared about us and our families."

Inmates who never attended worship services were coming to the Prison Fellowship Bible studies. Some came simply from a sense of obligation. Many came to Christ as a result.

Reports told of families being reunited. Wives would say, "He's never given them gifts before." Or "This is the first time he's done anything for those kids." Broken relationships were healed, and as women saw their husbands become Christians and change, they, too, made professions of faith. Beyond anyone's imagination, God's hand was clearly on the project—Angel Tree triggered a revival.

In June Mary Kay attended the PF national staff conference. She took copies of the forms Nina had made and told anyone who would listen about Angel Tree. The reception was not as enthusiastic as she had hoped. Most directors did not think it would go over as well in their states as it had in the south. Eventually a few committed to pilot an Angel Tree project in their state. Mary Kay returned to Alabama with a new project to begin.

The Prison Fellowship Community Service Project involved asking permission for the federal prisoners nearing release to be furloughed to perform community service. They would be housed in the homes of volunteers for two weeks. The Care Committee was committed to the project, but by July the person put in charge of the project in Alabama had not organized anything. Mary Kay did not have time to spearhead this project and perform her other duties; she needed more volunteers.

One new volunteer was a tall middle-aged man named Joe Don Beard. Prison Fellowship was full of ex-cons, ex-drunks, and ex-drug addicts; Don fit right in—he was all three. He had been sober less than six months when he arrived. His manner offended some—he seemed to bark words out—but his ready smile, sharp wit and wholehearted devotion to the Lord were impressive. Mary Kay respected his jolting honesty. His rough edges came from years of prison, living in the streets of New Orleans, and hard drinking and drugs. This did not bother Mary Kay; her rough edges weren't all smooth yet either. They became good friends.

Don worked in the PF office where his organizational skills and degree in accounting were badly needed. A hard worker, he knew how to get things done. In his first two weeks he called churches and arranged housing for the eight inmates being furloughed for the new project. He arranged training meetings for those involved, and made sure every detail was covered.

Don lived at the Salvation Army and had no vehicle, so Mary Kay let him use her car to transport the men. On the way to the work site in the morning, they stopped by a local church for a Bible study taught by a pastor or church member. At noon, they walked across the street to another church, where the women's group provided lunch for them. In the evening Don returned them to their host homes.

After the first week, everyone met for a big picnic and the inmates were introduced to their new host families for the second week of the project. Don had included as many different people as possible. The project was considered a success, and Don impressed the Care Committee with his efficiency.

Brenda had been with Mary Kay for two years now. When she learned her grandmother was not well, she wanted to return to Illinois. Mary Kay was reluctant, but she knew Brenda was a believer; her daughter had seen God's provision and learned a great deal about His love. She had grown into a strong young woman. Sad to lose her, Mary Kay agreed to let Brenda move to Illinois to live with her widowed grandmother and finish her senior year of high school.

Summer was the time to begin work on the next Christmas project.

"We probably won't do Angel Tree this year," she told Don one morning at the office. "It was so overwhelming and exhausting; we have to think of another project."

"You learned a lot last year. With proper planning and organization, I'm sure it would go a lot smoother. It's too good an idea to abandon."

"It *is* a good idea, but I don't think I could get anyone to commit to it."

She was wrong; without exception, everyone expressed the same thought— they wanted to try again. Everyone also agreed that the leadership must change; Mary Kay was too busy with her duties as director to run Angel Tree as well.

Hank allowed Nina to participate if she and Mitzi weren't in charge. As a military man, he was appointed to take charge of the project. Just as Don predicted, with Hank's direction and the lessons they learned the first year, the second year proceeded much more smoothly. He enlisted volunteers from churches to staff the tables in malls in Birmingham and Montgomery on a rotating basis in four- to six-hour shifts. Drayton's secretary, Marjorie, made large banners to hang above the tables and Christmas aprons for the volunteers to wear when they worked. The newspaper published photos of Nina, Mitzi, and Mary Kay wearing their aprons and holding angels.

In early November Mary Kay conducted a volunteer training conference at a church in Mobile and took several volunteers with her to conduct workshops. She asked Don to come and conduct a question and answer session on the needs and issues faced by ex-offenders upon their release from prison. During a break, she overheard someone in a group remark, "Mary Kay is just so great at everything she does, but she needs a husband."

Before she could respond, Don said, "I'll volunteer for that. I think I could handle her."

Everyone laughed and Mary Kay quipped, "And when I start believing you, they will send me to the mental hospital."

Immediately, Don's face darkened. "I'll have you know I don't lie about *everything!*"

He walked out of the room. What could possibly have offended him? She didn't mean to imply he was lying. She followed him to apologize.

Perhaps I should also gently reprimand him, she thought. *He was pretty touchy. I'll remind him that 1 Corinthians 13:4 says love is not easily offended.*

She began to imagine his becoming repentant and asking her forgiveness, which she would give, of course. She found him outside smoking.

"Don, I want to apologize for offending you. I certainly was not trying to hurt your feelings." She paused for effect. "But I don't really understand why you were offended; we were all just joking, weren't we?"

Before she could piously throw Scripture at him, Don responded. "I wasn't joking." He looked directly at her. "I don't know if I love you or not, but we have a similar background and we work well together. Will you marry me?"

Mary Kay was stunned and humbled. "Oh, I really *am* sorry, but . . . no."

"Will you pray about it?

She agreed to pray. An avalanche of feelings that she thought were long gone overwhelmed her—feelings of being unattractive and doubts about her desirability as a woman. Uncomfortable with her outward appearance, she relied on her skills in speaking and teaching to boost her confidence. She felt out of her element in a romantic relationship.

It won't matter, she thought ignoring the unwanted feelings, *He'll change his mind by the time we're back in Birmingham.*

The following week Don came into her office, closing the door behind him. "Have you been praying about it?"

"About what?" She knew exactly what he meant, but she wanted to hear him say it again to be sure.

"About getting married."

"You're really *serious!*"

"I certainly am. I'd appreciate it if you'd take it seriously and pray about it."

He left the room. Though she didn't admit it to him, she had actually thought of little else. He had not changed his mind—he really did want to marry her! New emotions welled up inside her.

I need to get away to think and pray, she thought. Her apartment was too crowded. Her sister Ilene and two of their nephews were now living with her. She decided that on Thursday when she went to Montgomery to meet with Angel Tree coordinators, she would stay the weekend to spend time alone with God.

She had been single for eleven years. She hadn't dated for a very long time because she assumed God wanted her single the rest of her life. As the mileposts between Birmingham and Montgomery flashed by, questions flew through her mind. One main concern kept recurring: Did God want her married and if so, why and to whom?

"I'm happy just serving You all the rest of my life," she told the Lord as she drove. "Why in the world would I want to get married again?"

After the meeting, she returned to her hotel and immediately began reading her Bible and praying. She knew that many in the church condemned remarriage after divorce, and she had heard many arguments on the subject. What did she believe? She asked God to guide her. As she read and prayed, she realized, "All of my sins, my thefts, my deceptions, even my divorces are included in the list of things for which God has forgiven and cleansed me. I am a new creation in Christ."[28] A deep conviction settled in—she was free to marry—but should she?

She was nearly thirty-nine; she wasn't planning to have more children. Wasn't marriage primarily for raising children to the glory of God? As she

---

[28] 2 Corinthians 5:17

continued to read in the Word, more thoughts formed.

"I'm involved in prison ministry, and because I am a single woman I must be very cautious—most inmates are male. As a married woman I *would* have more freedom, accompanied by a husband, to have greater contact with men in prison."

She remembered what Don had said: "We have similar backgrounds and we work well together."

It made no sense to her to marry Don, yet every time she prayed she sensed God telling her to do it. She argued with Him.

"What about the fact that he hasn't been sober even a year? I do *not* want to take that chance. I've seen too many women suffer with alcoholic husbands, and I cannot take that lightly. Also, he's a new Christian. I've been a Christian for eleven years—and I don't mean to be puffed up, Lord—but couldn't that be a difficulty? Besides, he's twelve years older; he doesn't even have a job. And I've already made poor choices in men twice before."

No, it did not make sense, no matter how she looked at it. Yet, she could not shake the impression that the Lord wanted her to accept. She could not believe He would tell her to do something that made so little sense. Then she remembered seemingly senseless things He had told some of His other servants. He told Joshua to leave his army behind and march with a band around Jericho. He told Abraham to leave his home and family and go live in a strange land. He told Hosea to marry a prostitute.

"Is this really what You want for me? I have to admit, I *am* attracted to Don, but do I love him? Lord, I'll do whatever You want and trust You with the results. Just make Your will very clear . . . *please*."

Over the next forty-eight hours, she continued to meditate and pray. God reassured her that this was His will, that He would do more through their marriage than if they stayed single. Finally, on Saturday afternoon, she felt that sweet, comforting peace of God, which settled all her doubts. She knew that she was to marry and that she was to marry Don.

She drove back to Birmingham and called him. He was on his way to an AA meeting but promised to call when the meeting finished. Later, he listened quietly as she told him that yes, she would marry him. However, the following Thursday was Thanksgiving, and the next day Angel Tree opened all over the state. She certainly didn't have time to get married in the middle of Angel Tree. His answer was a shock.

"Well, I've been praying this weekend, too, and I realize that I can't marry you!"

"What do you mean?" Her voice raised a pitch.

"Satan would always have a means to accuse me if I married you with no job. I would wonder if I married you just for creature comforts. So I have to find a job first."

Relief rushed over her. In that moment she realized she wasn't only willing, she *wanted* to marry Don.

The weeks ahead were filled with hectic, eighteen-hour days. Although it was exhausting, Mary Kay thrived on it. Don and Ilene both claimed she was crazy. Don continued to work in the Prison Fellowship office and frequently helped newly released inmates find jobs, but he could not find one for himself. Don was nearly fifty, and his college degree overqualified him for many jobs. He believed these factors were bigger hindrances than the fact that he was an ex-offender.

All the while, Angel Tree gifts accumulated quickly. Friends offered to store them in the back of their shoe store. Then one night the store was robbed—the gifts were stolen! The group was devastated; how could they replace all those gifts? They appealed to everyone they knew. Money started coming in, and volunteers began shopping. They went up and down K-Mart aisles filling carts with clothes and toys. People thought they were store employees stocking shelves and kept taking things out of their baskets. In the end, they were able to replace every gift stolen.

As Christmas grew closer, they needed a bigger place to sort and distribute the gifts; there were over eight hundred angels this year and thousands of gifts. The pastor at Homewood Church of Christ volunteered the use of their gymnasium on Friday and Saturday, but they had to be out of the gym by five o'clock when the youth group started.

They moved all the gifts in on Friday morning and taped numbers on the gym floor to correspond with each child, grouped by families. There were two copies of each application filed in large notebooks, one arranged alphabetically by the inmate's last name and the other arranged numerically by the number assigned to each child's application. Looking around the room, Mary Kay saw that there was a difference in the value of the gifts and that not every child had received all four gifts this year.

At nine o'clock the next morning, the caretakers were lined up at the door to present their ID's and be directed to a volunteer who would escort them to their pile.

The previous year, when the caregivers came to receive the gifts, they didn't know what to expect and were deeply grateful. This year, however, some complained when they saw a TV, bike, or expensive toy on one pile and not much for their own children. Or they were upset that there were gifts only for the inmate's children.

"Well, I've got six other children in my house, too, and they's not going to get nothin'. She's getting everything she wants and more." They didn't understand that the father or mother in prison had to sign a child up in order to be on the Angel Tree. The volunteers apologized and tried to explain. A few caretakers grumbled, but the children grinned; their eyes sparkling in eager anticipation of a real Christmas.

Across the gym, a fifteen-year-old volunteer named Laura was about to be tested. As she stood directing the small group of caretakers gathered about her, one woman spoke up.

"I'm here to pick up gifts for Joe Brown's[29] kids."

"Are your children Anthony and Latitia?" the girl asked.

"No."

"Are they Johna, Willard, and Henry?"

"Yes, those are mine."

Suddenly a woman stepped out of the line and marched to the front, glaring at the first woman, "*I'm* Joe Brown's wife and *I'm* picking up the gifts for his kids."

Before the volunteer could speak, another woman stepped forward and said, "Anthony and Leticia are *my* children and Joe Brown is their father."

---

[29] Name changed

Laura did not panic; she searched her clipboard of paperwork. Joe Brown had signed up all eight of his children by three different mothers, and they had all shown up at the same time, each unaware that the others existed. There were three twelve-year-olds listed under the same father!

The teenager quickly grabbed a volunteer walking past the group and said to the first woman, "You go with this lady. She will help you." Turning to the second woman she said, "You come with me and we'll get this sorted out." As they walked away she turned back to the third woman and said, "You stay here; I'll be right back." When Mary Kay heard the story, she was impressed with Laura's composure in the face of a potential firestorm.

When the Angel Tree was put up at Montgomery Mall, Mary Kay arranged for the Tutwiler prison choir to sing. Chuck Colson came from Washington to promote and observe the project. The local television station sent a cameraman and reporter. Four young children, ages three through eight and each an Angel Tree recipient, were invited to be on television. Their great grandmother raised the children while their mother was in prison. And their mother was in the prison choir.

Chuck talked with the oldest boy, helping him become comfortable with the microphone and lights. He told the boy how Christmas is about Jesus.

"Jesus is God's Son and He came to save all of us from our sins. If we ask Jesus to come into our hearts, we can live with Him in heaven forever. Have you ever done that?"

"No," said the little boy.

"Well, would you like to do that?" Chuck didn't really expect any response. "Now?"

"If you want."

The boy reached over and put his little hand in Chuck's big one and said, "Uh, huh."

Chuck, choked with emotion, prayed with the boy. When it was time to film, Chuck asked him, "What is the most important Christmas gift?" The boy was supposed to respond, "Jesus."

But he said, "To have my Mommy home for Christmas." A tear rolled down the boy's face, and his three-year-old sister reached up, patted her brother on the cheek, and wiped the tear away. Everyone watching in the mall, including Chuck, began weeping.

Chuck Colson fell in love with the whole concept of Angel Tree that day. Mary Kay presented it at the Prison Fellowship National Conference the next June, and Angel Tree became an official ministry of Prison Fellowship in the United States and eventually worldwide.

CHAPTER TWENTY-FOUR

Don still could find no work except temporary positions. One Saturday he dropped by Mary Kay's apartment after a morning AA meeting. He wasn't there five minutes when the phone rang.

"Hello is Don Beard there?" a voice asked. Mary Kay said yes and held the receiver out to Don.

"But no one knows I'm here."

"Well, he asked for you by name, so someone knows." She handed him the phone and walked into the kitchen. When she came back, Don sat on the couch with a dazed look on his face.

"Mary Kay, you are not going to believe this. That was Jim Swoager. While he was jogging, he was trying to think of someone to fill a staff position at the recovery center he runs. I came to his mind, and he thought he might call me next week. But he said he felt a strong impression that he was to call now. He knew he didn't have a quarter, but then the thought came: *Look in your pocket.* He reached in his pocket, and to his amazement he pulled out a quarter. He has no memory of ever keeping change in his jogging shorts. When this strong impression came the third time he argued, 'I'm on a residential street. There's no phone around here. I'll do it when I get home.' Jim is *not* accustomed to having this kind of conversation with God. Then he rounded the corner, and there in front of the library was a pay phone!" Don paused, his voice breaking at the notion of God working on his behalf like this.

"As Jim headed toward the phone booth, he thought, *I don't even know how to reach Don.* Then he recalled my introducing him to you. He couldn't remember your last name, but he looked up Prison Fellowship in the phone book, and there was your name and number. He asked me to come in

217

Monday for an interview. Can you believe that? No one has to tell me that was God!"

Don interviewed on Monday and started work the next day. After a few weeks of work, he said to Mary Kay, "We can get married now."

"What do you mean by 'now'?"

"I mean this week. We're not getting any younger, and we don't need a long engagement."

"I'm really busy this week, and so are you. The only night I have free is Thursday, and that's the night you work late."

"What are you doing on Saturday?"

"I'm going to Tutwiler Prison to lead a volunteer training seminar; I'll be there all day."

"Can I go with you?"

"Sure, it's for both male and female volunteers."

"What about the chaplain?"

"He'll be there. What about him?"

"Is he legally able to perform marriages?"

"Well, he's an ordained minister, so I suppose he could."

"Call him and see if he'll do it Saturday."

"You want to get married in *prison*?"

"I think it suits us, don't you?"

Mary Kay had to laugh. Don was right; it did suit them. She called Lennie Howard, and he agreed to perform the ceremony. They got a marriage license and blood tests that week during a lunch break, and on Saturday, January 28, 1984, they went to prison for a seminar and a wedding.

When the morning sessions were done, Lennie announced to attendees, "Y'all need to come back to the chapel immediately after lunch because Don and Mary Kay are going to get married."

Everybody laughed, wondering what the punch line would be. While everyone went to the dining hall to eat, Lennie stayed behind. When the volunteers came back to the chapel, they found he had beautifully decorated the altar.

"Look! They really are going to get married."

It was a solemn and beautiful ceremony. Lennie had put a unity candle and two tapers on the altar. Don and Mary Kay each picked up a taper and together they lit the large candle as they said their vows. They didn't exchange rings because Mary Kay didn't want cheap rings and they couldn't afford good jewelry yet. They served each other communion for their first meal as husband and wife.

Two volunteers in attendance that day were their friends Edwin and Ruth Messerschmidt. They were just as surprised by the wedding as anyone else. They eventually became mentors to Mary Kay and Don. No family or friends were invited; at the time, no one was pleased about their marriage. Nina was so against it that she cried when Mary Kay told her about their plans and begged her not to go through with it. She and Hank knew Don well; they knew about his former life, and they didn't trust him. They didn't speak to the newlyweds for three months after the wedding.

Following the ceremony, Don sat down and Mary Kay finished teaching the seminar. At three in the afternoon they left for Mary Kay's apartment, their new home. Ilene and the nephews had moved, but the fifteen-year-old daughter of an inmate was staying there. She had delivered a baby girl the first week of December, and her mother kicked her out because she had been unwilling to have an abortion.

She stayed with Mary Kay and Don for three months before she was placed elsewhere. Having houseguests became a pattern for them. From the day they were married, they usually had someone living with them: acquaintances, ex-inmates, their family members—somebody always needed a place. Through their work they often came into contact with people in desperate situations. They both agreed: How could they turn people away when they had the means to meet their needs?

Not that their means were luxurious. Don's mother discovered they were sleeping on a daybed and immediately bought them a double bed. They were willing to make do with less in order to share with others.

Don continued to work with Prison Fellowship, but he never confused their roles. At the office she was the director and he was the volunteer. One evening, shortly after they were married, they prepared to leave the office. She reached down to pick up her briefcase; she was used to working long hours and usually took work home.

"You can leave that here," said Don.

"But what will I do?"

"When we get home, you can just be my wife." It wasn't said unkindly or accusingly; it was matter of fact. Mary Kay put down the briefcase.

She appreciated Don's honesty and directness; he never hesitated to tell her exactly how he felt, whether positive or negative. Not having to guess what he was thinking or feeling gave her a sense of security. After quite some time, she began to believe him when he told her she was beautiful.

She knew God chose Don especially for her because she was becoming a better person through their marriage. Don made her question herself. She had fallen into the habit of excusing and overlooking negative aspects of her character. She easily put on a pleasant face for an audience, but she could not put on a face for Don. He made her aware of areas where she had begun to slip.

Sometimes people thought he was criticizing her, but she knew he teased her so she would not become arrogant. She might not agree with him, but she never doubted his intent; she trusted his heart to look out for her good.

One night Nina and Hank invited them to their home for dinner—and to apologize. Later, Nina and Mary Kay sat in the living room talking about people they knew. Suddenly Don called from the kitchen, where he and Hank were talking.

"Mary Kay, you're not talking anymore; you've gone to gossiping."

How rude, she thought, *especially in front of other people.* But she knew he was right, so she simply said, "Yes, dear."

Her irritation lingered until later as she did her night-time devotions. She bowed her head and poured out her feelings to the Lord; then she asked Him to forgive her and make her heart right. When she at last opened her eyes, they fell on a verse in Proverbs, "Wounds from a friend are better than many kisses from an enemy."[30]

She wrote in her journal that night, "Today I fell more in love with my husband. He loves me enough to keep me from sin."

---

[30] Proverbs 27:6, *New Living Translation*

CHAPTER TWENTY-FIVE

Several months after Don and Mary Kay were married, Don was hired to start a nonprofit organization, assisting released offenders in integrating into society. The Care Committee recognized the need for a job registry and believed Don would be the best person to create and build the ministry. As executive director, he recruited employers and interviewed inmates, matching each inmate to the best job. At the same time, Mary Kay and Don sensed God planting a vision in them for a residential facility for ex-offenders, a place emphasizing spiritual and social development as well as employment.

In the spring of 1985, Don met Clyde Wright, owner of three old houses in the Birmingham area. He told Don to look at the houses to see if one might be suitable for a residential home. The most promising structure was a large two-story that might be renovated to fit their needs. Clyde offered to lease it to them for the cost of the annual property taxes.

They sought the advice of their pastor. He supported the project and suggested they form a six-member advisory board, which they did. Working through the legal considerations of establishing a nonprofit organization took months. When everything was ready, they called the home Shepherd's Fold.

They decided Mary Kay would continue to work, and Don would quit his job in order to repair the house. Their own money would fund the project, but they knew much more was necessary to renovate the building to make it suitable for residents. Don was reading George Mueller's biography, and they decided to follow his pattern. They would not solicit funds; they would only pray about their needs and let God do the rest.

"Lord, if You'll bring in the funding, we'll go forward," they prayed every day. On a dark, dank day, Don was working alone at the house scraping years of filthy buildup from the walls. The magnitude of the project gradually overwhelmed him. He sank onto a low footstool and covered his face with his hands.

"Lord, what is the point of all this?"

Just as the prayer left his lips, the reply came into his mind, "Son, just as you are scraping years of garbage from these walls, this home will be used to clean up the years of garbage in people's lives and liberate them." Don's heart filled with joy and he jumped up, leaning into the work with renewed purpose.

To save time and money, they decided to leave their apartment. Don made two rooms in the house livable, and they moved in with a toaster oven, hot plate, and coffee maker. Repaired plumbing provided running water, but damaged gas lines meant it was never hot.

They moved in on March 6, 1986, allowing six months before they could make the place livable for others. However, by the first weekend, they had given their second room to three desperately needy women. Before the end of March, two men had moved in, and the number grew to eleven by mid-April. The rooms filled as fast as Don could repair and clean them.

Don borrowed a pickup truck from their pastor to haul away the mountain of trash accumulating in the backyard. Returning from the dump, he stopped to visit a member of the advisory board to report on the progress they were making.

"Come on," the man said. "Let me show you something." In the basement, he showed Don a beautiful dining room table, matching chairs, and other pieces of furniture. He gave it all to Shepherd's Fold, with a check for five hundred dollars. The truck Don had borrowed to haul trash away returned to Shepherd's Fold filled with furniture and money.

Mary Kay and Don agreed that any resident who was not looking for a job or working at one would help with the house repairs. They made the rule from necessity, but when they saw how healthy it was for the residents—how it gave them ownership, how it helped them develop responsibility—it became tradition always to have the jobs around the house done by the residents.

By November, hot water ran from the taps, and though there was still much to be done, the house was quite livable. The time had come for the final step of faith—Mary Kay resigned from Prison Fellowship to work full-time at Shepherd's Fold. Now they were totally dependent on God for their day-to-day provisions.

At one point, twenty-two men and women, not counting Mary Kay and Don, lived in the house. Eventually they decided fifteen was a more manageable number. Don and Mary Kay did not consider the nature of their crimes when interviewing them for residency—the men and women could not change that. However, their behavior during incarceration was an important factor, since it indicated whether they were moving in a positive direction. Don and Mary Kay did not want to manipulate someone into a false profession of faith, so they did not make Christian conversion a condition of acceptance. Altogether, their stipulations for residency were simple.

They settled on two main requirements. The first was that the person must recognize that his primary problem was himself. They met many inmates who still blamed their ethnic background, their poverty, their parents, or anything other than themselves for their situations. Those unwilling or unable to admit that they had played the most significant role in their own circumstances were not allowed to move into the home. Don and Mary Kay firmly believed that a person who is unwilling to acknowledge personal responsibility for his or her choices cannot be helped. The second requirement was a willingness to commit to a spiritual way of life; they must accept authority and exhibit openness to including God in their lifestyle.

Their rules were primarily based on 1 Corinthians 13. During the intake interview they explained why it is often referred to as the "Love Chapter" and that verses 4 though 8 describe the behavior of love. Whenever problems arose they would show how any group of people can live together as a family with justice and harmony by putting those verses into practice.

Of course, a strict policy of no drugs or alcohol was enforced. A simple contract was made with each person stating that Mary Kay and Don would initially supply room, board, and all necessary fees. Residents were required to actively seek work, to contribute to the expenses of the house once they did have work, and to save money toward moving out of the house. They did their best to remove every excuse for failure.

As a general rule, most residents were encouraged to stay at Shepherd's Fold no longer than six months. Don and Mary Kay believed that a real encounter with God means change. This criterion determined whether a resident was benefiting from his time at Shepherd's Fold—was there evidence of positive change as a result of an inner transformation?

Sharing meals in the house led to meaningful discussions. They required that everyone eat both dinner and breakfast together at set times. Even residents without jobs were expected to be out of bed by six-thirty for breakfast. For the morning devotional someone would read the chapter of Proverbs that corresponded with the day of the month. They collected prayer requests and took turns going around the table, each one praying for the person on his right. The evening devotional after dinner often led to discussions that stretched long into the evening.

All during that first summer in 1985, work on the house continued. The men from McElwain Baptist Church chose Shepherd's Fold as their weeklong summer mission project. During this time, they remodeled all four bathrooms and replaced the plumbing throughout the house.

The women and teens from this same church invited children in the neighborhood between the ages of five and twelve to a Front Porch Bible Club at Shepherd's Fold. The children enjoyed Bible stories, games, cookies, Kool-Aid, and singing. The boys and girls competed to see who could bring the most pennies for a mission offering. At the end of the week, the children had brought over twenty-six dollars. More than forty neighborhood children attended the Bible Club, and seventeen prayed to receive Jesus Christ as their Savior.

Mary Kay sent letters home with the children offering to take anyone to church who came to the house at nine on Sunday mornings. A nearby Episcopal church agreed to send their van and a team to take them to church. Each interested family was visited, and consequently, twelve adults received Christ and became members of Christ Episcopal Church. Shepherd's Fold was not giving the neighborhood a bad name; indeed, the ex-convicts proved to be very good neighbors.

Winters in Alabama are not harsh, but when temperatures began to fall into the thirties in mid-October, it was evident the furnace needed to be replaced. However, the cost was five thousand dollars; they didn't have a dime of it. Committed to their policy not to solicit contributions, everyone in the house began praying for God to provide a furnace. Meanwhile, a couple of kerosene heaters took the chill off the air in the common rooms. A visit to the thrift store provided sweat shirts for everyone, and donations of blankets and quilts trickled in.

At dinner one evening, the discussion focused on the popular topic of the cold weather. For the devotional passage, Don chose Philippians 4:19: "But my God shall supply all your need according to His riches in Glory by Christ Jesus."[31]

"What do you think God means when He says He will supply all our needs?" Don asked. "Will He supply a new furnace?" Some said yes, some said no, and a few said maybe.

"Is there some kind of criteria we have to meet? Does God only supply the needs of people He likes?"

"You have to be a Christian for God to supply your needs," offered one person.

"Do you mean if unsaved people have something, they got it from someone besides God?"

"No, every good gift comes from God."

"What is God trying to tell us by our not having a furnace?"

"That we don't need one?"

"God does not promise to give us everything we want," said Don. "He has provided heat for us, and even though we don't like the smell, these heaters are much more than many people throughout the world have. Sometimes by not giving us an immediate answer, God is trying to teach us to trust Him and to wait on Him.

"Mary Kay and I believe God was the inspiration for this house," Don continued, "However, if we are wrong, or if God simply decides that the time for Shepherd's Fold is past, He may be telling us that it's time to close. We made a commitment not to go into debt. We are trusting God to show us what He wants us to do."

---

[31] *New King James Version*

A hush fell upon the residents, and as they bowed to pray, several asked for wisdom and for God to keep Shepherd's Fold open. The next morning, a call came from one of the Board members.

"Don, can you stop by this morning?" asked Margaret. She was retired and her first husband had died suddenly, leaving a business with more debt than income. She had remarried Leonard, a widower, and they welcomed Don into their small riverside home.

"We have been praying fervently for you," Leonard began, "and we believe God's hand is in the work at Shepherd's Fold." Leonard looked at his wife. She handed a folded check to Don.

"I've been trying to pay off all of my debts, and God has been good. I have not finished yet, but I believe He wants me to give this gift to Shepherd's Fold as an act of faith."

Don took the check and glanced at it. He did a double take; his eyes filling with tears. "Margaret, this is for five thousand dollars!"

That evening, Don did not wait until after dinner to make his announcement. He told the group at Shepherd's Fold about Margaret's gift, and their eyes widened in disbelief.

"She gave the whole five thousand?" one of the residents asked.

"I thought we might get lots of little donations from a whole bunch of people," another said, "I never thought we would get one check for the whole thing."

"Wow!"

Someone began singing "What an awesome God we serve," and soon the entire group joined in.

CHAPTER TWENTY-SIX

The first anniversary celebration of Shepherd's Fold was filled with joy and thanksgiving; in addition to the house, many lives had been renovated as well. Soon afterwards, Mary Kay and Don were contacted by their former pastor, who had moved to Houston. He wanted help developing a home just like Shepherd's Fold in Texas. His church flew them to Houston to meet with the project ministry board. Mary Kay and Don spent the afternoon telling them the story of Shepherd's Fold and returned to Birmingham that same day.

The group in Texas had a building ready to renovate. Don was excited about participating in this new project, one with full funding; Shepherd's Fold was always hand to mouth. Mary Kay wasn't excited; she didn't want to leave her friends. Don suggested they put it before the Shepherd's Fold board and let God speak through them. Mary Kay agreed; she was sure the board would not want them to go.

When the board encouraged them to go to Texas, she was dismayed. Then, Mary Kay hoped, the board wouldn't approve the sole applicant for director of Shepherd's Fold; after all, he was a resident who had been there only six months. All hope of staying in Birmingham died when the board voted to hire him.

In November 1987, Don drove a truck to Texas to begin restoring the facility. They took only personal items, leaving most of their furniture and household goods behind for Shepherd's Fold. Mary Kay drove their car out the next week after a speaking engagement. The night before leaving for Houston, she and her sister Ilene stayed up late, eating chocolate and popcorn, watching television, and fighting off depression.

The next day, she drove into the night and then stopped at a motel. When she woke in the morning, the car battery was dead; she had left the dome light on. By the time she was finally back on the road, rain was pouring down. Suddenly, in the middle of the highway ahead, a woman stood, waving frantically. Mary Kay hit her brakes, hard, and watched in the rear view mirror as a semi-truck bore down on her.

"Dear God, I'm going to die!" Her voice was lost in the scream of truck brakes. She wrenched her steering wheel to the right and drove off the road. The semi followed her into the ditch, rushing by the right side of her car, missing it by inches. Mary Kay and the truck driver jumped out of their vehicles and ran to the woman to see what the emergency was. They both began yelling when they discovered she simply wanted someone to fix a flat tire.

Mary Kay was sure these must be bad signals—Texas was *not* going to be a good experience. She joined Don, who was staying with a couple from the church, Wyn and Nancy McCready. The two couples quickly became close friends—they would need good friends in the months to come.

Soon Don began to have serious doubts about the man working on the house with him. His first misgiving came when he saw the urinals installed in the men's bathroom; no average height man could reach them without standing on a stool. A second concern was the building permits; they should be posted visibly on the building, but they were not even on the property.

"They're at my office," the man explained, "I'll bring them over tomorrow." Every day he gave a new excuse for not bringing the permits.

"It's illegal for us to be doing remodeling without posting permits," said Don. Finally, he went downtown himself to get copies from the zoning office. There he discovered that permits had never been requested; they cost five hundred dollars, and the man had decided to save money by not getting them. While downtown, Don also learned that the building was zoned for commercial, not residential usage and that no inspections had been done.

When Don brought these issues to the attention of the board members, they seemed unconcerned. However, what they *were* concerned about was whether worship services would be held on Sunday afternoons. If there were at least one service a week, they would not have to pay property taxes.

"We're having a worship service to save on taxes?" said Mary Kay. Her prior misgivings about this project seemed prophetic. The heaviest blow fell when they discovered there was no money available for the project; there never had been. The board had simply presumed, based on a church member's past donation, that he would fund the entire renovation. They were wrong. In frustration, Don went to each board member individually to discuss his vision for the project. None of them had the same vision, neither with each other nor with Don and Mary Kay. Don resigned.

While this project was falling apart, Mary Kay was counseling people at the church. Very quickly a few hours a week became three or four days a week. Mary Kay and Don thought they had come to Texas to start a halfway house but they soon realized God had different ideas—He was building a counseling ministry. Over time, the ministry grew to five full-time counselors who saw approximately three hundred people each month. The church named it the Encourager Center for Biblical Counseling, and Mary Kay was appointed director. God was doing amazing things—marriages were restored and people were healed of deep emotional wounds.

The little church was also growing rapidly. They added a youth pastor to work with all the young people who were now coming. One morning the youth pastor's wife called him, frantic about their young son.

"Timothy can't breathe! I'm taking him to the hospital."

Brandon rushed out of the church to drive to the hospital. He came across his wife's car stopped on the highway. His wife was inside, giving Timothy mouth-to-mouth resuscitation. A helicopter arrived and took the boy across Houston to the children's hospital. Brandon followed in the car and arrived forty minutes after his wife and son.

"I'm sorry," said the doctor. "We've done all we can, but we couldn't revive him. There is no heartbeat."

"May I see him?"

The doctor took him to the room and left him alone with his son. Timothy remained hooked up to the useless equipment. Brandon put his hand on the boy's chest and began to pray, asking the Lord to give him his son back. Fifty-nine minutes had passed since he had stopped breathing. Suddenly, the heart monitor started to bleep and Brandon rushed into the hall. The doctor was amazed but not optimistic; Timothy had been too long without oxygen and would surely be brain dead.

"If God can start his heart, He can make him well," said Brandon. Timothy suffered minor damage to his motor skills and had to learn to crawl and then walk all over again. Years later, he still brings joy to his family.

The news spread all over the hospital, and doctors and nurses came to see the boy who had come back to life. Many hospital personnel began attending the church and seeking counseling at the Encourager Center. God was obviously working powerfully in this church.

Mary Kay mentored her friend Nancy as she studied to become a counselor. She had been an incest victim, and the Lord had done a mighty work in her heart. Eventually, through Nancy's example of grace and forgiveness, even her abusive father repented and became a Christian. Seeing what God had done in their lives, Mary Kay decided to hold a Saturday conference for victims of early childhood sexual abuse. She placed a one-inch ad in the *Baptist Standard*, which was distributed throughout Texas. The response was overwhelming; women called from as far away as Florida. A man called from Michigan and said, "I'm bringing my wife. Is there a motel nearby?"

The day of the conference, the place was packed, and Mary Kay had a raging fever. Don called the elders and asked them to meet him in the church office to pray for her. He helped her dress, carried her to the car, and drove her to the church. As they prayed, her fever broke. Her throat hurt badly, but she could speak; her voice sounded muffled inside her stuffy head.

Nancy gave her testimony, then Mary Kay got up to teach the women how to progress from victim to survivor to overcomer. She explained how each woman's identity was not as an abuse victim but as one of God's beloved creations that happened to have been abused. She stressed the importance of sharing the secret and rejecting the lie that it was their fault. She led them through the process of accepting responsibility, not for the abuse, but for any wrong attitudes and choices they had made as a result. She talked to them about the freedom of forgiveness and taught them how to forgive. At the end of the day, she challenged them to confront, not for the purpose of blaming, but only for reconciliation and healing.

God worked powerfully among the women in the audience; one lady in her sixties had never told anyone about her abuse until that day. Many others were freed of pain, guilt, and anger. When the conference was over, Mary Kay went home to bed with a bad case of pneumonia.

She wasn't the only one not feeling well; Don had been suffering with a headache for eight months. Try as she might, Mary Kay could not convince him to see a doctor. Finally, one day she asked him to go shopping with her.

"Why?" he asked. Her request surprised him; she had never asked him to shop with her before.

"It's important to me. Just come." They went to a dress shop, and she pulled two black dresses off the rack. "Which one do you want me to wear to your funeral?"

Don got the point and agreed to see the doctor. His blood pressure was very high, and the doctor prescribed medication. When Don returned for a follow-up visit a week later, his blood pressure was even higher.

"Mr. Beard," said the doctor, "we have to bring your blood pressure down. You are going into the hospital today. You are a stroke waiting to happen." Don stood up to leave the office. He intended to go home and pack a few things for the hospital stay.

"Sit back down!" ordered the doctor. "I'm putting you in a wheelchair. You're going to the hospital *right now*." He called an attendant, who wheeled him across the street to the emergency room. They called Mary Kay. When Don heard she was with a client, he asked them not to bother her. He was sure he would be released from the hospital before she left work that day.

As the nurse put an IV in Don's arm, she suddenly cried out, "Doctor, I need you—now!"

"They're really serious about this," Don mused. This realization was Don's last thought before he lost consciousness. By the time Mary Kay arrived at the hospital, he was waking up in the cardiac intensive care unit. Don had had a heart attack; they had almost lost him. However, by the grace of God, he experienced no serious damage and they were able to stabilize his blood pressure. He went home a few days later with strict instructions to keep taking his medications. He did not argue this time.

While working at the counseling center, Mary Kay continued to travel and speak. She spoke for Angel Tree, the Gideons, and at women's retreats. A group of softball players from Oregon paid for her to travel with them all over the country several times. They went into prisons, played softball, and ministered to the inmates. For two years they begged Mary Kay and Don to come to Oregon, and build a house like Shepherd's Fold. They flew the two of them to Oregon, where Don looked over their finances and discussed the project with them.

"You all can't afford to hire us. You need to get out of debt first." The group worked hard and did everything Don recommended. They called to tell him of their improved finances; Mary Kay and Don began to think this project might work. The counseling center was doing well, and Nancy was prepared to assume the directorship. They asked their prayer partners to seek God's direction. Every partner reported back the same thing—they should go. The church in Texas gave them three months salary as severance pay.

Unlike the move to Texas, this transfer to Oregon didn't worry Mary Kay. She knew that much of her anxiety about leaving Birmingham was because she had never been a Christian anywhere else. She worried about finding friends with whom she could be real. People don't always want teachers and leaders to be real, but she had found so many friends in Texas, she felt confident about moving to Oregon.

Before moving, they took a trip to Nashville to visit Don's brother, David, and his wife. One evening they went to a restaurant. Mary Kay noticed Don looked rather pale.

"Are you okay?"

"Yes, I just need to get something to eat."

As they sat down, the cardiac nurse who had cared for David during his own heart attack a few years before came by to greet him. They chatted a moment and then ordered the food. Don still looked pale and shaky. After a few bites of food, he suddenly threw up in his plate. David jumped up and ran for the nurse. She took one look at Don and announced she was calling for an ambulance.

"Just leave me alone," Don told her.

"Mr. Beard, I've seen people die who looked better than you."

"Please call the ambulance," begged Mary Kay.

Don was in the hospital for five days; this was his second heart attack. However, they moved to Oregon as soon as he was well enough to travel. They were so certain God wanted them there that they offered to earn their own income if the group would supply their accommodations. In September 1991, they drove from Houston to Salem, Oregon. A week after they arrived, the ministry director came to their apartment.

"We have decided we don't want to be in a house ministry after all."

Don and Mary Kay stared at her. "So what do you want *us* to do?" Mary Kay finally blurted out.

"You can go into the prisons with us if you want."

They were speechless. The woman picked up her bag; and as she left, she called back, "We hope you like Oregon."

They had been dropped like hot potatoes. Had they misunderstood God? What did He want to teach them in this? They were all alone in Oregon; they did not even have a church home yet. None of the group members ever invited them to attend a church with them.

Their housing was no longer covered; they needed to find work and quickly. Mary Kay had a few speaking engagements lined up in other parts of the country. Don offered to find a job so she could continue her ministry. The economy was bad, and jobs were not easy to find. He was finally hired as a substance abuse counselor in a state-run program, making less money than he had been offered eight years before as an intern. Mary Kay cleaned apartments in their complex to pay the rent. They barely made ends meet.

Three months after they arrived in Oregon, Don had another mild heart attack but refused to go to the hospital because he was concerned about money. Mary Kay couldn't force him so she just prayed.

Don's health continued to go downhill in Oregon. An itchy quarter-sized spot appeared on his wrist; he thought it was an irritation from his watch. The spot spread and the itchiness began to keep him awake at night. In desperation, he went to the doctor; it was psoriasis. The doctor gave him a prescription, which helped for a few months. Then it stopped working. He began a different treatment, which also stopped working after a few months. Psoriasis would plague him for the next twelve years.

In February a friend called to say that Peggy had died. This news struck Mary Kay hard. Several other friends had died within a six-month period. She began to slip into depression.

The manager's job at the complex where they lived was vacant. She interviewed for it, and the director seemed pleased with her. She drove forty miles to Portland for the second interview at the main office.

"Have you ever been convicted of a crime?" the interviewer asked.

"Yes."

The man looked up suddenly from the form he was reading. "What for?"

"Armed robbery." He nearly fell off his chair. Mary Kay calmly continued, "Bonding is not an issue. I am fully pardoned."

The next day, the interviewer called to withdraw their offer.

"You can't do that," exclaimed Mary Kay. "It's illegal. There is a federal program allowing ex-offenders to be bonded after a reasonable time."

He said he would look into it, but she didn't wait for him to call back. For the first time, she had been refused a job because of her past. She went to the state employment office. They knew nothing about the federal program. Mary Kay helped them find the paperwork in the big file of federal documents and helped them fill out the forms. The real estate management company that ran her apartment complex refused to take the papers. She had been out of prison for sixteen years and had never gotten into trouble since; it made no sense to her. She was honest with them about her past. An attorney at the church they were attending said she had a good case.

"You could probably win," the lawyer said, "but do you want to work for a company that doesn't want you?"

He was right; she decided not to pursue it. She had never before felt the rejection most ex-offenders experience. Later she learned that it was part of the humbling and brokenness God wanted to work into her. In years to come, she reached the point of being grateful for this experience; it helped her to identify with others who do their best and are still rejected.

She was not able to see it then. In her mind, it was just one more thing on the pile of troubles. She became so depressed she could hardly get off the couch. Don telephoned her friend Jean in Houston and asked her to call Mary Kay periodically. He knew that she needed to talk to another woman, and there was no one in Oregon for her.

A week later, a large check arrived from another friend, along with a note—*"I've never made good decisions when money was the primary issue. Maybe this will make it easier."* They talked about using the money as a deposit on a cheaper apartment. Within days another check arrived from a different friend. Both were unsolicited.

"We're not getting another apartment," said Don. "We're going home. I won't rest until we're on the other side of the continental divide!"

Mary Kay's spirits lifted immediately. "Isn't it strange," she remarked, "I was so sure moving to Texas was going to be bad and it turned out so well. Then I felt so good about moving to Oregon and it turned out so badly."

"I guess that's just another example," said Don, "of the fact that when it comes to decision-making, feelings cannot be trusted."

CHAPTER TWENTY-SEVEN

Thirteen months after they arrived in Oregon, they left and drove straight to Eldon, Missouri, where Mary Kay's sister Connie had offered to put them up. They unloaded their belongings into storage and went to Mama's house. All the family members in town came to welcome them—Ilene and her family, Bill and Kathy with Sean, and of course Connie and her family. Mama was waiting for them with a big pot of her famous homemade vegetable soup. It was so good to be home.

When their friend Janice Webb, the Prison Fellowship state director, heard they were in town, she called. "I'm so glad you're here. I have a job for you." She was on the board of a nonprofit ministry. "We're looking for a new director."

House of Clare in Jefferson City was an in-home alternative to incarceration for women started by two Catholic nuns. The residents had all violated their probations and were given one more chance before going to prison. Don was hired as director and Mary Kay as the housemother. They moved into the house on February 1, 1993.

The home was located two miles outside the city limits in a neighborhood of ranch-style houses. Jefferson City didn't want women like these residents in their town. The house was a split level. The drive sloped around to a basement with a garage, three small bedrooms, a bath, and the laundry room. Upstairs a large dining room, kitchen, living room, four bedrooms, and two baths finished the home.

The president of the board of House of Clare was a former warden. He arranged for them to visit the prison to do programs there, and Don became a volunteer assistant chaplain. They loved their work at the home, and Mary

Kay especially liked being near her family.

When Christmas drew near, every woman in the house received permission to go home for a few days. Rebecca, a former foster daughter, spent the holidays with Mary Kay and Don. On Christmas Eve, their family tradition was to gather at Mama's to enjoy homemade vegetable soup and to open gifts. Don had a cold that evening and decided to stay home.

A little after nine o'clock, Rebecca and Mary Kay left Mama's to drive back to Jefferson City. It was twenty-two degrees outside with snow in the forecast. About a mile from Mama's house, a vehicle in the oncoming lane suddenly turned left into their path. Mary Kay wondered, *Why are they turning? There isn't a road there.*

She glanced in her rearview mirror and moved into the left lane, but she could not avoid the pickup truck crossing the highway in front of them. She broadsided it and spun around three hundred sixty degrees, then another hundred and eighty degrees. Her car finally stopped on the opposite side of road facing the direction they had just come from.

Mary Kay was stunned. She heard Rebecca crying, "I'm hurt. I'm hurt," but she could not move to help her. Her knee was tingling, and the front end of the car was up against her chest. She looked out the window and saw that the truck, which had caused the accident, had plunged into a pasture.

She opened her door but could not get out, so she just held her hand out. Rebecca cried, "Don't leave me!"

"I'm not leaving you; I'm just waving at traffic."

"Why are you waving?"

"Because we're hurt. We need help."

A truck pulled up beside them, and the driver jumped out and rushed over to them. As soon as he saw them, he ran back to his truck and called an ambulance on his CB radio. Then he came back and knelt next to Mary Kay's door.

"Can I contact someone for you?" he asked.

"Please call my family, but don't tell my mother; tell my brother."

"Who is your brother?"

"Bill Petet."

"I know Bill. He's my neighbor."

The man was Larry Scrivner; he and Mary Kay had gone to elementary school together.

"Where is the other car?"

Mary Kay pointed to the pasture.

"I'd better go check on them, too."

Soon a police car, ambulance, and fire truck arrived. Two EMT's began work on Rebecca, two helped Mary Kay, and two went down the hill to check on the woman in the pickup truck. She was alone in the truck, and Mary Kay heard one of EMT's remark, "She's so drunk, she doesn't even know where she is."

The other driver's sister and the sister's boyfriend arrived on the scene shortly afterwards and tried to take the woman away. They told the EMT, "You're taking care of the people in the other car, and she's not hurt so we'll just take her on home."

The patrolman recognized the driver of the truck; he had ticketed her once before for driving under the influence. He was angry. "You won't take her anywhere." He turned to the ambulance driver, "I want her to go to the emergency room and I want a full tox screen on her."

"Please, just let us take her home, she's upset," the sister argued.

"You take her away and I'll arrest all three of you."

When Bill arrived, they were cutting apart the car to pull Mary Kay and Rebecca out. The engine had been pushed into the passenger compartment. When he saw them taking his sister out of the car, Bill was sure she was dead. He couldn't imagine how anyone could survive, based on the damage to the car. Mary Kay's foot had been caught under the brake pedal.

They were both placed on backboards and loaded into the same ambulance. The next morning, after a night of surgery, the orthopedic surgeon came into their room. He stood by Rebecca's bed.

"Your injuries are more extensive than Mrs. Beard's, but you will have a full recovery. You have a compound fracture in your leg, four broken ribs, and multiple cuts and scratches. You can forget about going back to work until September. Mrs. Beard, I have bad news. Your injuries don't appear as severe, but they are permanent. I'm not sure you will walk again on that foot."

As though from a great distance, Mary Kay listened as he continued, "Both joints are crushed; it's sawdust in there. There are not two pieces big enough to pin together. We've put the foot in a cast hoping it will meld together." *Why did his voice keep getting farther and farther away?* ". . . sublator and ankle joints crushed. I don't know if you will ever be able to walk again without some kind of special shoe or brace."

After the doctor left, Rebecca burst into tears, crying for both of them. Her sobs pulled Mary Kay's attention back to their hospital room and off the doctor's grim prognosis. She set about comforting her friend and calming her fears. She had learned in prison how beneficial it was to minister to someone else and thus take her focus off her own problems. Mary Kay thanked the Lord for the opportunity and left her damaged ankle in His hands.

Rebecca's concerns were not unfounded; she was single, and her job was her only support. Nine months without income seemed devastating. But soon she had more pressing problems; within weeks she developed pneumonia from her broken ribs and from lying flat in bed. The doctor kept her in the hospital until March. When she was released, her pastor and her employer flew her home to Pennsylvania in a private plane owned by one of the church members. The folks in her church cared for her until she was well enough to work again. Mary Kay was right; God did care for both of them, just as He had on the night of the accident.

The police officer told them their seat belts had saved their lives that night. When they left Mama's house, Rebecca unbuckled her seat belt and reached down on the floor for an audio tape to put into the tape deck. Seconds before the truck turned in front of them, she had put her seat belt back on. From then on both Don and Mary Kay were adamant about using seat belts.

There were deep purple bruises on Mary Kay's left side from her neck to her waist. The muscles and tendons in the sternum had torn. Breathing and sitting up were extremely painful. When the doctor saw the bruising, he winced.

"It will take about six months for the body to absorb the bruising. We need to watch it to make sure no lumps appear."

Don visited her in the hospital but quickly went home. He felt like his cold was escalating into the flu, but it was not flu—it was congestive heart failure. When they moved to Missouri, he did not see the doctor because they had no insurance. Janice Webb took him to the same hospital as Mary Kay. His pulmonary artery had the most severe blockage. Medication reduced the blockage, and then they treated his respiratory problems. Janice pushed Mary Kay in her wheelchair down to Don's floor to see him.

"We're a lovely pair!" Don quipped.

"Don't make me laugh. It hurts too much." Neither of them really felt like laughing anyway.

"We're going to have to quit our jobs," said Don.

"I guess you're right, but what will we do? We can't pay the hospital bills as it is."

"We'll do what we've always done—wait on the Lord," he replied.

"Of course, you're right, He is sufficient. He always takes care of us."

Don was released after a few days, but Mary Kay was transferred, on New Year's Eve, to the University Hospital by ambulance. In God's providence, a very good orthopedic surgeon there, Dr. Jon Gehrke, had spent an extra residency at Johns Hopkins studying ankle surgery. Besides her ankle, Mary Kay's right kneecap was broken in several places; the patella was broken in two. The doctor operated, and afterwards she was immobilized from her hip to her toes.

Two weeks after her surgery and six weeks after the accident, Mary Kay was released from the hospital and Don suffered another heart attack. A friend referred them to a Christian doctor who agreed to perform heart surgery and arrange a plan of reduced payments.

The board allowed them to live at House of Clare until they were well enough to move. Janice transported them both, in their wheelchairs, to the hospital for Don's surgery. He had told the hospital they could not afford the bills, and incredibly the hospital forgave Don's entire bill.

The other driver's insurance covered Mary Kay's bills. Their car had been totaled but the company would allow them only three thousand dollars toward the purchase of a new one. The agent thought Don was trying to weasel money out of them because he insisted they provide a rental car. From then on, they had difficulty getting any money from the insurance company. Only by suing the company were they finally paid, two years later. When it arrived, the check barely covered their actual expenses.

Their finances were as tight as they had ever been, but Don and Mary Kay seemed somehow to manage; they never had to dishonor any obligations. One afternoon the phone rang; Molton, a member of the Prison Fellowship Care Committee, was calling from Birmingham. They had not heard from him in over five years.

"Man, you folks are hard to catch up with. I just had you on my mind. What's this about Mary Kay being in a wreck?" Don told him the story.

"I believe you must need some money."

"Well, I'm certainly not going to look a gift horse in the mouth," Don said.

Molton sent them a thousand dollar check. Once again, they sensed God being involved in their situation.

"I like it this way," said Don as he looked at the check, "because I am still so conscious of my propensity to manipulate to get what I think I need."

When they were well enough, they moved in with Mama. Mary Kay was concerned about Don. With each attack, his endurance and energy level declined. He could no longer go to the gym. He used to exercise faithfully and vigorously; now he had trouble walking up stairs. The psoriasis worsened, covering him in red, scaly, itchy patches that kept him awake at night and miserable all day long.

Mary Kay wasn't sleeping well either, due to constant pain. Unable to lie flat because of bruising and muscle spasms, she spent many hours in the lounge chair. Her cast was non-weight bearing; the bruises made using crutches painful. Though she went to physical therapy three days a week, she saw no improvement.

"I didn't really expect improvement," said the doctor when she discussed it with him.

"Then why did you make me go to therapy for three months?"

"You needed to realize that it wouldn't get better just by exercising. We'll go in and fuse the ankle, but we need to wait until you can build your leg muscles back up. The ankle needs more time to heal on its own."

In September, they decided to move back to Birmingham. Don drove the moving truck, and Mary Kay, still wearing a cast on her foot, drove their new car. Unable to find a one-level apartment in the city, they moved to the suburb of Bessemer.

Mary Kay still traveled and accepted speaking engagements, hobbling on crutches and sitting to speak. She never asked for a fee, accepting only reimbursement for expenses and whatever a group offered or collected in a love offering. Some churches were generous, but some were not. She and Don lived on credit until the insurance settlement arrived. Their debt was wiped out, but little was left. They lived on what she earned from speaking and teaching, and contributions. They had established Encourager Ministries, Inc., a nonprofit organization.

Her foot became so painful, Mary Kay could not tolerate it. She was in constant pain. Even with the use of a cane, if she stood on her foot more than three hours a day, the pain increased significantly. Eighteen months after the accident, her ankle was fused at University Hospital in Missouri. The insurance company required that the procedure be performed by the same doctor, Dr. Gehrke, and Mary Kay was glad; she liked him.

She spent the summer in Missouri so that Mama, Connie, and Ilene could care for her. Don stayed in Birmingham. His psoriasis was alarming; it now covered over eighty percent of his body. The doctors determined that the beta blockers he had been given after his heart attack in Tennessee had triggered the condition. He entered a study at the University of Alabama at Birmingham where they tried different medications, but none helped.

Mary Kay returned to Birmingham at the end of the summer and spent the fall and winter traveling and speaking. In March 1996, they moved to Jacksonville, Alabama, to work with another ministry that wanted to establish a residential home for people coming out of addictive or destructive lifestyles. By August it was evident that the halfway house project would take much longer than anticipated. They accepted an invitation to serve as interim directors for three months at Palmera Home, a safe house for women and children in Double Springs.

Don's physical condition deteriorated rapidly; he was diagnosed with kidney disease and hepatitis C. Chest pains and dizzy spells plagued him. Several times they made the seventy-mile trip to Birmingham to see his doctor. In December they returned to Birmingham permanently to be near Don's physicians and a major hospital. Previously they had rented apartments, but now they rented a house near downtown. In this rough area, they felt right at home.

In January 1997, Don once again had open heart surgery. Their supporters were kind enough to continue to help them, though finances were no better than they had been in Missouri. In early March, Molton called Mary Kay about Impact Family Counseling, a program to help juvenile delinquents who were referred by family court. He was on the board of directors and offered Mary Kay the position of lead counselor. She and Don needed a steady income, so she accepted the job.

At Impact she developed a biblical counseling curriculum. The interactive program required parents to attend with their children. The goal of the class was to develop family relationship skills to accomplish conflict resolution without involving the courts. Many of the parents were single, having become parents in their teens, and had never seen good parenting skills modeled for them. Mary Kay led classes, saw individual clients, and taught an adult anger-management class to people referred to Impact by the courts. She recruited and trained volunteers and supervised college interns. The work was gratifying, and Mary Kay loved bringing families together, helping them bond and develop healthy interactions.

The director of the center knew Mary Kay was a hard worker and trusted her, so she enjoyed a flexible schedule. Since she spent so many weeknights working, she took days off to travel, continuing her speaking engagements. These took up most weekends in the fall, winter, and spring.

Her ankle healed more fully than expected. Although high heels were not allowed, she was able to give up the cane, the braces, and the special shoes. For the rest of her life, she would be careful not to spend too much time on her feet or the ache would return, but she was immensely grateful for how much mobility God had given her.

Don, however, was now unable to manage a job outside the home, due to his health. He became Mary Kay's administrator, managing her schedule, making travel arrangements, doing the bookkeeping, interacting with the different groups to whom she spoke, and running the household. He traveled with Mary Kay to speaking engagements occasionally, and they enjoyed the long drives to Missouri to visit Mama and the family.

At her speaking engagements, Mary Kay was frequently asked for tapes of her talks. Don knew the sale of these tapes could be a source of additional income for them. However, they were unable to afford the large amount of money they needed to get started.

Don attended a concert of prayer with Drayton Nabers, another friend from the Prison Fellowship Care Committee. Afterwards Drayton said, "I think I'm supposed to give you something. Get in touch with me. Don't disregard what I'm saying. Call my secretary. I want to see you."

When Don arrived in Drayton's office a few days later, Drayton told him, "I've been praying about this, and two thousand dollars keeps coming around. The only question I have is: Do you want me to write you a check for all of it, or do you want me to give it to you monthly over a year?"

Don was overwhelmed; it was exactly the amount they needed for the tapes. "Drayton, I don't have any divine leading on the matter. You just do what you want."

He gave Don a check for the full amount. Mary Kay's tapes were produced, and Don now had another job, managing sales and inventory. He found that being a help to Mary Kay was one of the most satisfying jobs he had ever had. He loved telling stories about how God used her in people's lives.

"Shades Mountain Baptist Church invited her up to speak," Don would begin, "and before the event she kept getting cards about how these women were praying. We were both pleased. At least these ladies knew that getting a rousing speaker is not enough; they knew they had to cover this in prayer. They had invited a real cross-section of women. After Mary Kay spoke, there were twenty-nine first-time professions of faith. I was so gratified to be married to the person that the Lord uses to do that. When you boil it all down, that's what it is all about—people who are going to bust hell wide open. One of the strongest things about Mary Kay is her commitment to be a witness of what God has done in her life. It's a great encouragement to me."

Testimonies from participants at Mary Kay's engagements encouraged them that God was in their work. At a women's retreat in Williams, Arizona, one of the women told how Mary Kay's message had impacted her. Sally Shanahan had attended a retreat five years before, where Mary Kay had also spoken.

"My neighbor and I lived three houses apart, talked every day and were as close as sisters. The Christian school our children attended had a split over an issue. My neighbor and I took different sides, and it destroyed our relationship. At the time of the retreat, we had not spoken in nine months.

"Our relationship was at a stand-off. There was a line drawn in the sand, and neither of us was going to step over it. The harder I dug my heels in, the deeper the root of bitterness grew. After listening to Mary Kay, God spoke to me and told me I needed to reconcile with my neighbor. The verses in 1 John 4:20-21 really pierced my heart—I was a liar because of the break in our friendship.

"After the retreat, I pulled up into the driveway, and my husband came to greet me. He saw the look on my face and asked what was wrong. I told him that God and I had some unfinished business.

"I didn't even take the bags out of the car. I took one of the longest walks I'd ever take in my life, just three houses down. I knocked on the door. I felt as if I had a bowling ball in my throat.

"She was on the phone, but she invited me in. I stood there quietly, with my head hung low until she finished her phone call. I asked her if she would forgive me for hurting her and said that I was sorry. I told her I loved her. She did forgive me, and she asked me to forgive her as well.

"We sat down for some iced tea, and I shared what I had learned at the retreat. Her husband walked through the door and did a double take when he saw us together. It has taken time for the relationship to slowly rekindle itself. We are not as close as we used to be, but we talk often and enjoy each other's companionship. It was the most freeing, liberating thing I have ever done."

CHAPTER TWENTY-EIGHT

Mary Kay never wanted to be tied down to a house; she wanted freedom to go wherever the Lord took her. The few things she had collected to personalize their homes were more than enough for her. Then Mama came to visit.

Owning a house was very important to Mama. She had worked hard to buy her home in Eldon, Missouri, and she wanted her daughter to have a home of her own. Mary Kay's friend Nina was a real estate agent, and before she left town, Mama told her, "Now, Nina, you find a house for Kay. She needs a permanent home."

Like everyone, Nina loved Mama, so she told Mary Kay, "I *have* to do this before your mother dies." Nina was on a mission, and Mary Kay's fax machine began to churn out information on different houses. They had moved so many times lately that their belongings stayed in storage for a year. Don's health was poor, and Mary Kay realized she could not do as much as she used to; each time they moved the packing and moving fell solely on her. Though her ankle was better, carrying heavy boxes was out of the question. Maybe a permanent home wasn't such a bad idea. Besides, they had a new addition to the family, one with four legs.

Suzanne[32], an ex-convict, had started a program in a Colorado prison. Her vision was to enlist violent offenders to care for and train puppies to be used to help children, the elderly, and the disabled. She believed the inmates would learn obedience and discipline themselves in the process. She chose puppies from the pound that would otherwise soon be put to sleep.

Inmates who volunteered as dog handlers also had to agree to attend

[32] Name changed

weekly Bible studies, take complete care of their puppies, including daily walks, and meet with professional dog trainers each week to learn how to train their dogs.

Mary Kay was invited to speak at the first graduation ceremony of Cornerstone Canines and their human handlers. The first class consisted of five dogs: Charlie, Moses, Aaron, Captain Pat, and Phoebe, the only female. Charlie had the rare ability to discern brain seizures before they occurred. He was placed with a group of several patients institutionalized with frequent, severe brain seizures. He would go get a nurse or aid when he sensed an impending seizure and was a vital help in preventing a medical crisis. For Suzanne, Charlie was a confirmation that the program had God's blessing.

Moses and Aaron were sent to a home for abandoned, abused children to comfort and befriend them in their moments of fear and rejection. Phoebe moved in with an elderly deaf lady; the dog let her know whenever the telephone, doorbell, or oven timer sounded.

Captain Pat, however, had to be removed from the program because, at six months, he weighed seventy pounds and was much too big to work with children, the elderly, or the disabled. When graduation was over, Suzanne offered the gentle black dog to Don and Mary Kay. They looked at each other and knew the answer immediately.

"We'll name him Cellblock so people will know where he came from," said Don. At the graduation ceremony, a local ABC affiliate arrived to film the occasion, and each time Cellblock completed one of the required exercises, the dog looked directly at the camera as if to say, "Did you see that?" He became the center of the news piece that evening. Redeemed from the pound, Cellblock fit right in with his new family, and Mary Kay and Don were thrilled to have such a personable, well-trained, and well-behaved pet.

Mary Kay found she liked their rental house much better than an apartment. She enjoyed working in the yard and didn't mind the upkeep of a house; it was relaxing to her.

If we had a house, I wouldn't have to pack up and move all the time and Cellblock would have a place, she thought. She began to study more carefully the faxes that Nina was sending; they helped narrow down and define what she and Don were looking for in a house.

Initially they considered purchasing a very large house, like Shepherd's Fold, so they could take people in and help them. But they realized that their increasing ages, Don's poor health, and her schedule would not allow time for the upkeep of a bigger house. They suspected this would be the first, last, and only home they would own, so they decided to look for something small that they could handle as long as they were physically and mentally able.

They quickly discovered they had very different tastes; she liked Victorian, and he liked ranch-style. An old neighborhood was fine, or a mixed one, and Nina never allowed them to consider an area where houses were depreciating. They talked to a mortgage company to find out their price range.

Finally, they decided—yes they *would* buy. They itemized the features that were important to them—one level, two bathrooms, fenced yard, gas heat. Don studied the fax sheets and on one he wrote, "possibility." Nina took them to see the possibility. As soon as they stepped inside they both knew this was exactly what they wanted. It met all the requirements, was in their price range, and had two added blessings: hardwood floors and a fireplace. It was a bit Victorian and a bit ranch-style. They made an offer.

On the first of May 2002, they moved into the first home Mary Kay ever owned. She never imagined it would mean so much to her. In June they traveled to Missouri for Mama's birthday and showed her pictures of the house.

"Well, we'll just have Thanksgiving at your place this year." Mama always chose the place, and Mary Kay was thrilled. She still felt like she didn't belong in her family, that they just tolerated her. She was surprised when everyone agreed to come. It reminded her once again—never trust feelings.

The upcoming family visit spurred her to hang her pictures on the walls and finish her decorating. They needed chairs in the living room; a recliner would be perfect for Don but a tough fit for her because she was so short. One store loaned their resident decorator to customers for free, with the purchase of a certain amount of furniture. Mary Kay felt she was artistically challenged, so she jumped at this chance for help.

The Petet family long ago began the tradition of celebrating their Thanksgiving on Veteran's Day weekend. This left them free to celebrate

Thanksgiving Day with other sides of their extended families. On the second weekend of November, Bill and Kathy came with their family; Tom came with his wife, Maureen; Mama, Connie, Ilene, and her boys came from Eldon, and Don came from Las Vegas. Everyone in the family couldn't come, but it was a rare year when all could make it.

The weather cooperated; a balmy autumn weekend greeted the company. Mary Kay set the table outside so they could eat on the back deck. They sat and laughed and talked for hours after the dinner was cleared away until it was time to start eating again. That day was one of the high points of her life.

Another Petet tradition on Thanksgiving is for visiting family members to help the hosts do work around their house. Mary Kay had been cleaning the lower edge of the yard where a creek cut along the border. She wasn't tall enough to trim some of the branches and bushes so she asked her brothers to help.

"You can use my chain saw," she said as she headed for the basement. They expected her to return with something small, like a hedge trimmer. She rounded the corner of the house lugging the real thing. "Maybe we *can* picture you toting a gun," they laughed.

Their support and encouragement warmed Mary Kay, and she mustered up the courage to introduce them to her alter ego, Maudie Mae. Sometimes at women's retreats, she would remove her partial plate, exposing a toothless grin. She would dress in an old dowdy dress with granny shoes and top it off with a floppy hat decorated with a big flower. She'd amble out on stage and present her comedy routine, imitating an old hillbilly woman. She loved to ham it up on stage. Don said she could go from ugly to beautiful faster than anyone he had ever met. Her family was shocked and delighted.

On Monday Connie and Ilene drove Mama back to Missouri. All the way home Mama talked about how lovely Mary Kay's house was and how glad she was that Mary Kay finally had a home of her own. On Friday Connie called to say that Mama had been admitted to the hospital with pneumonia, and the next weekend Bill called to say Mary Kay should come home.

She drove to Eldon the next day, crying all the way. She had always been strong and in control, but the thought of losing Mama undid her. When she arrived, however, she locked all the crying away. She could comfort the others, but she could not weep *with* them—she didn't know why.

Everyone thought they would have a funeral on Thanksgiving, but Mama rallied. When she wanted to go home, the doctor expressed concern. "As dehydrated as she is, she could die."

"Mama is the one who makes the decision," said Jean. "She *is* ninety, and she doesn't want extraordinary measures. All we want is to obey our mother's wishes."

"If the doctor thinks it's best, I will stay," said Mama. Connie and Mary Kay stayed at the hospital with her. Almost as though she willed it, Mama was soon rehydrated, and the doctor said they could take her home. She was calmer and more content in her own bed.

Mary Kay returned to Birmingham when the long weekend was over. Don was feeling ill again; his feet and legs were swollen. His kidneys had been functioning at only about twenty percent for months. His heart condition eliminated him as a candidate for a transplant.

"Eventually," said the doctor, "he'll have to go on dialysis."

Mary Kay was literally torn in two directions. During the week she spent as much time as possible with Don. Then on the weekends she made the ten-hour drive to Eldon. She was using up all her vacation and sick days, but her co-workers were wonderful, picking up the slack for her. Don insisted that she spend her entire Christmas vacation with Mama.

"I'll still be here when you get back," he said. "I have nothing to complain about, and even if I did, I shouldn't." He wouldn't let her consider staying in Birmingham for the holidays.

As with the previous trips to Missouri, she cried almost the entire six hundred miles, but once she arrived, her tears dried up. Mama had her good days and her bad days. She seemed to want to sleep most of the time. Sometimes Mary Kay lay on the bed and sang hymns to her. Mama mouthed the words along with her and smiled. Once she opened her eyes and said, "Oh, I'm still here." She was making the transition; she seemed to be more in heaven than on earth. Occasionally she would moan in pain, then catch herself in mid-moan and say, "But praise the Lord."

A few years earlier, each of Mama's children had made a square for a quilt.

Someone made a square for Ronnie. When they were sewn together there were nine squares, three squares across in three rows, in the order of their ages. That put Mary Kay's square in the center. In a stroke of divine inspiration, she stitched on her square, "Grace made the difference." These words were the testimony of her life—without the grace of God and the prayers of her Mama, Grace, she knew she would have been lost forever. Now as they gathered at Mama's home, Mary Kay told a story of those prayers for her.

"Mama was visiting me while I was in college in Auburn, and she attended a luncheon where I spoke. After the lunch, she stood beside me and answered questions. A woman approached and asked, 'How do you pray for a Mary Kay?' I knew she was really asking how you pray for someone who already knows about God but isn't living it. My curiosity was stirred; it had never occurred to me to ask *how* Mama prayed, I was just grateful that she *did*.

"In her soft voice Mama replied, 'I just asked God to put her somewhere she couldn't get away from Him, and that He would put someone in front of her that she would listen to.'

" 'Mama! You prayed me into jail!' "

" 'Well, that's what it took for you, Honey.' It took her twenty-eight years but Mama prayed me into the kingdom of God. I realized that Mama trusted that God knew me best and knew what was best for me as well. The more I have considered her reply, the more I realized that all the time I had been away from Him, Mama had been praying—in 1963, when I was an angry young teenage mother; in 1968, when I was still angry and running from everything I knew to be right, and in 1972 when I was finally arrested. Mama had prayed, and God had used everything that was happening around me to bring me to the place where I could no longer get away from Him. God always knew where I was, and Mama always loved me and prayed for me."

Mary Kay couldn't remember ever spending hours and days with her older siblings as she did that Christmas. As they took turns caring for Mama, she asked them what growing up had been like for them and was surprised to learn that it had been bad for them, too. But for each one of them, it was Mama that helped them through.

Christmas Eve was always spent at Mama's house. Family came from all over the country—children, grandchildren, and great-grandchildren. They gathered around Mama's bed to open presents and then sang Christmas carols. Bill suggested they pray. He had barely said amen when Mama began to pray. They were startled to hear her voice sounding stronger than it had in weeks. She prayed for each one, individually. Mary Kay's heart sang.

"Do you feel well enough to sit up?" Joyce asked when she was finished.

"Yes, I'd like that," Mama replied.

"We've been talking," Joyce said, "and no one knows the story of how you and Daddy got married. Do you remember your wedding day?"

Mama looked at Joyce as though she were crazy. "Of course, I do. There was a family picnic. Bud and I sneaked out and got married. Then we ran off to California."

"Why did you go all that way?"

"We had to get as far away from our families as we possibly could so they wouldn't come after us."

Mama sat up in bed for almost an hour reminiscing about her past. Finally she began to tire. "I know this is hard, but this is part of life. It's time for me to go on, but I want you kids to stick together. Take care of each other. Love each other. Whatever you do, do it in love and peace."

She was more ready to leave than they were to let her. Mary Kay knew how much it pleased Mama that after everything they could all be home, unified and loving. At the foot of the bed lay the quilt folded with Mary Kay's center square facing up. Everyone was together because Grace *had* made the difference in all of their lives.

Four days later, on Saturday, December 28, 2002, Grace Petet quietly passed away. Mary Kay said, "It felt like there was a black hole in the universe because Mama wasn't there anymore."

The funeral was on Monday. Each of her children said something about Mama. Mary Kay said, "I don't know anyone who laid down her life as much as Mama. She taught so many things by example. She worked very hard at menial labor jobs, but she never complained, never slipped into self-pity. She always seemed to have something to rejoice about."

All her life Mary Kay had wanted to have those qualities that made her

Mama so precious: her gentle spirit and her big heart. Mama's love was unconditional, she never said anything bad about anyone and she accepted everyone just as they were. At an in-prison seminar several months after Mama's death, an inmate asked Mary Kay, "How does it feel to be like your Mama?"

Mary Kay paused. Was she like Mama? She certainly had changed. She remembered God's promise in Ezekiel and the day she had knelt on the cold cement in a prison cell to submit her life to Him. She may not be exactly like Mama, but she knew one thing: God had truly given her a new heart.

EPILOGUE

As this book was researched, some points of family history fell into place. Jean wants to emphasize that their mother didn't marry a mean, abusive drunk. "She had a good life, she was happy with him in the beginning. Alcohol, fighting in the war, and his mother's death really changed him."

Mama never said anything against her mother-in-law; she always insisted her death was simply a sad accident. It tells a lot about Mama and about their father. Dad was mean and Mama was kind; Dad was vindictive and Mama was gracious and forgiving, Dad was tormented and Mama was at peace. Mary Kay and her siblings experienced the worst and the best.

Some might blame Mary Kay's difficulties on her father. She quickly points out that she was the only one of the nine who experienced such troubles. She readily admits that her actions were her own choice and *not* the result of her childhood.

"My father sinned against us all, but I sinned by how I responded to my upbringing, by the choices I freely made. Obviously my siblings made other choices."

While this book was being written, Mary Kay was asked repeatedly for crime stories. She simply said she'd think about it. Finally one day, when told that some details of her crimes had to be included, she answered:

"In prison one of the things the inmates do is sit around and talk about their crimes. It's like comparing war stories, and there is a lot of one-up-manship. Almost as soon as I got in, I sensed the Lord would not allow me to do that. He showed me I was not to talk about my sin by speaking to me through the verse in Ephesians 5:12. 'For it is shameful even to mention what the dis-

255

obedient do in secret.' It seemed that in order to grow spiritually, I was to put those things behind me. So, thirty years later it all just runs together." Eventually, a few memories of her criminal life surfaced.

Mary Kay has a good relationship with her daughter Brenda. When Mama died, Mary Kay said to Brenda, "I'm so sorry I never was to you what Mama was to me. I was far too self-focused and selfish to be a good mother to you."

"Oh, Mom," replied Brenda, "if it wasn't for you, I never would be the person I am today or have a job I love." Mary Kay has cherished those words.

Sean knows that Mary Kay is his biological mother, but she is still Aunt Kay to him; Kathy Petet is his real mother. He tried to find Paul, his biological father, when he was in his mid-twenties. He talked to the FBI, but they never had another lead on Paul Mahaffey after that day on the road in North Carolina.

Mary Kay's oldest son thus far has no interest in a relationship with her, which is a source of deep sorrow. When his son, her grandson, Nathan, turned twenty-one, Mary Kay sent him a letter. "Out of respect for your Dad, who didn't want to see me or have anything to do with me, I have not contacted you since I saw you at the airport when you were two. I don't know what you've been told about me but I'd like to get to know you if you'll let me." She has been in touch with him and his sister, Nancy, ever since.

The Petet family still meets together every year for their Veterans Day Thanksgiving. After Mama died, they decided to begin at the oldest sibling's, Jean, and move down through the ranks. Each host's home is the work project for the weekend.

Mitzi Hinde, Molton Williams, and Hank Hamilton have each passed away. Shepherd's Fold has grown into six homes, all updated, repaired, and run by former inmates.

Mary Kay no longer works for Impact Family Counseling. State grants were a major source of funding and in 2003 they were deeply cut. Left with only a part-time job, Mary Kay contacted Prison Fellowship and left Impact to become the field director of Mississippi, commuting from her home in Birmingham. She still travels the country speaking to various groups, and spends time promoting Angel Tree nationally. Chuck Colson says that Mary

Kay has always been part of the PF family, even when she wasn't on the payroll, because she has brought so many churches, volunteers, and funds into the ministry.

In early December 2004, Don was finally put on dialysis. After the first treatment, he was so violently ill that he told the doctors he would not go through another. They gave him two to three weeks to live and hospice came to care for him. Mary Kay took her vacation days to stay home with him. They were both at peace with Don's decision and believed that it was a joyous occasion to pass from this life of pain and suffering into the presence of Jesus.

Their friends, family, church, supporters, and even strangers all over the country prayed for Don and Mary Kay. When the holidays were over, Don was not only still alive but feeling better. They tested his kidneys and found they were functioning normally! For two years they had been operating at fifteen to twenty percent, and now they were normal. They also determined that his bone marrow had begun producing red blood cells again. Once again, God had graciously pulled him from the edge of death. Although he still has many health challenges, he continues to bring encouragement and humor to the lives of his loved ones.

The following pages contain helpful information, including how to contact Mary Kay if you would like her to speak at an event. If you ask nicely, she might bring Maudie Mae.

APPENDIX

AN INVITATION FROM MARY KAY

The following scriptures are found in the back of Bibles that are placed by Gideons in motels, schools, hospitals, and prisons, and are frequently referred to as God's Plan of Salvation. If you have never surrendered control of your life to God, it is my deepest desire that you do that, so that you will have freedom and love and joy and peace like I found.

—Mary Kay Beard

God Loves You

For God so loved the world that he gave his one and only Son, that whoever believes in him shall not perish but have eternal life. John 3:16

But God demonstrates his own love for us in this: While we were still sinners, Christ died for us. Romans 5:8

All Are Sinners

For all have sinned and fall short of the glory of God. Romans 3:23

As it is written: "There is no one righteous, not even one." Romans 3:10

God's Remedy for Sin

For the wages of sin is death, but the gift of God is eternal life in Christ Jesus our Lord. Romans 6:23

Yet to all who received him, to those who believed in his name, he gave the right to become children of God. John 1:12

For what I received I passed on to you as of first importance: that Christ died for our sins according to the Scriptures, ⁴that he was buried, that he was raised on the third day according to the Scriptures. 1 Corinthians 15:3-4

All May Be Saved Now

Here I am! I stand at the door and knock. If anyone hears my voice and opens the door, I will come in and eat with him, and he with me. Revelation 3:20

For everyone who calls on the name of the Lord will be saved. Romans 10:13

My Decision To Receive Christ As My Savior

Confessing to God that I am a sinner, and believing that the Lord Jesus Christ died for my sins on the cross and was raised for my justification, I do now receive and confess Him as my Lord and Savior.

NAME   DATE

Assurance As A Believer

That if you confess with your mouth, "Jesus is Lord," and believe in your heart that God raised him from the dead, you will be saved. Romans 10:9

I tell you the truth, whoever hears my word and believes him who sent me has eternal life and will not be condemned; he has crossed over from death to life. John 5:24

I write these things to you who believe in the name of the Son of God so that you may know that you have eternal life. 1 John 5: 13

But these are written that you may believe that Jesus is the Christ, the Son of God, and that by believing you may have life in his name. John 20:31

IF YOU WOULD LIKE TO LEARN MORE about Mary Kay and Don, visit their website at **www.marykaybeard.com.**

She is available for retreats, workshops, and special events. In addition to her sharing testimony, you may request a specific topic designed for your group or choose from her most popular. They include :

- Dealing With Bitterness
- What Forgiveness Really Is
- Building Your Self Esteem On Jesus Christ
- Recovery From Sexual Abuse
- Discovery (Addiction Recovery)
- The Exchanged Life Of Jesus Christ
- Gifted To Serve (Discovering Your Spiritual Gifts)
- Effective Communication In The Family
- other topics essential to parenting.

To schedule Mary Kay to speak at an event, you may contact her via the above website or by calling (205) 815-9991.

JODI WERHANOWICZ is a writer and speaker. She has her Masters in Counseling from Arizona State University and has been a volunteer for Prison Fellowship as a Bible study teacher and an instructor since 1994. Her previous work includes *Passionate Pursuit: Pursuing the One Pursuing You*, a Bible study designed for small groups. She lives in Phoenix, Arizona with her husband, Victor and their two sons, Casey and Jamie. To contact Jodi or to schedule her to speak at an event, call (602) 926-8217.

PRISON
FELLOWSHIP.

PRISON FELLOWSHIP

P rison Fellowship partners with churches across the United States to strike
at the very heart of crime—by offering prisoners the same hope and trans-
forming power of Jesus Christ that Mary Kay Beard discovered in prison.
Founded by Chuck Colson in 1976, PF is now active in every state of the U.S.
and in more than 108 other countries (for information on Prison Fellowship
International, see page 271). Churches and volunteers minister in a variety of ways
to help reconcile prisoners to God, to their families, and to their communities
through the power of Jesus Christ:

- **Seminars and Bible Studies.** Teaching introduces prisoners to
  Christ, deepens their knowledge and application of Scripture,
  and builds them into committed disciples able to live out that
  teaching—both in prison and when they get out.
- **Mentoring.** Volunteers offer prisoners friendship and spiritual
  "coaching" through ongoing one-to-one relationships.
- **Operation Starting Line™.** These lively in-prison evangelistic
  events—which include musicians, athletes, and dynamic speakers—appeal to even the most skeptical prisoners!
- **Pen Pal Program.** Volunteers minister right from home by writing to prisoners in need of healthy friendship and encouragement.
- **InnerChange Freedom Initiative®.** This program offers interested prisoners round-the-clock programming taught from a
  Christian perspective—beginning in prison and continuing after
  their release.
- **Church-Based Aftercare.** Churches come alongside released pris-

oners to help them make a successful reentry into their family and their community.

*   **Angel Tree®.** Founded by Mary Kay Beard, this program has grown into a cross-country network of churches that minister to children of prisoners.

In addition, Prison Fellowship's **Wilberforce Forum** tackles the cultural and moral conditions that can feed criminal activity. Through radio broadcasts, online and print publications, curriculum, legislative involvement, and other means, the Forum calls and equips believers to apply biblical truth to every arena of life.

Some of these ministries are described in more detail on the following pages. So please read on!

For additional information, complete and mail in the Response Card on page 273 to Prison Fellowship, P.O. Box 1550, Merrifield, VA 22116-1550. Or you may call toll-free 1-877-478-0100. (Spanish-speaking callers can call toll-free 1-800-279-7324.) Or you may visit www.prisonfellowship.org. Click on "local offices" to find the PF field office nearest you.

If you are a prisoner, please talk to your chaplain or prison program director to find out what Prison Fellowship programs are available in your facility.

ANGEL TREE

Mary Kay Beard launched Angel Tree in Alabama in 1982—rallying people to provide Christmas gifts to 556 local children of prisoners. Today Angel Tree® is one of Prison Fellowship's most popular and far-reaching programs.

Nearly all prisoners leave behind a family—children, spouses, parents—who suffer shame, loneliness, and financial hardship. More than two million children have lost a mom or a dad—or both—to prison.

Families have several strikes against them. Prisoners' children are at a very high risk of turning to destructive behaviors: promiscuity, drug abuse, aggressiveness, poor school performance, and crime. Incarceration plunges many families into economic hardship. Not surprisingly, most marriages of prisoners end in divorce—

either during the incarceration or within a year after the inmate gets out. And prisoners who have no supportive family when they get out are at greater risk of returning to crime.

But Angel Tree is helping make a difference! More than 12,000 churches across the U.S. now participate in **Angel Tree Christmas**, which reaches more than half a million children each year. Prisoners sign up for their children to receive gifts, and those applications are distributed to local churches in the families' communities. Church members purchase the gifts and deliver them on behalf of the imprisoned parent. They also share the Gospel.

Churches can also get involved in Angel Tree **Camping**—sending prisoners' children to Christian summer camps. And Angel Tree **Mentoring** matches caring Christian adults in more intense one-to-one relationships with the children.

But Angel Tree is really a door-opener for the church to extend its *ongoing* ministries to these families who are often shunned or forgotten. Prisoners' families benefit from churches' Bible teaching, fellowship, pastoral counseling, material assistance, and youth activities.

If you or your church would like to get involved with Angel Tree, please complete and mail in the Response Card on page 273. Or you may call toll-free 1-800-55-ANGEL, or visit www.angeltree.org. If you are a prisoner, the Angel Tree program works closely with prison chaplains. Please ask your chaplain if Angel Tree is available in your facility and how you can sign up for your children to receive Christmas gifts.

PEN PAL MINISTRY

In prison, "mail call" is a precious time for many prisoners. Every letter from family or friends is a lifeline, bringing light and hope into a dark and lonely place.

But for many other prisoners, mail call is just a painful reminder that everyone has abandoned them. Their name is never called; they receive no words of support and encouragement . . . no news from home to ease the loneliness inside.

For a long time, Calvin was one of those prisoners. "I felt so alone," he remembers. Until he got a pen pal named Chip.

Today Calvin is one of the thousands of prisoners who have been matched with caring Christian correspondents through Prison Fellowship's Pen Pal Program. These valued volunteers provide a special ministry to inmates longing for friendship, acceptance, and a connection with the outside. Through correspondence, they can also fulfill Jesus' command to visit those in prison (Matthew 25:36-40).

Volunteer pen pals don't need to be great biblical teachers or counselors. Primarily they offer Christian *friendship*—writing monthly to share about interests, hobbies, jobs and family life; giving hope through God's Word.

Prison Fellowship provides guidelines to help ensure healthy and appropriate correspondence; volunteers also have ready access to resources and answers to their personal questions through e-mail, phone, and the Pen Pal Program's Website.

Calvin says his pen pal Chip has taught him "to be wise. And he has showed me love and support—something that my family has not done for me since I have been locked up."

But Calvin has also added something special to Chip's life—reciprocal friendship. "How privileged we are to be used by God to reach His children," says Chip. "The reward so often comes in the form of those same children reaching back to us."

If you would like to volunteer to "share hope in an envelope" as a pen pal to an inmate, please **send in the Response Card on page 273 to receive an application.** Or you may call toll-free 1-800-497-0122; visit www.prisonfellowship.org; or e-mail penpal@pfm.org.

If you are a prisoner and would like a pen-pal friend on the outside, write for an application: The Pen Pal Program, Prison Fellowship, P.O. Box 2205, Ashburn, VA 20146-2205.

OPERATION STARTING LINE

Today's prison and jail population has reached a record high of more than two million inmates. Many of them would like to turn their lives around, but few really know how to do that. True liberation and transformation come only through Jesus Christ—but many prisoners never hear that message. Only 20 percent of prisoners attend regular chapel programs in prison.

This is why Operation Starting Line™ was developed—to attract that 80 percent of prisoners who would never set foot in traditional worship services. OSL's creative evangelistic events feature contemporary musical performances, athletic exhibitions, comedy routines, and dynamic speakers—all powered by Christ!

OSL is a collaborative effort of Prison Fellowship and more than 20 other national ministries that have joined together to help reach *every* prisoner in *every* state and federal prison with the Gospel. These national ministries—which include the Navigators, Campus Crusade for Christ, the Billy Graham Evangelistic Association, Crossroad Bible Institute, and others—share their particular areas of expertise to evangelize and disciple prisoners.

Each one- to two-week OSL campaign, covering several prisons within a state or region, also involves hundreds of local church volunteers from various denominations. These local volunteers, trained by Prison Fellowship, continue to disciple interested prisoners after the events are over.

God has blessed these efforts with tremendous impact! In OSL's first five years (2000–2005), it spread through 22 states, reaching about 556,000 prisoners in 684 prisons with the Gospel. Of those, 32,995 handed in response cards saying they accepted Christ as their Savior and Lord! Only God knows the total number of seeds that have sprouted into redemptive relationships.

By the end of 2010, OSL plans to take the Gospel message to the remaining 28 states. So OSL could be coming to your area!

For more information on Operation Starting Line, fill out and mail in the Response Card on page 273. Or you may call toll-free 1-877-478-0100 or visit www.prisonfellowship.org and click on "Operation Starting Line."

If you are a prisoner, ask your chaplain if Operating Starting Line is coming to your facility. If it's already been there, ask your chaplain of there are ongoing Prison Fellowship programs that you can attend.

AFTERCARE (REENTRY) SERVICES

Every year, according to the Bureau of Justice Statistics, more than 600,000 prisoners are released back into our communities. But most won't stay there very long. Within three years of their homecoming—despite many ex-prisoners' best intentions to "go straight"—67 percent will be arrested for new crimes and more than half will go back behind bars. For most prisoners, the so-called "free world" presents obstructions and enticements far too forceful to overcome on their own.

A major University of Pennsylvania study showed that Christian prisoners getting out don't fare much better than their secular counterparts, UNLESS they have a strong church-based support system helping with their transition to the outside.

Aftercare matters—not only to the success of the prisoners, but also to the safety of the community.

Ex-prisoners need the same kind of ministry most churches already provide: solid Bible teaching, a caring community, support groups that help members overcome struggles, material resources. But ex-prisoners also have unique needs and restraints that many churches have not encountered before. This is where Prison Fellowship comes in.

Prison Fellowship helps churches extend their reach to men and women coming out of prison by providing connections, specialized training and resources, and a team structure for planning and implementing ministry.

The training, in part, focuses on understanding the effects of prison life on ex-prisoners, working with people of other cultures, setting up support groups and mentoring relationships, and locating helpful community resources.

If you or your church is interested in helping Christian prisoners make a successful transition back into their families and their communities, contact Prison Fellowship for more information. **Simply complete and mail in the Response Card on page 273. Or you may visit www.prisonfellowship.org, or call toll-free 1-877-478-0100.** (Spanish-speaking callers can call toll-free 1-800-279-7324.)

If you are a prisoner nearing release from prison, please contact your chaplain to find out what Prison Fellowship services are available to you.

PRISON FELLOWSHIP
INTERNATIONAL

PRISON FELLOWSHIP INTERNATIONAL

P rison Fellowship International (PFI) is a global, trans-denominational association of Prison Fellowship (PF) ministries. It was formed in 1979 by representatives from existing PF groups in Australia, Canada, England, Northern Ireland, the Bahamas, and the United States and is based on principles of national leadership and national development.

PFI is the world's largest and most extensive network of Christians involved in criminal justice ministry. PFI is active in every continent of the world with a network of more than 100,000 volunteers in 108 countries. As a non-governmental organization (NGO), PFI maintains consultative status (Category II) with the UN Economic and Social Council and is an active participant in the UN Alliance of NGO's on Crime Prevention and Criminal Justice.

With offices in the U.S., Switzerland, South Africa, New Zealand, and Singapore, the PFI secretariat serves member PF organizations through on-site consultation, leadership training, programme development, communications and international representation.

Secretariat Offices of Prison Fellowship International
General Offices and Administration
Caribbean & Latin America Liaison Office
Centre for Justice and Reconciliation
P.O. Box 17434
Washington, DC 20041 USA
TELEPHONE: (1-703) 481-0000 • FAX: (1-703) 481-0003
E-MAIL: info@pfi.org • WEB: http://www.pfi.org

International Services and Leadership Training
Asia Liaison Office
Kitchener Road
P.O. Box 0122
SINGAPORE 912005
TELEPHONE: (65) 6472-0867 • FAX: (65) 6472-0045
E-MAIL: Asia Office - asia@pfi.org • ILF Office - ilf@pfi.org

European Liaison Office
Les Vernettes
1081 Montpreveyres
Lausanne, SWITZERLAND
TELEPHONE: (41 21) 903-0270 • FAX: (41 21) 903-0272
E-MAIL: europe@pfi.org

Africa Liaison Office
Postnet Suite #152
Private Bag X3
Northriding 2162
SOUTH AFRICA
TELEPHONE: [+27-11] 794-7721 • FAX: [+27-11] 794-5245 (Telefax)
E-MAIL: africa@pfi.org

Pacific Liaison Office
P.O. Box 40270
Upper Hutt
Wellington 6007
NEW ZEALAND
TELEPHONE: (64 4) 528-7341 • FAX: (64 4) 528-7341
E-MAIL: pacific@pfi.org

RESPONSE CARD

Yes, I am interested in getting more information about Prison Fellowship!

_____
NAME

_____
ADDRESS

_____
CITY   STATE   ZIP

_____
PHONE   E-MAIL

I am interested in learning more about volunteer opportunities in the following areas (check all that apply):

- ❑ In-prison ministry—BRIPM
- ❑ Aftercare (reentry) ministry—BRAFT
- ❑ Ministry to prisoners' families/Angel Tree—BRMPF
- ❑ Operation Starting Line—BRSL1
- ❑ Pen Pal Program—BRPP1
- ❑ I would like to be a part of Prison Fellowship's Intercessory Prayer Team—VIPYR (You can also sign up online at www.prisonfellowship.org/prayer.)
- ❑ I would like to make a financial gift to Prison Fellowship's ministry. Enclosed is $_____ (check made payable to Prison Fellowship).

Please mail this card to:

Prison Fellowship
P.O. Box 1550
Merrifield, VA 22116-1550.

You may also call 1-877-478-0100 or visit www.prisonfellowship.org. To contact the PF field office closest to your area, visit our homepage and click on "local offices."

000-4205   GNMKBRSPN